MOMENT OF TRUTH FOR PROTESTANT AMERICA

INTERCHURCH CAMPAIGNS FOLLOWING

WORLD WAR ONE

MOMENT OF TRUTH FOR PROTESTANT AMERICA

INTERCHURCH CAMPAIGNS FOLLOWING

WORLD WAR ONE

by

ELDON G. ERNST

Published by

AMERICAN ACADEMY OF RELIGION

and

SCHOLARS' PRESS

DISSERTATION SERIES, NUMBER 3

1974

Distributed by

SCHOLARS' PRESS
University of Montana
Missoula, Montana 59801

MOMENT OF TRUTH FOR PROTESTANT AMERICA

INTERCHURCH CAMPAIGNS FOLLOWING

WORLD WAR ONE

by

Eldon G. Ernst
Graduate Theological Union
Berkeley, California 94709

Ph.D., 1968
Yale University

Advisor:
Sydney Ahlstrom

ISBN: 0-88420-120-1

Library of Congress Card Number: 74-16567

Printed in the United States of America

Printing Department
University of Montana
Missoula, Montana 59801

TO JOY

CONTENTS

The Interchurch World Movement demonstrates
how the churches patterned their life
according to business principles and, in
turn, were supported by powerful businessmen.

Analysis of the social gospel impulse during
the explosive period of post-World War I
social upheaval; the shifting of popular
Protestantism away from progressivism and
social gospel idealism after the war; yet
the Interchurch World Movement social
involvements through surveys and investigations, most noteably the investigation of
the great steel strike of 1919-1920.

The postwar campaigns are waged as the
nation's mood shifts away from crusading
enthusiasm and optimism; the demise of the
Interchurch World Movement portrayed with a
sense of disillusionment and uncertainty
about America's future.

Analysis of forces which worked against the
success of the Interchurch World Movement
and would dominate religion in the 1920's;
a description of Protestantism within the
religious culture of the 1920's; a concluding brief interpretation of subsequent
American Protestantism fitting the World
War I experience and the 1920's into the
past half century.

PREFACE

On March 29, 1920, the *New York Times* carried a story
announcing a banquet to be held at the nation's capitol. Invitations were sent in the names of Vice President of the United
States Thomas R. Marshall, Speaker of the House of Representatives
Frederick H. Gillett, Secretary of the Navy Josephus Daniels,
General John J. Pershing, Senators Sheldon P. Spencer and Warren
G. Harding, and former Secretary of State Robert Lansing. It may
seem unlikely that men of such diverse political views and loyalties could find reason to sit together socially in the Spring of
1920, one of the most disruptive election years in American history. Yet these men had a common concern that transcended their
social, political, and economic biases--the cause of American
Protestantism.

The April 5th dinner, at which Robert Lansing presided in
his first public appearance since leaving the State Department
several weeks before, was a promotional observance on behalf of
the Interchurch World Movement of North America, the most spectacular and widely publicized American religious event of the
immediate post-World War I period. This study examines the story
of the Interchurch World Movement within its historical religious-
cultural context.

The Interchurch World Movement, a single religious organization lasting two years, seems at first glance an unlikely topic of
lengthy historical examination. Despite an interesting human flavor and intrigue to the subject, I would be hard pressed to justify
the telling of the story simply for its own sake. Rather, I found
in the Interchurch World Movement an entree into the religious life
of the American people, specifically the people of Protestant
heritage, at a significant period in their history. This aspect
of the American religious experience provides the broad subject
matter and occasion of this study.

In retrospect, the post-World War I years were transitional
in American religious history. For a century Protestantism, as
the majority religion, had been a dominating spiritual force in
American culture. Despite ecclesiastical, theological, regional,
ethnic and racial divisions, American Protestants of many stripes

entered the twentieth century sufficiently conscious of sharing
a common national vision and ideological platform to allow later
historians to speak of a Protestant America. The Interchurch
World Movement, rising in the wake of great wartime enthusiasm
heavily flavored by the Protestant America ethos, gave climactic
expression to the crusading spirit, the lofty idealism, the optimism and popular organization which long had characterized popular
Protestantism. But the fate of the Interchurch World Movement
demonstrated the dynamic forces at play in American religious life
and, indeed, the changing place of Protestantism among the religions in America. My study of the Interchurch World Movement as
a chapter in American religious history has swayed my judgment
to the side of those historians who view World War I as a turning
point in American history.

The purpose of this study, however, is not to trace the
course of social change in twentieth century America and the
coincident change in religious life and thought. That massive
task, in my judgment, has yet to be accomplished by American
religious historians. My more modest aim is to examine a critical
and hitherto neglected moment in the American Protestant community's awareness of, and attempts to relate to, large changes occur-
ring in the cultural context of their faith. Something of the
essence of what later historians and theologians have termed,
imprecisely, "post-Protestant" or "post-Christian" America was
sensed by many Protestants and non-Protestants alike during the
1920's. This awareness brought about various kinds of responses
in religious circles which contributed to the longer range patterns of religious life and thought in twentieth century America.
The problem of religious self-identity in an increasing cultural
pluralism, the quest for religious unity within diversity, the
conflict inherent in religious involvement in the social problems
of modern technocracy: these are some of the dimensions of post-
World War I American Protestantism which this study examines.
The Interchurch World Movement provides a significant instrument
through which to portray Protestant America at the doorstep to
the 1920's.

Sources for this study uncover the concerns and mood of a
broad spectrum (though not all) of the American Protestant community, both in its ecclesiastical (denominational) and

non-ecclesiastical (voluntary societies) manifestations. Official
proceedings and reports, correspondence, religious journalism,
religious material in secular newspapers and magazines, and books
about religion and the contemporary world are included in the
list. Because this is not an intellectual history, technical
theological works of the period are not treated as sources.
(Twentieth century Protestant theology in America is a subject in
itself only indirectly related to the popular life of religious
communities and to the churches. The popular and public religious
phenomena comprise the subject matter of this study.)

Many published books and articles in the field of American
religious and social history have contributed to my knowledge and
understanding of the subject matter in its details and in its
larger context. Whereas documentation in footnotes is limited
almost exclusively to primary sources, the bibliography includes
a selected list of relevant books on American religious history.

This study began as a Ph.D. dissertation in Yale University (1968) entitled "The Interchurch World Movement of North
America 1919-1920." Since then, the study has continued and the
manuscript in its present form is a thorough revision. Throughout this process, many persons have provided assistance and in-
sight. A few deserve special mention.

Sydney E. Ahlstrom, Raymond P. Morris, Charles W. Forman,
and Daniel W. Howe of Yale University, Winthrop S. Hudson of
Colgate Rochester Divinity School and the University of Rochester,
Robert T. Handy of Union Theological Seminary in New York, Samuel
McCrea Cavert of New York City, James H. Smylie of Union Theologi-
cal Seminary in Richmond, Virginia, Leonard J. Trinterud of the
San Francisco Theological Seminary, Edwin S. Gaustad of the Uni-
versity of California at Riverside, and Robert H. Ferrell of
Indiana University have commented helpfully on the manuscript at
its various stages. Special assistance came from librarians at
Yale Divinity School, Union Theological Seminary in New York,
The Research Library and the archives of the National Council of
Churches of Christ in the U. S. A., The American Baptist His-
torical Society, The Presbyterian Historical Society, The Board
of Missions of the Methodist Church, The University of California
in Berkeley, and the Graduate Theological Union Library in
Berkeley, California. The secretarial staff of the American

Baptist Seminary of the West in Berkeley--Marjorie Stultz, Lorene
Martin, and Elsa Nielsen--assisted in preparation of the manu-
script; Joann Burnich of the Religious Studies Department at the
University of Montana typed the final copy. Finally, I am in
large debt to my faculty colleagues and graduate students in the
Graduate Theological Union who always help me grow.

CHAPTER I

CRUSADING AMERICAN PROTESTANTISM: 1885-1918

In 1918, when America was in the throes of a great battle
to "make the world safe for democracy" and to "end all wars,"
the Methodist Book Concern published a volume entitled *The
Christian Crusade for World Democracy*. The Methodist Episcopal
Church was preparing to celebrate the one hundredth anniversary
of the beginning of its missionary program. Planned to coincide
with this 1919 celebration was the start of a five-year Centenary Movement for the expansion of Methodist world missions. The
new book, written by two outstanding Methodist leaders, S. Earl
Taylor and Halford E. Luccock, portrayed a great opportunity for
American Protestant missionary expansion which the Centenary
campaign was geared to meet.

"It is a crusade that is God-timed," said the authors,
"timed, it is true, in days of burden and stress, but timed to
a day when men are thinking in larger terms and there is a moral
sacrificial temper in the hearts of men and a larger horizon to
their minds than ever before." Furthermore, the year 1918 showed
signs of being a turning point in history, and Taylor and Luccock
detected "a widespread unanimity of opinion that only one date
has surpassed in importance to mankind these days in which we
live"--the life of Jesus Christ! In fact, they thought, "the
future will in all probability look back on these years, not
merely as a turning point in history, but as determining the
destiny of mankind for ages to come."[1]

What accounts for such audacious statements by American
religious leaders in 1918? American Protestants long had been
used to interpreting events and conditions of the world in spectacular, earth-shaking terms; but especially was this true for
the thirty or so halcyon years preceding World War I. That was
"the age of crusades" in America.[2] Crusading American Protes-
tantism--its missionary impulse, its wartime mentality, and its
institutional dynamics set the mood, the mind, and the methods
which led climatically to the great Interchurch Campaign following World War I.

1

During the quarter century preceding World War I Protestant Americans became increasingly conscious of entering the threshold of a new era in national and world history. The urban-industrial revolution, new immigration of masses of diverse peoples, the emergence of new secular philosophies and social-scientific thought, and scientific discoveries and inventions presented a "spiritual crisis" fraught with new problems and opportunities for American religion.[3] In a new kind of world Protestant church life, theology, inter-church relations, and extra-church religious activities, but especially missions and evangelism were due for a re-examination, a restructuring, and revitalizing. Furthermore, as the United States became a world power with colonial interests, home and foreign missions became vitally and concretely involved in the notion of American manifest destiny. Together they helped inspire a crusading zeal in American Protestantism which grew in intensity as the century closed and became normative and institutionalized during the progressive era in American history.

In some ways Protestant leaders entered the twentieth century prepared to enjoy the best of all possible worlds. During the last quarter of the nineteenth century--especially the last decade--churches and preachers were at their height of popularity and influence in a nation apparently destined for a golden future. Phillips Brooks, one of the most popular and influential preachers of his day thought in 1890 that "the world was never better than it is today." He believed that Christians everywhere ought to be optimistic, but especially those in America.

> We live in the completest theater of God's
> work. We are Americans. I do not know how
> any man can be a Christian and an American
> and despair . . . When a man is both a
> Christian and an American, then he ought
> absolutely to glow with hope and the enthu-
> siasms of humanity.[4]

There was much to be happy about. The frontier continued to be churched with rapid thoroughness, while city churches were prospering in numbers and wealth. Without being legally established, Protestants had succeeded not only in maintaining their churches as the majority religious force but in molding the basic institutions and the culture of the land. Could there be any doubt that America was a Christian nation, churchmen thought. Had not hurdles been overcome, enemies defeated, and crises met? Had conditions ever before been "so favorable to the advancement of Christ's Kingdom and so encouraging to faithful Christian effort"?[5] Was not, in fact, the Kingdom of God at hand? American Protestants of the gilded age came as near to answering "yes" to these questions as had any churchmen in all of American religious history.

Persons of such opinion remained mindful of great obstacles before their goals, however. The publication in 1885 of Josiah Strong's best-selling study of *Our Country* by the American Home Missionary Society had captured the latent spirit of the times. Strong had succeeded in reiterating traditional American Protestant convictions and relating them to the conditions and events of a new day. Dramatically he characterized a new "crisis" which presented the "opportunity" necessary to revitalize the American Protestant missionary impulse.[6]

The central theme of *Our Country* often had been expressed by American Protestants, but it assumed new proportions in this book. Referring to "the time factor," Strong noted that

> There are certain great focal points of history
> toward which the lines of past progress have
> converged, and from which have radiated the
> molding influences of the future. Such was the
> Incarnation, such was the German Reformation of
> the sixteenth century, and such are the *closing
> years of the nineteenth century*, second in
> importance to that only which must always
> remain first; viz., the birth of Christ.

These, in other words, were "extraordinary times," and Strong proposed to demonstrate the "dependence of the world's future on [his] generation in America."[7]

Strong's conclusions about the American Protestant mission were based both on his ethnocentric theological convictions and on scholarly sociological historical analysis. On the one hand, no one before or since has been more certain than was Strong that Americans of his generation were destined to "occupy the Gibraltar of the ages which commands the world's future." Greatly influenced by the popular Social-Darwinian doctrine of "survival of the fittest," Strong sought to give scientific respectability to the widespread (white) American Protestant belief that "the extinction of inferior races before the advancing Anglo-Saxon" was inevitable.[8]

On the other hand, Strong was aware of the industrial revolution taking place in the United States and the world. He believed that it presented a grave crisis to American Protestantism, but also a great opportunity. Had his book ended after

the early chapters which warned against the usual "perils" of
intemperance, sabbath-desecration, "Romanism," Mormonism and
general secularism, it probably would have made no unusual impact. But *Our Country* went beyond the traditional nineteenth
century moral concerns to what was becoming known in some Protestant circles as "the social question." With its concern for
social justice and reconstruction as a religious responsibility,
the book played an important role in the rise of the social
gospel.

Our Country brought a new social urgency to the attention
of evangelistic-minded Protestants and thereby helped undergird
the social gospel with their crusading spirit. The real significance of Strong's book, in fact, is the way in which it set
American Protestant home missions in the context of the social
gospel and the world revolutionary forces with which the social
gospel dealt--a development which in 1914 H. P. Douglas called
the "social redirection" of home missions.[9]

Josiah Strong recognized both the crisis and the opportunity inherent in America's new urban-industrial frontier. If
there were new "perils" to be overcome, there was also great
Christian potential in a powerful industrial nation. America
was fast becoming the economic power of the world in agriculture,
natural resources, inventive genius, and industrial development--
in sheer wealth. "Has not God given us this matchless power that
it may be applied to doing [his] matchless work?" asked Strong.[10]

If so, then the American money power had to be Christianized, which meant not only a new emphasis on stewardship but the
most constructive use of every aspect of America's wealth and
power for the world's betterment.

Convinced that "the world is to be Christianized and
civilized," Strong believed that "it is fully in the hands of
the Christians of the United States, during the next ten or fifteen years, to hasten or retard the coming of Christ's kingdom in
the world by hundreds, and perhaps thousands of years." They
could hasten that day by Christianizing and civilizing their
own land. "During this crisis," Strong declared, "Christian
work is unspeakably more important in the United States than
anywhere else in the world."[11] His book apparently was read and
believed, for never were American Protestants more busy doing
"Christian work" than during the decades following the publication of *Our Country*.

Home mission crusading continued to be a great unifying force in American Protestantism during the progressive era. Progressivism itself has rightly been described as "a latter-day Protestant revival,"[12] for it was closely related to the American Protestant missionary impulse directed toward new social conditions. In 1889 the American branch of the Evangelical Alliance met in Boston and devoted its discussions to national needs and remedies; and in the years following, popular reformism was carried on by nearly all segments of Protestantism.[13] Even city revivalist Billy Sunday, who from pulpit and platform thundered a crude "old-fashioned" (nineteenth century) Gospel, directed his campaigns toward civic "clean-up" reforms.[14] The great body of American Protestants, moreover, identified with the nation-wide social gospel crusading of the Men and Religion Forward Movement. They had come to understand their home mission task in light of changing conditions of the day, as expressed in a speech delivered at the 1910 Buffalo Conference of the Movement:

> We are living literally in a matchless age, in
> an age utterly unlike any other; and the age
> that gives the world the wireless telegraph and
> the flying machine must also give the world an
> adequate interpretation and representation of
> Jesus Christ.[15]

American Protestants were trying hard to become what Josiah Strong had said they could and should become--"God's right arm in his battle with the world's ignorance and oppression and sin."[16]

Almost contemporaneous with Josiah Strong's summoning of American Protestants to their home mission task, a new chapter began in the history of American Protestant foreign missions in July of 1886 with the first meeting of what was to become the Student Volunteer Movement for Foreign Missions. For the next three decades this movement, formally organized in 1888 at the Northfield Conference, with remarkable enthusiasm enlisted some of the ablest American college students for missionary service throughout the world.[17]

Among the many outstanding persons associated with the Student Volunteer Movement, none became more influential in twentieth century American Protestantism than John R. Mott. Mott's life spanned nearly a century (1865-1955), from the Civil War to the post-Korean War period. Especially during the middle third of his life Mott was literally Protestant America's representative to the world, and also a representative of world Christianity to America. He was the ideal Christian statesman

of his day, taking a leadership role in many national and international religious movements and organizations. Mott, very much
aware of world events and conditions, was highly optimistic in
his hopes for the world's evangelization. Considered by some to
have been the foremost Protestant leader of the world, he embodied a style of progressive Protestantism, viewing critical
moments in history as a call for large religious programs.

The Student Volunteer Movement envisaged a large program
indeed. One of the most potent expressions of idealistic zeal
and optimism which appeared during the progressive era was the
Volunteers' motto, which Mott made the title of his great book--
The Evangelization of the World in This Generation. In this
book, written in 1900, Mott defined the motto and discussed from
several angles the real possibility of its fulfillment.[18]

The evangelization of the world in a single generation
was a bold plan, but men of Mott's mind in 1900 were inspired by
what they considered to be an unparalleled opportunity to carry
it off. Political changes in many nations were opening new doors
to missionaries, while developments in transportation and communication were making far-distant places accessible. Furthermore,
Protestantism had passed through "the great century" in missionary expansion[19] and showed no apparent signs of slowing down.
Mott, having studied Josiah Strong's book *Our Country*, knew that
American churches had the skills and knowledge, the personnel and
the wealth to evangelize the world. "Everything," concluded
Mott, "seems to be ready for a general and determined engagement
of the forces of Christendom for a world-wide proclamation of
the Gospel." There were great obstacles, of course; but Mott,
a product of traditional American Protestant mentality, believed
that "difficulties are not without their advantages, for they
are to call forth the best that is in Christians."[20]

Mott defined the American Protestant foreign mission task
in 1900, and during the next fifteen years he restated his message with greater clarity and urgency. To the great world
missionary conference in Edinburgh in 1910 he spoke optimistically of "the decisive hour of Christian missions":

> In the history of Christianity there has never
> been such a remarkable conjunction of oppor-
> tunities and crises on all the principal
> mission fields, and of favoring circumstances
> and possibilities on the home field.[21]

It was during the next four years, however, that Mott
came to realize how decisive the hour really was. In 1914 he

wrote his most prophetic and mature book, *The Present World Situation*. In this book the urgent summons surpassed all that came before, even Josiah Strong's call in 1885. Mott, who traveled extensively throughout the world, believed that during the years following the Edinburgh missionary conference there had developed an "openness and responsiveness in the non-Christian world."

> Where, after China, is there another nation of
> four hundred millions of people to turn from an
> ancient past and to swing out into the full stream
> of modern Christian civilization? Where after
> India is there another vast empire to be swept
> by the spirit of unrest and to be made peculiarly
> accessible to the reconstructive processes of
> Christianity? Where after Africa is there
> another continent for which Mohammedanism and
> Christianity can contend? Where after Turkey
> and the Nile Valley is there another keystone
> to the vast arch of the Mohammedan world, with
> seams of weakness, which make possible the dis-
> rupting of the whole structure?

Add to this the "shrinkage of the world" and other factors favorable to Christian missions; and, above all, consider the crusading zeal of American Protestants. Mott believed that the providential call of the moment was clear: "God sees that there are now on the earth those with whom He can trust a situation world-wide in its sweep." It was a time of "rising spiritual tide," Mott concluded, and "it is always wise to take advantage of a rising tide."[22]

Bringing American Protestantism into a successful confrontation with the non-Christian world meant incorporating the social gospel into foreign missions and extending it beyond American shores. Social activities had always been a part of Protestant foreign missions. Medical, educational, and agricultural missions, various social reforms, and other humanitarian works were common throughout the nineteenth century. After the turn of the century the expanding foreign missions enterprise kept pace with the progressive impulse at home by an increasing stress on the social aspect of missions.[23]

The full implications of the social gospel, however, reached beyond benevolence, humanitarianism, and even charitable social service to include the regeneration and reconstruction of the social order itself. This was a more practical goal for home missions than for foreign missions, since American Protestants could scarcely hope to mold the social structures of foreign lands to the degree that they could their own. Yet as

the United States became a world power, increasingly involved in
the extension of Western social-economic activity into non-
Christian lands, the social gospel became more relevant to
foreign missions.

According to Mott's analysis in 1914, the un-Christian
aspects of the impact of western civilization on the non-Christian
world had become a great hindrance to the success of foreign
missions. He mentions aggressive colonialism of western nations
and their ignoring of treaties with weaker states; their frequent
unscrupulous commercial exploiting of underdeveloped nations; the
corrupt lives of western traders and merchants, and departures
from normal ethical standards by tourists; the exportation of
western vices such as dope addiction, alcoholism, and illicit
houses; and finally the circulation of books containing the
atheistic or otherwise un-Christian philosophies of certain
western infidel authors (Huxley, Spencer, Nietzsche, Haeckel,
and Schopenhauer).[24] All of these forces worked together,
thought Mott, to make non-Christian peoples bitter toward western
civilization--including its Christian religion.

Mott strongly believed that Christianizing the impact of
western civilization on non-Christian nations was part of the
social task of foreign missions. As representatives of the
Christian elements in American life, missionaries were in a
position to propagate the social and cultural benefits of
Christianity to non-Christian peoples. This entailed on the one
hand an even more aggressive application of social Christianity
at home: for "no one," stated Mott, "can easily overstate the
power of the apologetic which a thoroughly Christianized America
would present and exercise in the non-Christian world."

> Only a Christianity powerful enough to dominate
> all our social, national and international life
> and relationships will finally commend itself
> to the peoples to whom we go.

On the other hand, it was the peculiar task of foreign
missions to carry that kind of Christianity to the world, which
entailed the Christianization of American foreign relations.
American civilization, claimed Mott, too often had been mis-
represented in its contacts with other nations by the expression
of its worst elements. Therefore American Christians must "see
that a Christian impression is made upon other lands by their
country."[25]

By the time *The Present World Situation* was published in
1914, a catastrophic war had broken out in Europe which, according

to Mott, "lent a peculiar timeliness and meaning" to his treatment of the subject of foreign missions. As the war developed,
Protestants were forced to re-think their conception of America's
proper role in international affairs as a Christian nation. They
had a strong tradition upon which to draw their conclusions,
though the dimensions of World War I would put all traditions to
an unprecedented test.

Wartime Mentality

American traditions had been weighed in 1898 during the
"little war" against Spain. Standard nineteenth century ideology
portrayed the United States as a special nation, providentially
chosen and equipped to beam the light of Christian democracy
before all peoples. Americans were responsible to exemplify and
promote peace in the world on the basis of freedom and justice,
economic fulfillment, and human brotherhood. A perfecting example
rather than active intervention in other nations' affairs was the
American ideal; but if intervention would appear to be the only
way to prevent injustice and oppression, how far could the passive
isolationist ideal be maintained? For Protestant churchmen the
problem implied the complex relationship between "Christianizing
America" (home missions) and carrying American Christianity into
the world (foreign missions).

In 1898 the United States' sense of trusteeship in the new
world of the Americas won the day as she took to guns against
Spain in the Caribbean. The majority of American Protestant
spokesmen embraced the venture, though they debated the nation's
responsibility toward peoples "liberated" by military victory.
If the American tradition basically had rejected wars of conquest
and acquisition of colonial territory, it was becoming clear
that the old isolationism was not a viable absolute in twentieth
century foreign policy. In the process, however, the Protestant
missionary impulse and patriotic wartime mentality increasingly
coalesced.[26]

Protestant leaders applauded the war for religious reasons. Their missionary concern and their nativist bent made them
interested, for example, in rooting out of the new world what
they believed to be despotic Roman Catholic vestiges of the old
world. American Protestants always had looked upon Roman
Catholicism in their midst as a foreign, tyrannical force to be
feared and opposed. It represented to them a grave threat to

10

American democratic freedom and to the home and foreign missionary
cause of their own churches. The war, therefore, was popularly
evaluated in idealistic, moral terms, with the United States pictured as the saviour of peoples enslaved under Spanish misrule
and Roman Catholic Authoritarianism. Victory apparently would
clear the way for expansion of American influence and of Protestant missions in Cuba, Puerto Rico, and the Philippines.

What in retrospect appears to have been largely political,
economic, and cultural imperialism, Protestant leaders celebrated
as a religious event. In his 1898 Thanksgiving Day sermon, for
example, Baptist social gospel leader, Walter Rauschenbusch, told
his Rochester congregation that during the war God and Americans
were on the same side, the people experiencing "a deep sense of
destiny, of a mission laid upon us by the Ruler of history."
Moreover, this popular evaluation of American accomplishment persisted long after the event. Typical of many Protestant spokesmen was Fred B. Smith, a noted interdenominational and Y.M.C.A.
leader, who wrote in 1913 that,"There was need for some power to
be raised up for the delivery of seven millions of people who were
in the vicious tyrannical grip of an unscrupulous system."[27]
The significance of their memory of national virtue in the Caribbean military adventure against Spain soon would become apparent
as Protestants faced the prospect of American involvement in a
European battlefield, especially since by 1913 an increasingly
popular peace movement had captured their imagination and reduced their crusading zeal.

The nearly century-old anti-imperialist American peace
movement, having joined in a strong minority protest against war
in 1898, flourished with the tide of progressivism. Its adher-
ents, increasing in number annually, took part in peace conferences at The Hague in 1899 and 1907. Inspired by the conviction
that world-wide Christian forces could affectively "mobilize for
a warless world," they likewise believed that America must promote
and extend her ideals in the world by being an example *par ex-
cellence* of a peaceful Christian nation. In 1914, therefore,
when the interfaith Church Peace Union was formed in America
through an endowment by Pittsburgh steelmaster Andrew Carnegie,
and when the World Alliance for International Friendship through
the churches first met in Constance, Germany (on August 1, the
very day World War I began), much of American Protestant thinking was geared optimistically to the practical goal of permanent
world peace.

When fighting broke out in Europe in 1914, many Americans were shocked and bewildered that modern European Christendom could degenerate to a state of such barbarism. The prevailing sentiment was that America ought to remain neutral and expand her role from that of silent example to that of an exemplary, disinterested arbitrator among belligerent nations. The United States, however, was not disinterested culturally or economically, due to long ties and commercial trade with Britain. Still, most American religious communities publicly supported the ideal of neutrality. They applauded President Wilson's attempts to act as an arbitrator in Europe, but as German-American relations deteriorated, the ideal of America remaining a peaceful onlooker became untenable. Angered by incessant German submarine attacks on American ships (which continued to supply Britain) and by reports of German atrocities in Belgium (which British propaganda effectively exaggerated), Americans became increasingly less neutral and emotionally more prepared for war.

Still the Church Peace Union continued its crusade, producing various kinds of literature, holding conferences and organizing local peace groups. But its members were divided over what action the United States should take as German aggression increased. In 1915 it issued a message to American churches calling for "moderation, persistence, faith, national righteousness, brotherhood, sympathy, and constant prayer for the nation and the nations." In 1916 it passed a resolution deploring increased American armament; but the subsequent train of events, culminating in the American declaration of war, caused a diversity of opinions and an ethical confusion which stifled further attempts by the Church Peace Union to formulate theological-ethical resolutions on the problem.

After Congress declared war, however, most advocates of the peace movement joined other Americans in whole hearted support of the nation's effort. The peace movement never had been dedicated primarily to pacifism and hence could support war with patriotic zeal in the cause of ultimate world peace. Peace was the end, not necessarily the means; and a peace crusade could be made compatible with a particular war. Accordingly the Church Peace Union redirected its crusading energy to promoting support for a post-war League of Nations and to "educating the people of the United States in the aims of this war," which were set in President Wilson's idealistic terms: to "make the world safe for democracy" and to "end all wars."[28]

Among Protestant-influenced Americans, at least, a general consensus regarding "the moral necessity of war" had emerged. According to theologically conservative John Henry Jowett of New York's Fifth Avenue Presbyterian Church, "there is an interest which has priority over peace, which . . . is the parent of all real peace." Speaking before the Interchurch Clerical Conference in New York in April of 1918, Jowett confirmed his colleagues' conviction that, "We are all lovers of peace, but we value righteousness, in a sense, as higher worth than quietness, and we esteem our honor as more precious than our peace."[29] A people accustomed to thinking of themselves as bearers of the world's peace thus would weigh their religious priorities and justify their belligerency.

There is nothing unusual about religious leaders giving moral and patriotic support to their nation during time of war: Englishmen, Frenchmen, Russians, Austrians-Hungarians, and Germans did the same during the Great War. However, American Protestants of diverse confessional traditions in every public way made extraordinary moral claims for the Allies and frightful judgments of "Kaiserism" and the "Huns." They converted a political-economic international war into a national religious crusade. Indeed the historical problem is not to prove but to explain the rabid wartime nationalism of American Protestants.[30]

One large factor was the increasing extent to which the nineteenth century Protestant missionary impulse had flirted with notions of American manifest destiny, reaching a near merger by the turn of the century--the very years when the United States was becoming conscious of its increasing world power. This allowed Protestants idealistically to interpret America's participation in an international war as a religious obligation to repress evil abroad and to promote American value and ideals in the world.

Wholehearted endorsement by Protestant leaders of America's claim to magnanimity in entering World War I crossed nearly all theological and confessional barriers. Beneath their differences they shared with Americans from nearly all schools of thought a national experience involving a romantically cultured civic religiosity which endowed "America the beautiful" with a sacred conscience and an eternal soul. The nineteenth century amalgamation of Protestantism with American national ideology and commitment conditioned American Protestants to feel peculiarly threatened religiously when the security of national values and

ideals became challenged by war. On just such occasions the
Battle Hymn of the Republic called the churches to arms, and
Christians compared their dying "to make men free" with Christ's
death "to make men holy."

The national decision to take up arms in World War I,
therefore, was a traumatic cultural-religious experience for the
American people, and Protestants interpreted the action in transcendent terms. The United States, they thought, had tried to
stay out of the barbaric European conflict, but old world problems persisted in spilling over into the new world. The war
came to America from without, from causes for which Americans
felt little responsibility. As the nation was drawn into battle,
Protestants became convinced that the European skirmish had
developed into a decisive show-down between the forces of good
and evil. Once it became apparent to them that America must
fight, they read the heavenly signs, recognized the enemy of their
nation and of their God, and with great self-assurance set themselves to the task providentially thrust upon them. Walter Laidlaw, an American delegate to the 1914 peace conference in Constance, summarized the widespread belief among Protestant Americans in 1918: "the war was a crusade to save Christian civilization."[31]

Fighting a war to *save* Christian civilization was not quite
the same as the previous war in the Caribbean to *extend* it, even
though Americans claimed that their motive in entering the World
War was to pave the way for world democracy. While the ideals at
stake may have been similar in the minds of Americans, the German
army appeared to be--and indeed it was--a greater threat to the
preservation of those ideals at home than Spain had been. Consequently, Americans sanctified the First World War more avidly
than they had the war with Spain, and many clergymen joined the
ranks of the hysterical.

Conservatives and liberals alike admitted little or no
doubt that God was helping to fight their battle, since to them
"democratic" America represented the army of Christ and "autocratic" Germany the army of the devil. For fundamentalist revival
preacher, Billy Sunday, whose words were heard with great respect
in many Protestant circles, it was "Hell against Heaven," with
Germany representing the former by having "turned from Christ to
Krupp and from the Cross of Calvary to the Iron Cross." Sunday's
wartime revivals were saturated with religious patriotism, well
described in a conservative Baptist publication shortly after

America had entered the war:

> On Sunday afternoon, coming like a flash and
> fitting gloriously into an impassioned perora-
> tion, Mr. Sunday called upon the vast audience
> to stand up, raise their right hand and pledge
> loyalty to God, to country, to the flag and to
> Jesus Christ. More than 20,000 people jumped
> to their feet, and there were no slackers.[32]

Commanding more sophisticated language than Sunday's but expressing a similar confidence in American wartime virtue was Lyman
Abbott, who popularized liberal religion from his Plymouth Congregational Church pulpit in Brooklyn. "A nation is made
Christian," preached Abbott, "by the spirit of love, service,
and sacrifice. When did a nation ever show so much of the spirit
of love, service, and sacrifice as the American Nation does today."[33]

Still, not all preachers presented arms in the same mood.
Many German-Americans, for example, were not convinced of the
total superiority of American culture over German. One of the
most striking examples of a second-generation German-American
finding little in the war for which to crusade was Walter Rauschenbusch, widely acclaimed spokesman of the social gospel who
in April of 1917 (the same month that America entered the war)
delivered the Nathaniel W. Taylor Lectures before the Annual
Convocation of the Yale School of Religion. Rauschenbusch did
not glorify an all-out war against Germany as he had the comparatively minor scuffle with Catholic Spain in 1898. Though he
recognized the necessity of an allied victory, he entertained no
illusion that such a victory would eliminate evil from the world.
There could be no such "smooth road" to paradise. The Great War
was a catastrophe, and no more or less than a "catastrophic stage
in the coming of the Kingdom of God." Generations would feel its
effects, and the effects of war would prove to be constructive
only if they included "the social repentence of nations" as "the
foundation for a new beginning."[34] Most social gospelers had
adjusted their hopes for the Kingdom of God on earth to the glar-
ing reality of war, many finally concluding that Germany was a
last great obstacle to the progress of human society. But
Rauschenbusch, who died in 1918, was not able to conform his
thinking to the war being waged as a Christian crusade, for which
lack of patriotic zeal he received the hostility of many of his
former friends and followers.

By the time Rauschenbusch's lectures were published, few
who had heard them at Yale were sympathetic to his wartime

feelings. Whereas the Yale faculty desired not to settle for
rabid patriotism--nor did they wholly agree among themselves--
their differences were mainly variations on a religio-patriotic
theme.[35] Liberal theologian Douglas Clyde Macintosh, for example,
offering one of the more objective interpretations of the war,
nevertheless concluded that America was "fighting on the side of
God, as well as for the true well-being of humanity." But he
wanted nothing to do with self-righteous, militant nationalism.
He found especially vulgar the abundance of patriotic-religious
statements couched in military terminology and conceptions, often
undergirded by some crude, violent Old Testament passage which
transformed Christian ethics into a "warfare theory of morals."[36]
That theory found all words of compromise anathema in the single
warfare between good and evil powers; for victory would come, many
thought, only if Americans stood fast on moral lines and used
whatever means were available to accomplish their ends.

Yale Divinity School's Dean, Charles R. Brown, reflected
this militant response, though like his colleague Macintosh, he
wished to avoid patriotic extremes. After noting that Americans
"are a peace-loving people," Brown said with "no apology . . . as
a Christian minister" that "the conscience of the country must
become militant. The moral sense of our nation must be arrayed
against the gigantic system of barbarism which is now parading
as the Imperial Government of Germany." No apologies were necessary because the war had proved to be a "clear cut, definite,
moral issue." Brown's only concern was whether or not America
"in this great issue" would prove good enough to accomplish the
purpose for which . . . it is called of God."[37]

Believing with Brown that America had been "called of God"
to battle, Protestant leaders commonly identified the nation's
"cause" with Christ's "great commission" to take the Gospel into
all the world ("Go Ye therefore, and teach all nations." Mt.
28:19). Even Robert E. Speer, revered Presbyterian leader in
foreign missions, believed that since their aims were the same,
"the war was the greatest proclamation of foreign missions which
we have ever heard."[38] These words of one of the more theologically conservative representatives of the Reformed Tradition in
America suggests the degree to which popular Protestantism had
become confused with militaristic national consciousness as the
United States fought in World War I.

The militant, moral certainty of wartime American Protestantism fit in well with the progressive, crusading spirit of the

early twentieth century. Christians were supremely confident that
with the help of God, for which they prayed and which they believed
they deserved, they could accomplish their goals. In striking contrast with the notion of "impossible possibility" which guided the
sober "crisis theology" of Reinhold Niebuhr during World War II
was John R. Mott's belief in the "possible impossible" as the
Christian standard.[39] This too was crisis theology. It was a
theological thrust of sorts in which churchmen of Mott's missionary conditioning expected to meet and overcome crises by means of
Christian democratic ideals set in organized motion through
divinely-guided energy.

The World War I experience, during which the churches were
engaged in manifold ministries to the armed forces and the civilian
population, intensified an already strong popular American Protestant conception of Christianity as essentially life and work,
spiritual experience and moral living. What really mattered,
religious leaders thought, was marshalling an unashamedly patriotic wartime emotion and delineating common ideals and ethical
principles upon which Christians of diverse theological tendencies
could work together and get things done with business-like
efficiency. This would provide a policy of action for the churches
which could achieve the most practical good during a period of
international crisis.

By the time World War I began, nearly all major denominations had formulated "social policies" which were very similar
in tone and content. Most of them resembled the "Social Creed
of the Churches" set forth in 1908 by the Federal Council of the
Churches of Christ in America, which represented thirty denominations.[40] Recent scholarship suggests that during the war the
Federal Council tried to maintain a responsible Christian social
policy which would be consistent with its pre-war social positions. It labored toward the extension of the Church's united
ministry in the world, called for correction of abuses in the
social and industrial order, furthered international relations
of the churches, and called for prayers of penitence and forgive-
ness on both sides of the battle.[41]

The Federal Council's wartime policy of action helped to
placate the Christian conscience by providing a service of
practical moral support of a "just cause." For Christians who
never saw the battlefield, there were plenty of opportunities
at home to contribute their time and energy, their money and
prayers to the nation's military effort. The American Protestant

mind was thus conformed to war. It remains to be seen how Protestant institutions were geared to the war's demands.

Institutional Dynamics

The activism and practical-mindedness of American Protestants during the quarter-century preceding World War I were matched by their genius for organization, which together produced many new movements for a host of causes and objectives. During the progressive era, which witnessed the increasing importance of science and business, churchmen successfully channeled their missionary passion and their crusading spirit into functionally efficient institutions. Moreover, as Protestants sought to increase the efficiency of their religion, they looked increasingly toward cooperative union.

Cooperative union long had been a common pattern of American Protestant institutions. Early in the nineteenth century the tension between denominational structures and the need for united Protestant action was partly overcome by means of nondenominational, extra-ecclesiastical voluntary societies whereby churchmen of different denominations joined together for missionary, humanitarian, and reform objectives. More comprehensive than other voluntary associations was the American branch of the Evangelical Alliance, organized in 1867. The Alliance not only intended to bring about a union of Protestant work in America, but it represented an international fellowship of Evangelicals on a common doctrinal platform. The American branch progressed steadily until the turn of the century, when its doctrinal restrictions conflicted with the increasingly non-theological temper of American Protestants. Furthermore, the Alliance had never attempted to reach churches through official denominational bodies, which limited its influence among denominationally-minded churchmen (as all voluntary societies were limited). The turning point in the Alliance's popular success can be traced to its 1893 conference at the Chicago World's Fair, when speeches by President McCosh of Princeton, by President Hyde of Bowdoin, and especially by the aged Philip Schaff called for increased development of federative union within American Protestantism. [42] They voiced the sentiment of many who felt that Protestant unity must become ecclesiastically oriented.

In 1893 a significant step was taken in Protestant unity with the first meeting of the Foreign Missions Conference of

North America. This was the first consultative interdenominational conference of foreign mission boards and societies representing the United States and Canada. During the next twenty
years the formation of several other agencies added strength to
the federative movement in American Protestantism: the Home
Missions Council, the Council of Women for Home Missions, the
Federation of Women's Boards of Foreign Missions, the Council
of Church Boards of Education, the Sunday School Council. Most
significant of all was the organization in 1908 of the Federal
Council of the Churches of Christ in America as an interdenominational or interchurch federation comprehensive of all church
activity, functionally the twentieth century successor to the
Evangelical Alliance. These federative agencies, made up of
"official" representatives from denominational bodies, forecast
a new day in American Protestant cooperative union; but they
could not institutionalize satisfactorily the crusading spirit of
the Progressive era.

There were four distinct "movements" prior to World War I
which did institutionalize progressive dynamics within American
Protestantism: the Student Volunteer Movement, the Missionary
Education Movement, the Laymen's Missionary Movement, and the Men
and Religion Forward Movement. These movements most completely
expressed the world missionary impulse, the complex nondenominational structure geared for quick action, and the promotional
techniques of crusading American Protestantism during the three
decades preceding World War I.

The Student Volunteer Movement promoted cooperation and
unity among American Protestant missionary forces. Although
directed specifically to college and university students, its
influence extended far beyond the campus. Moreover, the birth
and development of the Movement linked nineteenth century revival-
istic evangelism with the new kind of campaigns common in the
early twentieth century. The Movement was born in a July, 1886,
gathering of 251 undergraduates to consider foreign missions,
led by city evangelist Dwight L. Moody at his school, Mount
Hermon, in Massachusetts. The Conference soon produced a group
of twenty-one students meeting "to pray that the spirit of missions might pervade the conference." By the end of the conference, this group of "volunteers" had grown to a massive prayer
meeting of one hundred, all declaring that "it is my purpose, if
God permit, to become a foreign missionary." By the time of the
organization of the Student Volunteer Movement in 1888, two of

its advocates, Robert P. Wilder and John N. Forman, had toured
167 schools and secured volunteer declarations from twenty-two
hundred students.[43]

The purpose of the Student Volunteer Movement was to enlist students to be sent out by existing denominational mission
boards. It formed no competitive missionary agency, but operated
solely for the benefit of existing church agencies, yet undenomi-
nationally--without official ecclesiastical control. The movement grew tremendously, soon becoming international in scope,
enlisting hundreds of missionaries, stimulating popular study of
foreign missions, planting missionary libraries, publishing
missions text books, and helping to increase financial giving
to missions. Most important was the manner in which the Movement captured the crusading spirit of the day in large mass-
meetings of students and directed it into concrete missionary
channels. The quadrennial conventions "drew students from more
institutions of higher learning in the United States and Canada
than any other gatherings for any purpose, secular or religious."[44]
Moreover, it created a new generation of fervently committed Protestant leaders of whom John R. Mott was only the best known.

Similar to the Student Volunteer Movement, but more
denominationally controlled, was The Missionary Education Movement.[45] Founded in 1902 as The Young People's Missionary Education Movement, this organization purposed to educate and enlist
young people outside of colleges and universities. In 1911
"Young People's" was dropped from its name, while the Movement's
appeal and scope were enlarged to include adults and to deal with
home as well as foreign missions. It published many study books
and other literature and held educational and inspirational
conferences regularly.

The real prototype of large nondenominational movements
during the progressive era in America, however, was the Laymen's
Missionary Movement, a product of Student Volunteer enthusiasm
for missions. The Laymen's Movement was organized in 1906 by a
meeting in New York's Fifth Avenue Presbyterian Church of seventy-
five laymen on the occasion of an interdenominational gathering
to commemorate the one-hundredth anniversary of the beginning
of the organized foreign missions movement of North America.
The original inspiration came to one John B. Sleman, who had
attended the quadrennial convention of the Student Volunteer
Movement in Nashville, Tennessee, early in 1906. Sleman became
deeply moved by the inability of mission boards to support

financially the increasing number of students desiring to become missionaries. He thus conceived of a plan to organize laymen for the purpose of raising money for the boards.[46]

The Laymen's Missionary Movement, which became a "clearing house" of information about denominational foreign missionary work, was an almost instant success. It was a spontaneous movement, quickly developed and highly organized, geared to reach high goals quickly. As a missionary movement of laymen organizing into a promoting agency to facilitate work already under way, the Movement introduced a new kind of American Protestant pattern of high-pressure, systematic financial campaigning.

Gaius Glenn Atkins has stated correctly that the Laymen's Missionary Movement standardized large-scale campaign organization and technique: "a central committee (chosen partly for the prestige of the names), an inner executive group, a budget, publicity . . . literature, selected speakers . . . local organization across the continent, a schedule of dates . . . an inaugural meeting in a strategic city."[47] This propaganda method was structured into large city conferences, lasting three or four days with great attendance and commanding the attention of the whole community. Conferences began with large "crusade dinners" addressed by notable men from all fields, including politicians Roosevelt, Taft, and Wilson.

> Largest halls were filled and pulpits through the land were made available. Business and industrial hours were shortened so that more men might attend the sessions. Boards of Trade, Chambers of Commerce, and luncheon clubs called special meetings to hear representatives of the movement. Universities, colleges, and high schools received speakers. Breakfasts, luncheons, and dinners were utilized to reach special groups. The secular press gave considerable space to the campaign.[48]

The enthusiasm generated by these sedate but highly organized descendants of the nineteenth century camp meeings and city revivals was expected to cause increased financial giving through regular denominational channels, and positive results were forthcoming. In addition to special campaigns, the Laymen's Missionary Movement greatly advanced the recently developed "every member canvass" for financial giving and made it a regular church program. In this way the Laymen's Missionary Movement combined business methods with crusading religion, and helped make local church finances more efficient.

During the first decade of the twentieth century, Protestant crusades in America became even more efficient and complex, reaching a certain climax in the Men and Religion Forward Movement. Here organized mass emotion reached a new height, described by Mott as loving God with "our nervous energy." Twenty years later Gaius Glenn Atkins judged the movement to have been "by far the most considerable joint enterprise the religious forces of the nation had ever undertaken . . . a statesmanlike conception effectively organized, brilliantly advertised, and carried through to the finish."[49]

The original vision of the movement came to Harry W. Arnold, a recent graduate of Otterbein University in Ohio who went to work in Maine for the International Committee of the Y.M.C.A. Arnold helped to federate organized Christian men's work in Maine, culminating in 1907 in a Portland convention which turned into an evangelistic rally. After this success, plans were laid for a city-wide campaign in Cleveland, Ohio, in November of 1909. Led by Fred B. Smith and Clarence A. Barbour of the Y.M.C.A., over fifty meetings reaching twelve thousand men and boys were held in Cleveland churches, Y.M.C.A.'s, schools, and factories. The time seemed to be "ripe for some great movement which should enlist all Protestantism."[50]

In this state of mind, 274 men from seventy-one cities representing the Y.M.C.A., various denominational church brotherhoods, and the International Sunday-School Association met in Buffalo on May 18, 1910, to plan a great nation-wide evangelistic movement. To the delegates such a movement seemed providential, "in harmony with the eternal currents and with the leadership of the Divine Spirit," thus calling for "a religious campaign for the men and boys of America, upon a magnitude and with a comprehensiveness of ideal never attempted on this continent or on any other continent,"

> a program big enough, masterful enough, stalwart
> enough, comprehensive enough, far-reaching enough,
> to fit into the superb greatness of Jesus Christ,
> to fit into the marvelous wonders of this century,
> to appeal to the biggest man alive in this age of
> intellectual and commercial giants . . . . The
> greatest program that the Christian Church has
> ever considered [ushering] in a new epoch in
> Christian history.[51]

The Men and Religion Forward Movement, lasting officially from October, 1911, through April, 1912, reached 1,492,646 persons in sixty towns, through 7,062 meetings and 6,349 personal interviews. Campaigns followed the pattern set by the Laymen's Missionary Movement, only on a grander scale. In the new

22

Movement business and religion became partners in operation:
"the composite of those forces which have produced cooperation
in business and philanthropy, progressivism in politics, and
efficiency in all administration." After weeks of preparation
in each city, national leaders in various fields of religion were
brought in for eight days to act as a team of experts, meeting
with local men in planning "Institutes." After each campaign
came a follow-up period ending in a "conservation day." While
"headquarters in the various centers swarmed with men and hummed
nervously with big business," however, operations were church-
oriented and run by local church leaders. Furthermore, the
movement never developed into a permanent organization but served
only "as a tonic" for existing institutions.[52]

If the Men and Religion Forward Movement was "severely
practical in its scope," it was also comprehensive of all religious concerns. In addition to utilizing periodicals published
by other non-denominational organizations, it produced a great
amount of its own literature covering many subjects.[53] Work
departments were formed including Boys' Work, Bible Study,
Evangelism, Community Extension, Missions, and most important,
Social Service.

The great thrust of the Movement, which "rallied the
audiences and brought men under conviction of dereliction," was
its social message. From the earliest stage of planning social
problems were a prominent concern, and in all subsequent meetings
"emphasis was put as never before upon the social service of the
church." Rauschenbusch thought that "the movement has probably
done more than any other single agency to lodge the social gospel
in the common mind of the church;" and Washington Gladden, father
of all social gospelers, declared with great emotion: "I have
seen come to pass in six months what I had despaired of seeing
come in my lifetime--the nation-wide preaching of the Gospel as
a great social message." The key social leaders of the Movement,
however, were Graham Taylor, President of the Chicago School of
Civics and Philanthropy, who provided intellectual acumen, and
Presbyterian Charles Stelzle who acted as a kind of social gospel
administrator. They built a social program upon a scientific
survey of the sociological and religious conditions of seventy
cities. Yet the Movement remained intensely evangelistic, combining the emotion common at Billy Sunday revivals with modern
methods of social organization.[54]

The crowning glory of the Men and Religion Forward Movement, however, was its world vision which brought foreign missions into distinctly social gospel concerns. After the official close of the Movement at a Christian Conservation Congress in New York, April 19-25, 1912,[55] plans were made for a world tour by a Men and Religion team. The team, made up of seven men led by Fred B. Smith, was convinced of being God's special messenger from America to the world. The men left San Francisco in January of 1913 and carried the Men and Religion campaign to Honolulu, Japan, China, the Philippine Islands, Australia, South Africa, the European Continent, and London, returning home six months later. Everywhere they preached on social issues, calling for legislation in labor and housing and other areas needing reform. At Melbourne, Australia, Christians noted "the wedding ceremony of Evangelism and the social service message which the Men and Religion Movement was performing." Fred B. Smith, amazed at "the world-wide influence" of the Movement, concluded that "what takes place religiously in North America becomes immediately of world information and interest."[56] The historian can at least agree that, prior to World War I, the Men and Religion Forward Movement marked the peak of crusading American Protestantism reaching out to the far corners of the world.

The world at war, however, presented a new challenge. American Protestants had faced the twentieth century determined to spread their faith throughout their homeland and the world. The war with Spain made them more aware of their world role as a nation and as churches, while new movements toward Christian ecumenicity (world-wide unity) were increasing their world contacts. The World War, therefore, did not initiate but simply increased American Protestant world-awareness. However, by disrupting plans for international Christian gatherings and restricting foreign missions, the war blocked American Protestant world contacts while forcing churchmen to concentrate on their institutional development at home. National self-awareness was as much intensified by the war as was international awareness.

One of the necessities of modern warfare made apparent in 1914-1918 was complete national mobilization, including civilians and religious institutions. Doubtless the impact of this reality was partly responsible for the literal militarization of churches and churchmen. With great patriotic gusto Protestants went so far as to convert their churches into military recruitment centers, into promotion agencies selling Liberty Bonds, and into instruments of Government propaganda.

Aside from the militaristic emotion which swept religious
America during the war, as significant for subsequent American
church history was the degree to which the war emergency brought
about a consolidation of religious institutions and enabled
churches to unite for cooperative action. The spirit of joining
forces in a great crusade was not new; thirty years of organized
religious campaigning had paved the way for wartime methods. Yet
the number of religious agencies arising for various purposes
during the war is amazing.[57] Even more remarkable is the degree
to which they were consolidated into one great machine. In the
process the Federal Council of Churches emerged as the most useful and enduring unitive force in American Protestantism.

As denominations, interdenominational and non-denominational
agencies began to organize special wartime commissions, the Federal Council took the initiative to coordinate their work by forming on September 20, 1917, a General War-Time Commission of the
Churches, with Robert E. Speer as Chairman and William Adams Brown
as General Secretary. Closely related to permanent Federal Council
Commissions, and cooperating with both the National Catholic War
Council and the Jewish Welfare Board, the General War-Time Commission enabled diverse religious groups to work closely and efficiently with Government wartime programs.[58] Together they enlisted soldiers, chaplains and other war-workers; together they raised
money and provided for the moral welfare of workers in communities
engaged in the manufacture of munitions and other vital products.
"Serving as a clearing house of information, a coordinating agency
and, when desired, as a means of joint administration and common
expressing," therefore, "the General War-Time Commission of the
Churches enabled the churches to present a united front in facing
new problems and responsibilities."[59]

In adjusting to the institutional demands of war, the
churches also transferred their pre-war patterns to the new
situation. For example, the National Committee on the Churches
and the Moral Aims of the War utilized methods of pre-war religious crusades in carrying on an educational propaganda campaign,
"interpreting the moral aims of the war to the people of the
United States, and arousing their consciences to the point where
the contest could be concluded in a decided victory for righteousness." The Committee rapidly organized an army of "minute men"
who traversed the nation addressing mass meetings in and out of
churches.[60] Likewise, the use of extensive surveys to determine

and meet social and religious needs in local communities was
greatly developed during the war by the Joint Committee on War
Production Communities.[61]

One of the most remarkable wartime achievements by the
civilian population, however, was the raising of vast sums of
money for war purposes and for relief at home and abroad through
many religious and secular agencies. The Red Cross alone, for
example, increased its assets from two hundred thousand dollars
at the start of the war to a total intake of four hundred million
dollars by the war's end. In 1917 the Y.M.C.A. asked the public
for thirty-five million dollars, and received over fifty million
dollars. It was estimated that between three hundred and three
hundred fifty million dollars were contributed in 1917 alone for
philanthropic objects connected with the war, which was "ten times
as much as the United States had ever given before in any one year
for similar purposes." Most striking, however, was the interfaith
United War Work Campaign launched November 11, 1918 (Armistice
Day) by the National Catholic War Council and the Jewish Welfare
Board (counter-parts of the General War-Time Commission of the
Churches), plus the Y.M.C.A. and the Y.W.C.A., the American
Library Association, the War Camps Community Service, and the
Salvation Army. The $175,500,000 secured by this campaign may
well have been, by a single endeavor, "the largest amount of
money ever offered voluntarily in the history of the world."
Most of these wartime financial drives were handled in the fashion
already proved successful by the Laymen's Missionary Movement,
relying on large-scale, highly organized, businesslike
approaches.[62]

American Protestants were learning from the war experience
how rapidly and efficiently their divided denominational and
interdenominational forces could be organized into a single campaigning unit to raise money, propagandize the masses, and enlist personnel during a great emergency for a righteous cause.

The churches thus became militarized along with American
society as a whole as the war for American ideals became a war
for religious truths. The war to end all wars had become something of a religious battle with millennial dimensions, a crusade
for the salvation of the world. "Patriotic loyalty and Christian
devotion," for immeasurable numbers of American people, became
"indistinguishable twins."[63] Wartime prophetic voices reminding
Americans that their nation, as all nations, might be judged for

its mixed motives in the muddy waters of human warfare, were extremely scarce. American nationalism of a Protestant flavor had come dangerously close to becoming nation-worship, as church-men later were to recognize with anguish and a yearning for some kind of religious normalcy.

Military warfare, however, could not be the final means of Christianizing the world. American Protestants, even at the height of their wartime fervor, never regarded war as the ideal method of evangelism. They continued to believe that only the church contained the ultimate spiritual power capable of preserv-ing world peace and evangelizing the nations. Therefore the churches, their leaders thought, were divinely obligated to com-plete the battle which the allied armies had so gloriously begun in battle. For this task, a program and a crusade surpassing all previous dreams would be necessary, and the military victory left American Protestants with little doubt that the church likewise would be victorious.

NOTES TO CHAPTER I

1. *The Christian Crusade for World Democracy* (New York, 1918), pp. 11, 30.

2. *Religion In Our Times* (New York, 1932), p. 156.

3. Paul A. Carter, *The Spiritual Crisis of the Gilded Age* (DeKalb, Ill., 1971).

4. "Need of an Enthusiasm for Humanity on the Part of the Churches," *National Needs and Remedies* (New York, 1890), p. 301.

5. Samuel Harris, *The Kingdom of Christ on Earth* (Andover, Mass., 1874), p. 255.

6. The first edition of *Our Country* sold 130,000 copies, was published (in part) in newspapers in the United States, Canada, London, and Glasgow, was translated into at least one foreign language with plans for translating it into others. References that follow are from the second (1891) edition of *Our Country: Its Possible Future and Its Present Crisis*, ed. Jurgen Herbst (Cambridge, Mass., 1963). The 1891 edition is especially useful because it was slightly revised according to the important 1890 census.

7. *Ibid.*, p. 13.

8. *Ibid.*, pp. 215, 218.

9. H. P. Douglas, *The New Home Missions, an Account of their Social Redirection* (New York, 1914).

10. *Our Country*, p. 220.

11. *Ibid.*, pp. 26, 218, 253.

12. Richard Hofstadter, *The Age of Reform from Bryan to F.D.R.* (New York, 1955), p. 152. See also S. P. Hays, *The Response to Industrialism* (Chicago, 1957), p. 93, where progressivism is described as "a veritable Protestant religious crusade."

13. See the discussions of the General Christian Conference held in Boston, Mass., Dec. 4-6, 1889, in *National Needs and Remedies* (New York, 1890).

14. William G. McLoughlin, Jr., *Billy Sunday Was His Real Name* (Chicago, 1955), p. 228.

15. F. L. Thompson, "Men and Religion: The Programs," *Men and Religion* (New York, 1911), p. 3.

16. *Our Country*, p. 253.

17. John R. Mott, *Five Decades and a Forward View* (New York, 1939), pp. 1-29, is an account of the organization and development of the Student Volunteer Movement by one who participated in it.

18. The classic statement is *The Evangelization of the World in This Generation*, pp. 1-16. See also *Five Decades and a Forward View*, pp. 23-24.

19. Kenneth Scott Latourette devoted three of his seven volumes *History of the Expansion of Christianity* (New York, 1937-1945) to "The Great Century," 1800-1914.

20. Mott quoted Strong in *The Evangelization of the World in This Generation*, p. 118. See also pp. 50, 131.

21. Mott, *The Decisive Hour of Christian Missions* (London, 1910), p. viii.

22. *The Present World Situation*, pp. 4-5, 15, 19-55.

23. There appeared during the period several books on the subject by qualified spokesmen. In 1908, for example, Arthur Judson Brown, an outstanding leader in interdenominational foreign missions, wrote *The Why and How of Foreign Missions* (New York, 1908). Four years later Alva W. Taylor, Professor of Social Service and Christian Missions in the Bible College of Missouri, published *The Social Work of Christian Missions* (Cincinnati, 1912). See also the speeches included in the *Report of the Proceedings of the Conference on Cooperation and Promotion of Unity in Foreign Missionary Work, January 12-13, 1914* (New York, 1914).

24. *The Present World Situation*, pp. 102-121.

25. *Ibid.*, pp. 121-123, 148.

26. According to Sydney E. Ahlstrom, "Never have patriotism, imperialism, and the religion of American Protestants stood in such fervent coalescence as during the McKinley-Roosevelt era." *A Religious History of the American People* (New Haven, Conn., 1972), p. 880. On the Protestant response to the war, see Winthrop S. Hudson, "Protestant Clergy Debate the Nation's Vocation, 1898-1899," *Church History*, 42 (March, 1973).

27. Rauschenbusch's entire sermon was published in the Rochester *Post Express*, November 25, 1898. Fred B.

Smith's words are found in *Extracts of Letters from Mr. Fred B. Smith Relating to the World Tour of the Men and Religion Forward Team* (n.p., 1913), p. 77.

28. On the Church Peace Union and the World Alliance for International Friendship through the churches, by a participant, see Charles S. MacFarland, *Pioneers for Peace Through Religion* (New York, 1946), especially pp. 17-23, 33-41, 46-56.

29. Portions of Jowett's speech quoted by Walter Laidlaw, ed., *The Moral Aims of the War* (New York, 1918), pp. 13-14. The Interchurch Clerical Conference, of which Laidlaw was organizing chairman, was promoted by the National Committee on the Churches and the Moral Aims of the War, representing jointly the Church Peace Union and the League to Enforce Peace.

30. Ray Abrams, *Preachers Present Arms* (New York, 1933), documents the public hyperpatriotism of American Protestant leaders during World War I.

31. Laidlaw, Executive Secretary of the New York Federation of Churches, was arrested when fighting broke out and held prisoner for several weeks in Germany. He edited *The Moral Aims of the War*, *op. cit.*, now a valuable collection of Protestant interpretations of the war.

32. *Watchman-Examiner*, April 19, 1917, p. 497. Sunday is quoted in William G. McLoughlin, *Billy Sunday Was His Real Name*, p. 258.

33. Lyman Abbott, *The Twentieth Century Crusade* (New York, 1918), pp. 56, 101.

34. The Taylor lectures by Rauschenbusch were entitled *A Theology for the Social Gospel* (New York, 1917)--an intellectual landmark in the American Protestant social gospel movement.

35. For interpretations of the war by Yale faculty members see Elias Hershey Sneath, ed., *Religion and the War, by Members of the Faculty of the School of Religion, Yale University* (New Haven, 1918).

36. "God and History," *ibid.*, pp. 23, 30.

37. See Brown's address in Laidlaw, *op. cit.*, pp. 62-73.

38. Robert E. Speer, *The New Opportunity of the Church* (New York, 1919), p. 89.

39. Niebuhr, *The Children of Light and the Children of Darkness* (New York, 1944), p. 187; and Mott, *The Present World Situation*, p. 171.

30

40.   See C. H. Hopkins, *The Rise of the Social Gospel in
       American Protestantism 1865-1915* (New Haven, 1940).

41.   John Franklin Piper, "The Social Policy of the Federal
       Council of the Churches of Christ in America During World
       War I," (Ph.D. dissertation, Duke University, 1965).
       Piper describes the Federal Council as having made a real-
       istic assessment of America's role in the war and of the
       Christian's responsibility in that role. It accepted the
       war but without enthusiasm. However, if Federal Council
       leaders had doubts about the purity of America's cause,
       they rarely expressed them publicly.

42.   Shaff's famous address, "The Reunion of Christendom," is
       discussed in Elias B. Sanford, *Origin and History of the
       Federal Council of the Churches of Christ in America*
       (Hartford, 1916), pp. 95-97. For a recent account of the
       emerging federative movement in American Protestantism at
       the dawn of the twentieth century, see Samuel McCrea
       Cavert, *The American Churches in the Ecumenical Movement
       1900-1968* (New York, 1968), chapter one.

43.   Mott, *Five Decades and a Forward View*, pp. 3, 6, 22.

44.   Kenneth Scott Latourette, *The Christian World Mission in
       Our Day* (New York, 1954), p. 41. From 1899 to 1902, 780
       new missionaries sailed from North America; 1,000 sailed
       from 1903 to 1906; from 1907 to 1910 1,275 sailed; and
       1,466 sailed from 1911 to 1914. See Mott, *Five Decades
       and a Forward View*, p. 12.

45.   The missionary boards of the principal denominations
       founded the Movement, and denominational representatives
       formed the board of managers. Yet it was not properly an
       interboard federation, but a separate movement sponsored
       by various boards.

46.   See Mott, *Five Decades and a Forward View*, p. 32.

47.   *Religion In Our Times*, pp. 162-163.

48.   George A. Salstrand, *The Story of Stewardship in the
       United States of America* (Grand Rapids, Mich., 1956), p.
       50.

49.   *Religion In Our Times*, p. 160. Mott is quoted in "Men
       and Religion: The Cost," in *Men and Religion* (New York,
       1911), p. 18.

50.   Allyn K. Foster, "The Dream Come True," *Making Religion
       Efficient*, ed. Clarence A. Barbour (New York, 1912), p. 9.

51.   F. L. Thompson, "Men and Religion: The Program," *Men and
      Religion*, pp. 1-15.

52.   See Charles S. Macfarland, "The Men and Religion Forward
      Movement--Its Significance and Duration," *The Homiletic
      Review*, LXIV (Sept., 1912), p. 180; and Foster, "The
      Dream Come True," pp. 7-8, 21-22.

53.   Atkins, *Religion In Our Times*, pp. 162-163, discusses the
      Movement's literature.   Existing periodicals used included
      Foreign Mail and *The Student World* of the Y.M.C.A., *The
      Intercollegian* of the Student Volunteer Movement, *Men and
      Missions* of the Laymen's Missionary Movement, and the
      International Review of Missions of the Edinburgh Continua-
      tion Committee.   Barbour, *Making Religion Efficient*, pp.
      164-166.

54.   Charts showing the survey results appear in Barbour, *op.
      cit.*   See also Hopkins, *The Rise of the Social Gospel*, p.
      298; Jane Addams, "Introduction" to Graham Taylor, *Religion
      in Social Action* (New York, 1913), p. xxxiii; Capen,
      Foreign Missions and World Peace, p. 20; Foster, "The
      Dream Come True," pp. 11-12; and Rauschenbusch, *Christian-
      izing the Social Order* (New York, 1912), p. 20.   Gladden
      is quoted in R. B. Guild, *Practicing Christian Unity*
      (New York, 1919), p. 3.   For Taylor's views see "The
      Social Emphasis," in *Men and Religion*, pp. 138-154.

55.   Reports made at this conference were preserved in *Messages
      of the Men and Religion Forward Movement* (7 vols.; New
      York, 1912).

56.   The record of Smith's world tour in 1913 is *Extracts of
      Letters from Mr. Fred B. Smith*.   He discussed the Men and
      Religion Forward Movement in his autobiography, *I Remember*
      (New York, 1936), pp. 90-111.

57.   Most of the official denominational and interdenominational
      agencies are listed and described in Margaret Renton (ed.),
      War-Time Agencies of the Churches--Directory and Handbook
      (New York, 1919).

58.   According to Slosson, *The Great Crusade and After, 1914-
      1928* (New York, 1931), pp. 63-64, some efficiency on the
      local level was sacrificed by the Federal Government to
      allow for the generation of popular enthusiasm by the
      spontaneous growth of local committees and councils.   The
      same could be said about local churches; yet diverse
      religious organizations were remarkably coordinated with

government operations, while popular enthusiasm added much
to the feeling of religious unity in America.

59. Renton, *War-Time Agencies of the Churches*, p. 155. The
Federal Council Bulletin provides much information on the
General War-Time Commission of the Churches, especially I
(January, 1918), pp. 3-9; II (May, 1919), p. 75; and II
(June, 1919), p. 98. See also Piper, "The Social Policy
of the Federal Council of the Churches...During World War I.

60. R. B. Guild, *Practicing Christian Unity*, pp. 56-57; Renton,
War-Time Agencies of the Churches, pp. 212-216; and *Federal
Council Bulletin*, II (January, 1919), p. 5. The National
Committee was made up jointly of the League to Enforce
Peace, The Church Peace Union, the World Alliance for
International Friendship, and the Federal Council Commis-
sion on International Justice and Goodwill.

61. See W. M. Tippy, "Back to the Working People: Story of
the Word in War-Industry Centers," and Edmund de S.
Brunner, "A Year of Cooperative Work in the Rural Church
Field," in *Federal Council Bulletin*, II (February, 1919),
pp. 27-28, 30-31. The joint Committee was organized by
the Federal Council, the Home Missions Council, and the
Council of Women for Home Missions.

62. See Merle Curti, *American Philanthropy Abroad: A History*
(New Brunswick, N. J., 1963), pp. 248, 258; J. L. Murray,
The Call of a World Task in War Time (New York, 1918),
pp. 96-97, 176; and *World Outlook*, V (February, 1919),
pp. 3-5.

63. "Missions and Patriotism," *World Call*, II (May, 1920),
p. 31.

The history of missions shows that long war periods
characterized by great suffering have been among the most pro-
ductive years in the way of launching and expanding the missionary movement.   Such should prove to be the case in this fateful
and tragic hour.   If this is to be the result, however, it will
not come as a matter of magic, or of chance, and will not be
due to the war as such, but will be because the leaders of our
churches take advantage of conditions occasioned by the war and
furnish the requisite leadership, guidance and contagious
enthusiasm to influence the corporate sacrifice of the various
bodies of Christians.

John R. Mott, 1918

CHAPTER II

POST-WAR OPTIMISM: THE FULLNESS OF TIME FOR PROTESTANT AMERICA

The prevailing mood of Protestant America at the close of
World War I was expressed well in the 1918 Christmas number of
World Outlook, a magazine published by the Methodist Home and
Foreign Missions Boards but avowedly non-sectarian in its appeal
to a broad spectrum of progressive-minded churchmen. Illustrating
the magazine's theme for the month--"a cheerful world outlook,"
the front cover pictured a smiling Santa Claus wearing American
army boots and a battle helmet and carrying a large globe upon
which a sign read: "safe for democracy." Nothing could have
been more appropriate. Much of the religious and secular press,
saturated with idealistic interpretations of the war and of the
proposed League of Nations, announced that the United States had
saved the world from doom and prepared the way for a new age of
democratic, Christian peace and good will.

While not alone in their anticipation of a lasting world
peace facilitated by a League of Nations, Americans were able to
maintain an optimistic hope for the immediate future not shared
by the peoples of Europe who for nearly five years had dwelt in
the midst of destruction and poverty. The United States, an
ocean away from the fields of battle "over there," actually had
enjoyed a wartime industrial boom, which, combined with increased
exportation of goods and financial loans to Europe, enhanced the
nation's prosperity and secured its economic predominance over
the rest of the world. Moreover, the Americans had escaped over
three-fifths of the war before taking up arms and consequently
had suffered comparatively few casualties. In almost every way
the United States emerged from the war stronger than did the
European countries.

Some Americans, among them many religious leaders, viewed
this state of affairs with slightly mixed emotions. Fully cogni-
zant of the wide gap between American gains and European losses
from the war, they perceived with satisfaction their heightened
national power and prestige in the battle-fatigued world. Yet
their pride was tempered by the rather embarrassing facts of the

situation. "We must remember," wrote Willard Price, editor of
World Outlook, "that for a long time the other nations fought for
democracy while we made money out of the fight. Much of the
wealth needed to wage this war for liberty and democracy has
flowed into our pockets. The United States now stands war-bloated
with a prosperity unequaled in the history of the nation or the
world. We have not yet assumed our full share in the real sacrifice for democracy."[1]

If such apparent post-war economic derangement pricked the
American religious conscience, however, these feelings were offset by the strong conviction that America's ideals and good fortune forecast the world's future blessing. From within the
popular manifest destiny tradition, the rationale that "as goes
America, so goes the world" tempered serious alarm over the glar-
ing contrast between an enriched America and a pauperized Europe
at the end of 1918. So long as American idealism did not falter,
Protestant spokesmen argued, the world would benefit from America's
prosperity; and they could note that during the war Americans had
displayed their idealism with unusual vigor.

Seldom, indeed, had a people so fervently embraced a military venture as a national religious crusade in terms of absolute
good against absolute evil. The war's outcome proved where
righteousness lay. For example, Episcopal Bishop Charles H.
Brent, chief of chaplains in the American Expeditionary Force,
attributed the military victory to "superior vision which fired
everyone from statesman to child, from housewife to doughboy,
with a common purpose." This common understanding of American
domestic wartime enthusiasms led to the conclusion that while
"this nation emerges from the war with a maximum of glory at a
minimum of sacrifice," in the words of popular Protestant layman
Fred B. Smith, "the world should rejoice that America's vision
has not dimmed." The world's undisputed economic giant--a giant
of unshaken idealism--could now shoulder its full share of the
sacrifice for democracy by taking the lead in rebuilding war-
stricken lands. Just as an evil power nearly had destroyed
Europe, the argument ran, so a righteous nation would restore
it.[2]

Those who claimed victory for idealism in the war rested
their case on what they believed to be uncontestable evidence
that the American people had proved their moral superiority and
humanitarian ambitions. For example, they could point to the
hundreds of millions of American dollars given for relief abroad.

Even more striking was the public support of wartime prohibition, bringing a halt to wasteful (in foodstuffs and manpower) production of liquor in the land; while at the same time these people voluntarily rationed themselves to send grain to Europe.

The centrality of prohibition in American Protestant moral concerns of the day can hardly be exaggerated. Aside from the war crusade itself, nothing so united the minds and emotions of diverse churchmen. The Federal Council of Churches, for example, had waged its "Strengthen America Campaign" on the assumption that "the liquor traffic wastes food stuffs, labor, efficiency, money, and human life, the arguments being based upon economic facts and supported by reasons which [would] appeal to head, heart and conscience."[3] An additional appeal to popular patriotic emotions pitted prohibition legislation with the forces of righteousness against the evil fruits of German "Hun brewers." Hence wartime prohibition, a temporary measure passed by Congress in 1918, was acclaimed by many religious leaders a moral act—a great moral advance for the nation and the world. Americans, then, not only had fed the world with bread and soup; they also had assumed responsibility to provide the world with moral sustenance.

Protestant leaders were caught up in the popular conception of America's magnanimous attitude and performance during the war. Not only did they believe that history had never witnessed soldiers who fought more honorably and valiantly with their backs to the wall than did the Americans, and that civilians at home had never given more generous, concrete support to their fighting men; but many were also satisfied that they had done it all solely for the sake of humanity. Wiliston Walker, Yale's highly acclaimed church historian, expressed popular doctrine when he wrote in 1918 that "no action in which the nation has ever been engaged has been so unselfish." This theme was repeated time and again in a variety of popular expressions, such as the boasting by the editor of *Watchman-Examiner*:

> We had no vision of territorial enlargement, of financial gain or of political aggrandizement. We coveted no foot of land and no dollar of wealth belonging to another nation. We were moved by no passion save the passion for righteousness and liberty. For humanity's sake we bowed our shoulders to the burden, we bared our breast to the storm, we stretched out our hand to the sword.[4]

Here was thought to be an unprecedented example of national virtue, so impressive, in fact, that religious leaders announced

a regeneration of "true religion" in soldiers and civilians who
had abandoned self-interest for the well-being of mankind.   "The
struggle itself, from our American standpoint," declared Methodist
Bishop Edwin Holt Hughes of Boston who had witnessed the battle
front, "had in it a nobleness that was close to personal religion."
Moreover, this "nobleness" could be applied to other Allied
countries in the belief that nations and peoples had been divinely
inspired to join the forces of good in a battle for high ideals at
great sacrifice of life and resources.   "There never was a victory
over the powers of evil so widely shared," declared the editor of
The Congregationalist and Advance.   Victory for such as these
could be interpreted as both the sign and the embodiment of a new,
righteous world society.   "This is a day of the new affirmation
of our Christianity," proclaimed Charles L. Thompson in his pre-
sidential message to the annual meeting of the Home Missions
Council in January of 1919.   He considered the greatest product
of the war to be the world's "louder declaration of God."   Indeed
Germany's defeat proved to many that "God reigns."[5]

Despite the widely held assumption that Germany's defeat
spelled victory for Christian democracy, however, few believed
that the world's crises ended with an armistice.   On the contrary,
many felt they were entering the most critical period in modern
world history.   True, an attempt by autocratic powers to capture
the world by force had been thwarted; but Americans saw a new
threat in the rising tide of radical socialism spreading from
the 1917 Bolshevik Revolution in Russia into Europe and, most
important, into the United States.   The destruction of one power
and ideology had left a vacuum which, it seemed, was being filled
by another equally undesired power and ideology.   "Bolshevism has
arisen where autocracy fell," warned a Presbyterian editor early
in 1919 as a great "Red Scare" began to sweep the nation.[6]   Social
upheavals during the months following curbed earlier expectations
of a quick emergence of world peace based on Christian democracy,
yet great optimism continued throughout the year.   Though there
were still many enemies to be countered, the decisive victory was
believed won.

The war also increased what American Protestants long had
called the "plasticity" of the world, by which they meant that
the minds of peoples and the character of nations were "malle-
able"--open to the molding force of new ideas, be they socialistic
atheism or democratic Christianity.   For at least thirty years
prior to the world war, American intellectuals and social leaders

had sensed the dawning of a new era defined not only by revolu-
tions in industry, science, and urbanization, but also by the
social and intellectual awakening of non-Christian and comparatively non-industrial peoples hitherto subjected to western colonial powers. The war and its aftermath intensified the conditions
of social and intellectual change. Of immediate consequence, it
brought diverse peoples into intimate contact in an already
shrinking world, thereby introducing them to traditions and ideas
not their own. In which direction their commitments finally would
be directed was the question of the day for American churchmen of
world missionary vision, a question they believed soon would be
settled. "The titanic furnaces or forges of the war have been
made," declared layman John R. Mott, Methodist statesman and
ecumenical missionary leader. "The world is molten; it is ready
to run. In what mold shall it be cast?"[7]

     Such leaders of Protestant America thus interpreted the
World War I armistice as a precarious, transitional moment in the
world's history. They intended to communicate the delicateness
of the world situation to their constituent religious communities
without casting shadows upon popular idealistic hope for the
future. More than ever convinced of America's providential role
among the nations, and unswayed in their belief that the forces
of good had only begun to fight, with their great military victory behind them, they also looked hopefully upon the year 1919
as "the threshold of a new, fresh day"--an opportunity equal to
the crisis.[8]

     According to this interpretation of events, therefore,
World War I helped give birth to a new era in world civilization,
the nature of which had yet to be determined. To the American
victors this understanding meant that the war had been a constructive force toward world betterment, since it prepared the way for
the world-wide extension of Christian democracy--according to many
Protestant analysts the one means by which world peace and brotherhood might be preserved. Put most succinctly, they believed
that the war had "placed the world in a position to be saved."

     Moreover, it seemed apparent that the war had placed
America--specifically American churches--in a position to do most
of the saving. With Christian Britain and Europe impoverished,
American Protestants would have to shoulder an ever greater share
of the world missions enterprise than they had before the war,
which had been considerable. For example, in 1919 Great Britain
and Europe, with four times as many Protestant communicants as in

the United States, supplied fewer foreign missionaries than did
the Americans and contributed only a small fraction of the amount
of money given by the Americans for foreign missions. These statistics led to the conclusion that European Protestants had "not
yet been captured by the ideal of the completion of the Kingdom
of God on Earth."[9] Consequently American churchmen were prepared
to extend the United States' "role among the nations as the wheat
bringer" to a larger task which, in the words of Methodists S. Earl
Taylor and Halford E. Luccock, entailed "spreading the Bread of
Life before the world and bidding the lame, the half, the blind
of the East and West to sit at the great democratic feast of
God."[10]

Missionary leaders were ecstatic over the opportunity for
evangelism which they saw. John R. Mott had become persuaded
that the postwar world presented an opportunity for evangelization
even greater than his famous turn of the century vision ("the
evangelization of the world in this generation"). "Never has
there been a time," proclaimed Mott, "when simultaneously all
over what we call the home field, and throughout the vast stretches
of what we call the foreign field, the doors were as open as they
are today."[11] Mott's Presbyterian counterpart, Robert E. Speer,
was no less convinced that "the opportunity beyond precedent is
here"; while S. J. Corey of the Disciples of Christ, and president of the Foreign Missions Conference of North America, found
it "impossible adequately to describe the opportunities and obli-
gations which face the Foreign Mission Boards now that the war
is over."[12]

To those sharing this vision of the church's overwhelming
responsibility the time seemed ripe for action. "This one year
will shape the thousand years that follow after," President W. H.
P. Faunce of Brown University told a national Protestant gathering
in May of 1919. "The world is a molten mass, and before it cools
Christianity may stamp upon it the image and superscription of
God."[13] But only if the church went immediately to work! Ernest
De Witt Burton, President of the University of Chicago and a
leader in Northern Baptist affairs, phrased the urgent summons
in glorious terms:

> Never since the days of Paul has a universal
> religion seemed so within the range of practical
> possibilities as it does today. All barriers are
> down. All doors are open. All religions are in
> the melting pot. All systems are being tried by
> the test of their effects. If, as we believe,
> Christianity is adapted to the whole human race,

> if it can solve the perplexities, meet the needs,
> and promote the welfare of all nations, now is
> the opportunity of its adherents as never before
> to prove this and to win their way among all
> peoples.[14]

Protestant leaders girded their loins to meet a new challenge. The war had caught the churches somewhat unprepared for
what they were called upon to accomplish; yet, by utilizing hitherto unsuspected resources, they felt that they had risen to the
occasion. Now the quick end of the war was likewise baffling.
No sooner were the churches geared for war than the battle ended,
leaving them to ponder the task of post-war reconstruction. Feeling ran high in many circles that some large-scale emergency program was needed if the church and the nation were to meet the
demands of the hour.

For the Protestant leaders of the World War I generation,
developing massive programs in a brief time for specific goals
had become a way of life. Involved first with the tide of progressivism and then swept with the wartime crusade, churchmen had
learned to confront the unusual conditions of modern urbanized
and industrialized society aggressively and optimistically. They
did it in part by cooperating in their efforts to tap material and
human resources in barnstorming campaigns and highly organized yet
charismatically led movements. The Student Volunteer Movement,
the Missionary Education Movement, the Laymen's Missionary Movement, and the Men and Religion Forward Movement were outstanding
expressions of this form of religious organization which combined
social gospel and evangelistic goals, revival techniques, and big
business principles of operation. Then, as crusading American
Protestantism reached its apex, the world war burst upon the scene.
During the war a phenomenal number of religious agencies created
for the emergency became consolidated into a great religious
machine which worked closely with government programs, raising
large sums of money, recruiting soldiers and chaplains, waging
educational propaganda campaigns interpreting "the moral aims of
the war."[15] Such was the precedent for religious organization in
a crisis atmosphere within which Protestant Americans faced the
post World War I world.

Actually church leaders had been concerned about the post-
war emergency for some time. For example, delegates at the
January, 1918 meeting of the Foreign Missions Conference of North
America heard James M. Speers, Chairman of the Laymen's Missionary Movement, discuss the means by which "the new measure of

beneficence" brought about by the war experience could be maintained and directed into missionary channels after the war.
About the same time William Adams Brown, Executive Secretary of
the General War-Time Commission of the Churches, advised the members of the Home Missions Council at their annual conference to
"plan in the near future to hold a nation-wide gathering of all
the agencies engaged in Christian work within [American] borders,
to take account of the lessons which the war has taught, to consider our joint responsibilities for the future, and to generate
the enthusiasm which will make it possible to carry our conclusions into effect."[16]

Moreover, before the armistice Protestant energy was being
garnered into programs projected towards various post-war objectives. To begin with, on April 2, 1918, the Committee on the War
and the Religious Outlook was formed by joint action of the General War-Time Commission of the Churches and the Federal Council
of Churches. With the armistice still in the indefinite future,
Federal Council leaders gathered together a group of far-sighted
men "to consider the state of religion as revealed or affected by
the war, with special reference to the duty and opportunity of
the churches, and to prepare these findings for submission to the
churches."[17] Led by William Adams Brown, professor of systematic
theology in Union Theological Seminary and Executive Secretary of
the General War-Time Commission, the Committee set itself to the
task of providing a knowledgeable foundation for the churches'
post-war work. As "an experiment in cooperative thinking," it
made extensive studies of several aspects of Protestant endeavor
in light of changing social and religious conditions. The result-
ing publications proved enlightening and influential in the American Protestant conception of its position and role in the world
of the 1920's. But at the end of 1918, because of the limited
scope of its task, and because its inquiries were not scheduled
with an early end of the war in view, the Committee appeared to
many to be inadequate for the emergency confronting the churches.
It promised to add enlightened clarity to the churches' call to
evangelistic battle, but its sound was long in coming and its
rallying power limited.

Somewhat more resonant with the vibrant clamors of the day
was the Interchurch Emergency Campaign, initiated at the war's
end by leaders of the General War-Time Commission of the Churches.
During 1918 the Commission's expense had been met by subscriptions
from denominational wartime commissions and from individual

contributors. In addition to supporting the General War-Time Commission, each denominational budget included funds for its own commission's war-work. With the quick coming of the armistice, however, many feared that financial support for these commissions would cease if a popular feeling were allowed to emerge that because the war had been won all further extraordinary effort was unnecessary. An Interchurch Central Campaign Committee was thus formed as an inspirational and promotional organization to insure the continuing church support of wartime commission activities. During January of 1919 the Central Committee held fourteen inspirational conferences across the nation, attempting "to impress upon the church and the public the fact that the church has an after-wartime mission."[18]

Fourteen denominations finally became related to the campaign, each with one elected representative on the Central Campaign Committee. They set aside February 16, 1919 as "Interchurch Sunday," when each denomination appealed to its constituency for funds and the General War-Time Commission made a general appeal for contributions. The cost of carrying on the united campaign was met directly by the General War-Time Commission, but the Commission received compensation and general financial support for the year 1919 from the participating denominational war commissions. The campaign actually raised around two hundred thousand dollars for the General War-Time Commission and its affiliated committees, out of which a special fund of twenty thousand dollars was set aside to help finance the Committee on the War and the Religious Outlook.[19]

The Interchurch Emergency Campaign secured large sums of money through united effort, and it helped to maintain wartime enthusiasm for after-wartime work. But its goals, its short-term projection, and its narrow field of concern made it a modest endeavor in light of the post-war enthusiasm that existed. By the end of 1918 more ambitious church leaders had become convinced that the Federal Council and the General War-Time Commission had no plans for the kind of Protestant advance necessary to meet the challenge of the post-war world.

Far more promising were developments within the separate denominations, many of which by the time of the military armistice, or soon thereafter, were making plans for ambitious forward movements to increase their resources and expand their programs. The Congregationalists, for example, had begun in 1915 to prepare for an International Congregational Council in 1920 to coincide

with the Tercentenary celebration of the arrival of the Pilgrims
at Plymouth (1620). But the Council would look to the future as
well as to the past, analyzing the overall role of Congregationalism in the post-war world. To coincide with this celebration the
American Congregationalists planned a Pilgrim Memorial Fund campaign to raise five million dollars, largely for endowment of the
denomination's Annuity Fund for ministerial needs (disabilities,
pensions, etc.).[20] Even though this campaign embraced directly a
narrow field, it was projected as part of a larger forward advance
of the denomination's whole field of labor. It placed the Congregationalists in the mainstream of ambitious Protestant activity at
the close of World War I.

The Congregationalists were but one denomination among many
planning forward movements of a similar nature. Four such movements, however, stood out from the others because of their peculiar
and formative contributions to the movements as a whole, and because of their public recognition. The Disciples of Christ began
earliest and introduced the methods. Their Men and Millions Movement secured pledges of over seven million dollars and demonstrated
how a complex nation-wide organizationcould be created in a brief
period, rallying the whole denominational constituency to give a
sum of money unprecedented in their history.[21] The Methodists'
Joint Centenary Campaign took over the methods and expanded them
into the most grandiose of all denominational programs with a goal
of eighty million dollars.[22] The Northern Presbyterians included
local church as well as denominational budgets in their New Era
Movement and forged ahead with post-war fervor second to none.[23]
Finally, the Northern Baptists staged two large campaigns entirely
under the planning and direction of laymen, convinced that "as a
denomination we can accomplish almost any kind or size of task, if
we will only go at it in the right way, pull together, not be
afraid of organization, and not fail to utilize the experience of
others accumulated in the many campaigns of recent years."[24]

Such was the frame of mind not only of Baptists, Presbyterians, Methodists, and Disciples at the end of World War I but of
the majority of American Protestant leadership. The various organizations for post-war social and religious work did not satisfy
but simply increased the ambitions of many who envisioned a program
of quick action on a world-wide scale utilizing the combined forces
of American Protestantism. Persons of this mind were strongly
represented a few days after the World War I armistice of November
11, 1918, in a significant annual meeting of the Executive

Committee of the Board of Foreign Missions of the Presbyterian Church in the United States (Southern Presbyterian) in Nashville, Tennessee. Led by chairman James I. Vance, preacher of national repute, author, professor, and leader in contemporary inter-denominational religious affairs, much of the discussion focused on the recent earth-shaking events in Europe and on the church's task in the post-war world. After "earnest and prayerful consideration of the situation," the Committee unanimously adopted a resolution calling for the American Protestant churches to cooperate in the raising of funds sufficient "for equipment and support of all their Foreign Mission work, and to recruit a sufficient force of evangelists, teachers, doctors and nurses to go to the front, that the non-Christian world may be immediately evangelized, and Christian education, medical and sanitary work, and social service may be adequately done in non-Christian lands."[25]

Incorporating this resolution in a letter of invitation to American Protestant Foreign Mission Boards dated November 19, 1918, Vance explained the Committee's conviction "that the world situation confronting the church as the war closes calls for a bigger program and correspondingly increased resources." The Presbyterian executives believed that the war experience justified "Protestant Christianity in launching a united drive for world evangelism." Moreover, wrote Vance, "the fact that the Christian message is the only hope of creating permanent peace conditions should invest such a movement with a powerful appeal at this time."[26]

The appeal of Vance's letter proved to be even stronger than he and his colleagues anticipated, its proposal meeting a large and enthusiastic response. The denominational forward movements promised to fulfill the wildest ambitions, save at one point: they were unrelated and presented no united Evangelical front. The situation could be remedied, many thought, by structuring a coordination of disjointed efforts and a pooling of accumulated knowledge and experience--a united forward movement of Protestant denominations. That is precisely what the Southern Presbyterian resolution suggested to foreign mission boards. But sentiment clearly demanded an even more inclusive program. Replies to James I. Vance's letter from foreign mission leaders not only favored an interdenominational conference, but asked that invitations be sent to home mission boards and missionary agencies of every type.

This done, the wheels of the Interchurch World Movement began to turn, a dramatic cultural-religious event whose brief and stormy life would manifest the latter days of the century-old Protestant empire in America and forecast the emergence of a new age.

NOTES TO CHAPTER II

1.   "How Europe is to be Rebuilt," *World Outlook*, IV (December, 1918), p. 8.

2.   Charles H. Brent, *The Nation for Christ Campaign* (New York, 1919), p. 1; and Fred B. Smith, *The New Church for the New Day* (New York, 1919), p. 3. For another typical essay dealing with the supposed increase in idealism due to the war and America's responsibility to extend it in the world, see Cornelius H. Patton, "The Rise of the New Idealism," *World Facts and America's Responsibility* (New York, 1919), pp. 179-200.

3.   *Federal Council Bulletin*, I (January, 1918), p. 6.

4.   *Watchman-Examiner*, January 2, 1919, p. 5. Walker's comments were published in E. Hershey Sneath (ed.), *Religion and the War by Members of the Faculty of the School of Religion, Yale University* (New Haven, 1918), pp. 150-51.

5.   Quotations taken from the following: Edwin Holt Hughes, "Pershing's Crusaders as World Rebuilders," *The Christian Advocate*, March 13, 1919, p. 332; *The Congregationalist and Advance*, December 26, 1918, p. 729; Charles L. Thompson, "The Year of the Home Missions Council," *Proceedings of the Twelfth Annual Meeting of the Home Missions Council, January 14, 15, and 16, 1919*, pp. 43-44 (henceforth referred to as Home Missions Council Proceedings); and *The Christian Advocate*, May 15, 1919, p. 610.

6.   *New Era Magazine*, I (January, 1919), p. 5.

7.   John R. Mott, "The Present Advantageous Position of Christian Missions," *Foreign Missions Conference of North America, Report of the Boards, January 13-15, 1920* (henceforth referred to as Foreign Missions Conference Report), p. 96. On the "plastic" world situation see, for example, W. H. P. Faunce, "The Church and Social Reconstruction," *The Standard*, May 21, 1919, p. 989.

8.   Such was the tone, for example, of Federal Council of Churches President Frank Mason North's address to the General Wartime Commission of the Churches in September of

1918, "The Church and the Problems of the Future," *Federal Council Bulletin*, I (November, 1918), p. 3.

9. *World Survey by the Interchurch World Movement of North America*, Revised Preliminary Edition, vol. 2 (New York, 1920), pp. 17, 53.

10. S. Earl Taylor and Halford E. Luccock, *The Christian Crusade for World Democracy* (New York, 1918), p. 190.

11. From a speech delivered in Atlantic City, New Jersey, on November 5, 1919, in "History of the Interchurch World Movement of North America," I, p. 50 (a typewritten collection of documents henceforth referred to as IWM Documents). See also *Interchurch Newsletter*, November 13, 1919, p. 1.

12. Robert E. Speer, "World's Need of Christ Revealed by War," *New Era Magazine*, I (January, 1919), pp. 20-21; S. J. Corey, "The Foreign Fields and Post-War Conditions," *World Call*, I (January, 1919), p. 8.

13. W. H. P. Faunce, "The Church and Social Reconstruction," *The Standard*, May 31, 1919, p. 989.

14. Ernest De Witt Burton, "The Challenge of the Present Crisis," *The New World Movement* (New York, 1919), p. 10.

15. Most of the organizations are described in Margaret Renton (ed.), *War-Time Agencies of the Churches--Directory and Handbook* (New York: General Wartime Commission of the Churches, 1919).

16. Speer's address, "The War's Lessons in Giving," published in *The Missionary Review of the World*, LXI (March, 1918), pp. 202-05; Brown's address printed in *Home Missions Council Proceedings, January 15-17, 1918*, pp. 105-12.

17. W. A. Brown, "Report of the Committee on the War and the Religious Outlook," *The Churches Allied for Common Tasks, Report of the Third Quadrennium of the Federal Council of the Churches of Christ in America 1916-1920*, ed. S. M. Cavert (New York, 1921), p. 35.

18. *The Interchurch Emergency Campaign* (New York, 1919). A pamphlet published by Campaign Headquarters.

19. See *Federal Council Bulletin*, II (January, 1919), p. 24; and II (May, 1919), p. 75.

20. See "The Pilgrim Memorial Fund," *The Congregationalist and Advance*, November 29, 1917, pp. 767-68; and *The National Council of the Congreational Churches of the United States, 1917* (Proceedings), pp. 38-41, 48 ff.

21. See *Year Book of Churches of Christ (Disciples), 1918*, pp. 57, 448; "The Men and Millions Movement: History and Report, 1913–1919," *World Call*, I (September, 1919), pp. 54–60; and *The Whole Church Lifting the Whole Task: One Thousand Workers, Six Million Dollars* (Cincinnati, n.d.).

22. See "Minutes Joint Centenary Commission;" *The Christian Advocate*, September 27, 1917, and January 23, 1919; *The Centenary Bulletin*, April, 1919, p. 2; and "Report of the World Program Committee" (special unpublished account).

23. See *Minutes of the General Assembly of the Presbyterian Church in the United States of America, 1918*, p. 67; and *New Era Magazine*, I (January, 1919), pp. 18–19, I (February, 1919), pp. 67, 74–75, I (March, 1919), p. 116.

24. See *Annual of the Northern Baptist Convention*, 1918, pp. 202 ff; 1919, p. 41, 47; and *The Standard*, May 31, 1919, pp. 997–1000.

25. IWM Documents, I, p. 1. See also *Annual Report of the Executive Committee of Foreign Missions of the Presbyterian Church in the U.S. for the Year Ending March 31, 1919* (Nashville, 1919), pp. 26–28; and *New Era Magazine*, I (May, 1919), pp. 238–39.

26. For Vance's letter, see IWM Documents, I, p. 2.

CHAPTER III

PROTESTANT CRUSADE, 1919: THE MOVEMENT BORN, THE BATTLE PLANNED

The interchurch bandwagon began to roll on December 17,
1918, as one hundred and thirty-five representatives of American
Protestant mission boards and related agencies gathered in a
second floor room at the headquarters of the Foreign Missions
Conference of North America in New York City "to consider the
advisability and feasibility of a united campaign."[1] In the
spirit of popular Protestant piety, the meeting opened with
"devotional exercises" which were led by Robert E. Speer. Speer,
rigidly organized in mind and action, was a reverently stern yet
deeply thoughtful advocate of the doctrinal orthodoxy he had
learned at Princeton, and a charismatic transmitter of experiential
piety through the spoken word--most notably through eloquent missionary addresses and moving public prayers. No other Protestant,
John R. Mott included, could have by his mere presence so digni-
fied and solemnized a gathering of diverse Protestant church
leaders.

Appropriately James I. Vance, who had penned the invitations, presided over the Conference. His opening remarks confirmed the expectations and spiritual tone which the delegates
brought to New York. "The Church has come to the greatest hour
in its history," he declared. "Will it measure up or fall down?
It remains to be seen. No such task has challenged the Church
since Calvary as that which confronts it today. No such hour
has struck in human history as it is striking today."[2] This awe-
some sense of the moment's decisive historic significance, described by witnesses as comparable in spiritual intensity with
Apostolic gatherings, left a deep imprint on one participant who
later described those present "in the upper room on that momentous
December day when the Interchurch World Movement was born." Thus
reminiscing, William Adams Brown noted that "they had seen a
vision--the vision of a united church in a divided world, and
under the spell of what they saw all things seemed possible.
Difficulties were waved aside, doubters were silenced. In the

face of an opportunity so unparalleled, there seemed but one thing to do, and that was to go forward."[3]

Setting aside all reservation and doubt, the exuberant churchmen had no difficulty materializing their visions in the form of resolutions and a committee. First came reports on the various denominational forward movements already in progress, which reinforced their optimism. Then they set to work formulating the meeting's mind in a resolution to begin organizing a massive campaign. Thereupon chairman Vance appointed a Committee of Twenty (including himself) to prepare a plan for submission to the interdenominational mission agencies scheduled to meet in or near New York City during the next month.[4] With this the conference came to a close, and the Committee of Twenty went vigorously to work.

In less than a month, the Committee of Twenty completed its task. The plan called for the organization of an Interchurch World Movement of North America "to present a unified program of Christian service and to unite the Protestant churches of North America in the performance of their common task, thus making available the values of spiritual power which come from unity and co-ordinated Christian effort and meeting the unique opportunities of the new era." The scope of the proposed movement would "cover all those interests . . . outside of the local church budget which are naturally related to the missionary enterprise." (This could be interpreted to include almost any church-related activity.) Organization, suggested the Report, should reach from a General Committee of about one hundred, a small Executive Committee, and a Cabinet on the national level to inter-church committees or federations on state and local levels.

Regarding methods, there should be "a thorough united survey of the home and foreign fields of the world for the purpose of securing accurate and complete data as to what ought to be done by the combined churches to meet the needs of the hour, and of at least the next five years." Then should follow "a thoroughgoing educational publicity campaign to carry the facts of the survey to the entire Protestant church constituency in America and to every mission station where the churches of North America are at work." Eventually the field campaigns would be geared to stimulating the churches to provide the resources in men and money which, on the basis of surveys, would be proved necessary to meet the world's needs. These campaigns would culminate in a great united financial drive in the spring of 1920.[5]

Here, then, was the plan; and the interboard conferences approved it overwhelmingly. One agency after another, upon hearing Committee of Twenty chairman S. Earl Taylor's elaborate presentation of the proposed movement, voted its enthusiastic and unanimous endorsement of the plan. Each of them then appointed a committee of five to meet with the Committee of Twenty for further planning. On January 16, Taylor sent a telegram to the Foreign Missions Conference, meeting in New Haven, stating that, "Five bodies without a dissenting vote have now approved most momentous program since beginning of modern missionary movement."[6]

Encouraged by such approval, the Committee of Twenty met with the twenty-five elected representatives of the five interboard agencies (called the Cooperating Committee) on January 17 and 18 to create a General Committee. By the time all of the nominations were made, the number had reached 137. All were elected, and the General Committee was given power to increase its numbers as it saw fit. With this organizational groundwork thus laid, the General Committee took charge of the Interchurch World Movement.

The General Committee first met on February 5 and 6 at Wallace Lodge in Yonkers, New York, with seventy-nine members present.[7] Despite a heavy agenda of organizational business, the whole first day was devoted exclusively to prayer—so powerful was the evangelical piety which suffused all of these endeavors. Nevertheless, they completed their work. They added fifty-five new members to the General Committee, and they formed an Executive Committee of fifteen members (later to be raised to twenty-one) with John R. Mott elected chairman. S. Earl Taylor, Executive Secretary of the Methodist Centenary Movement, who had served as chairman of the Committee of Twenty, was elected General Secretary of the Interchurch World Movement—the chief executive officer. So the great machine began to function, its product yet uncertain. "The clock has struck for the Church of God," announced one editor of missionary news, "can she campaign on a world scale?"[8]

It had become apparent that a full year of planning and organization would be necessary in order to wage the various campaigns intelligently. During this period (the year 1919), the Interchurch World Movement developed from the rudimentary organization formed in New York on February 6 to a highly complex, nation-wide Protestant machine of many departments and divisions, with working parts operating even in local churches. Its scope

and goals mushroomed to enormous proportions, including practically
every aspect of American Protestant activity in the world from
revival meetings to investigations of social and industrial conditions, and seeking "nothing less than a complete evangelization
of all of life." In a phrase, the objective (and motto) became
"the giving of the whole gospel to the whole world by the whole
church."[9]

The Interchurch program was projected around a comprehensive survey of the world's religious needs and (consequently) the
church's task. On the basis of facts, the churches would be
educated in their mission and inspired to activate their latent
resources. Moreover, the survey was inextricably caught up on
the whole question of scope and objectives of the movement. Survey work had to begin immediately, therefore, and it became the
major element in the year's preparation and organization. All
activities centered around the survey organization, which quickly
became the largest, most complex department of the Interchurch
World Movement. From the first General Committee meeting in
February, when a Committee on Objectives was appointed to do the
preliminary organizing of the survey program, through a veritable
maze of conferences across the nation, to the great World Survey
Conference in Atlantic City on January 7-10, 1920, the gathering
of data dominated Interchurch World Movement concerns.

But there were other matters of pressing importance which
directed the movement's activities during the first year. The
Interchurch organization had to be ever more clearly defined to
the satisfaction of participating and cooperating agencies,
especially regarding its role as a unitive force in American Protestantism and its precise relation to the churches. The movement
also had to be promoted and sold to American Protestants; it had
to be made acceptable to all kinds of churchmen in order to gain
their enthusiastic support.

Activities of the Interchurch World Movement during the
first year fell generally into three main periods. The first
five months were devoted to preliminary or preparatory work: a
"feeling-out period" of announcing, explaining, discussing the
movement, and of securing a sufficient number of endorsements to
warrant proceeding with surveys, organization and money-raising.[10]
This kind of activity continued throughout the year and well into
1920, but the first few months were critical in getting the movement off the ground. During February and March, a series of
nation-wide regional conferences were held for ministers and other

religious workers, where all aspects of the movement were discussed. The general responses were overwhelmingly and enthusiastically favorable. Next came an important Pastors' Conference
held in Pittsburgh on April 23 and 24. Upon being nominated by
their respective denominations, 115 of the nation's outstanding
ministers were invited to go over the Interchurch World Movement
with a fine-tooth comb.[11] Debates were long and vigorous, and
it was significant that this pulpit elite finally unanimously
adopted the report of a Committee upon Message and sent it to
every Protestant pastor in the country.

The culmination of this preparatory stage in the Interchurch World Movement came at a large Interboard Conference held
in Cleveland on April 30 and May 1, 1919. Five hundred representatives of missionary, educational and benevolent boards heard
detailed presentations of the nature and objectives of the new
movement. "Here the idea of the movement was threshed out; every
angle was considered; questions were asked and freely answered."
And here the Interchurch World Movement was "officially" defined:

1. To undertake a scientific survey of the world's needs
   from the standpoint of the responsibility of Evangelical
   Christianity.
2. To project a cooperative community and world program to
   meet the needs as revealed by the survey.
3. To discover and develop the resources of men, money,
   and power necessary for the accomplishment of the
   program.[12]

The findings report of this largest and most representative
gathering of American Protestant leaders up to that time demonstrated the widespread support of the Interchurch World Movement.
The conference leaders proclaimed their intention to "fling our-
selves without reserve into a unified program to redeem the world,"
and the delegates applauded. "They were all with one accord in
one place," one observer described the scene. "They had learned
the lesson of the war. They had gone over the top in many a
patriotic drive. They were afraid of nothing. They realized that
a combination of forces with a common purpose and an uncommon
leader could do things in the higher life never tried before."[13]

During the summer months of 1919--the second period of
preparatory work--Interchurch leaders staged several more series
of conferences across the nation, intending further to promote
the movement and secure more endorsements. Additional regional
conferences in May met with the same enthusiasm that had marked

56

the earlier ones. During midsummer, the Interchurch World Movement sponsored and directed the annual camp-conferences of the Missionary Education Movement, reaching nearly two thousand persons. On September 19, in New York City, came an important conference of denominational forward movement leaders, whose approval of the Interchurch program and vision could not have been more fervid:

> We believe that the opportunities arising out of
> a united simultaneous financial campaign for the
> missionary and benevolent interests of the
> agencies of the evangelical churches of North
> America are so far reaching in their significance,
> and their reaction upon the life of the church
> and the welfare of the world so profound that
> they strike a most wonderful hour in the history
> of Protestant Christianity; and that the duty of
> carrying on such a campaign is inescapable.[14]

By this time, the denominational forward movements, instrumental in the formation and development of the Interchurch World Movement, were looked upon correctly as "prophetic forerunners" of the allied campaign--"the big apprentice movements of the day." Thirty denominations, so far, were involved in some kind of forward expansion movement, the sum total of which had induced progressive visions in nearly the whole spectrum of American Protestantism.[15] The Interchurch World Movement gathered momentum with the formation of each new denominational campaign. But none approached the grandeur of the Methodist Centenary Movement; it set the pace.

The Methodist Centenary Movement was extremely important in the development of the Interchurch World Movement. The editor of *The Christian Advocate* correctly predicted in January of 1919 that the Methodist Centenary would "serve as a demonstration field, which will test methods, yield the fruits of experience, and supply a contingent of trained workers to the Allied staff."[16] The Interchurch leaders used the Methodist surveys as models, organized the Interchurch departments along the lines of the Centenary Movement, and borrowed or purchased many of the Methodists' office and educational materials. No other denomination furnished as many key leaders for the Interchurch World Movement as did the Methodists, most of them assuming Interchurch roles similar to the positions they held in the Centenary. On top of this, the tremendous success of the Methodist Centenary immeasurably stimulated the optimism of other denominational and Interchurch leaders. Financially the Centenary Campaign went "over the top," raising subscriptions of over $113,000,000 for the Northern denomination

and over $53,000,000 for the Southerners.[17] So influential were
the Methodists that the Interchurch World Movement, as expressed
in its literature and programs, came to resemble a huge interdenominational version of the Methodist Centenary Movement.
Methodist prestige and influence in American Protestantism has
never been greater.

The General Committee meeting in Cleveland, September 24-26,
marked the end of the second period of preparation and the start
of a third. During these days, every aspect of the Interchurch
World Movement received careful attention, and significant policy
adjustments were made dealing primarily with relationships to
other Protestant bodies. Most of the general introduction of the
movement to representative Protestant gatherings across the nation
had been completed; it was now time to begin more specific training for the massive campaigns planned for the coming year. Thousands of lay people had to be trained to lead the educational,
evangelistic, recruitment, stewardship, and financial campaigns
on the regional, state, and local levels. Hence from October
through December the nation witnessed a barrage of Leaders' Training Conferences.[18] They all led up to, and culminated in, the
great Atlantic City World Survey Conference in early January of
1920--the peak moment in cooperative American Protestant enthusiasm during the post-war years.

Anticipating the World Survey Conference, John R. Mott,
on November 5, 1919, had addressed a gathering of denominational
forward movement leaders in Atlantic City. The purpose of the
conference, said Mott, would be "to make vivid the wholeness and
oneness of the task now confronting the Protestant church"; to
agree on a guiding principle of a united effort; to determine a
united budget; to launch the campaign itself; "to facilitate putting intelligently and therefore solidly behind the Interchurch
World Movement the constituencies and cooperating bodies and
agencies"; and "*to create atmosphere*." Mott compared the projected conference favorably with the great international missionary conference at Edinburgh in 1910: "Never in the history of
American Christian churches has a group of men been called together
to consider so many great issues. . . . None of the many great
war boards created by the government had a piece of work comparable with the task of the Interchurch World Movement."[19]

Even Mott's high expectations were surpassed by what
transpired at Atlantic City on January 7-10, 1920, at this

58

gathering of seventeen hundred religious, educational, and social workers--the controlling forces of American Protestantism.[20] For three long days they heard technical but extravagant presentations of the preliminary results of the nine months of surveying everything surveyable. They heard and discussed lengthy reports from several reviewing committees (on surveys, finances, field activities). They learned that during the previous year "140 different boards representing thirty-four Protestant denominations, covering the entire range of Christian activity" (and maintaining between eighty and ninety per cent of all American Protestant missions) had affiliated themselves with the movement, and that twenty major interdenominational and nondenominational agencies had given their endorsement. A consensus emerged that this was "one of the most glorious achievements in the history of the church, the proper and inevitable response of God's people to the appalling needs of our age." And then "the conference rose spontaneously and unanimously in expression of its enthusiastic approval." The Interchurch World Movement, it seemed, was plainly providential: "The ideal of the whole Church facing the whole task appeals to us as scriptural and practicable." Moreover, according to one reporter, "The enthusiasm was infectious. Personal differences and petty difficulties were submerged under the paramount determination to carry the banner of Christianity through to victory."[21] American Protestants could ask for nothing more.

They sensed a significant moment not only for the Interchurch World Movement, but for the Protestant America it represented. Optimism abounded. The Interchurch World Movement had been gloriously accredited. The churches were prepared to put their ideals on the line, to throw in all of their chips: a month of prayer (January), a month of stewardship (February), a month of missionary recruitment (March), a month of evangelism (April), and finally a great financial ingathering with an immediate goal of some three hundred million dollars and a five-year goal of one and a third billion dollars.[22] They extolled the movement without limit. Mott had already called it "the greatest program undertaken by Christians since the days of the Apostles," and a program for whose consummation "anyone ought to be willing to die." Speer had referred to it as "a supernatural cause." Others envisaged "the greatest revival in history"; God's "crowning movement of His purpose for the churches of Jesus Christ"; "the beginning of the greatest forward movement for evangelical Christianity in the history of the world"; "a new epoch in the history of Christianity." The churches had marshalled their forces; they had "ascended the mountain top and cast their eyes over the whole world."[23] Their hour had come.

The churches going to battle seemed natural in 1919. American religion had been so thoroughly enmeshed in the web of national militarism during World War I that armed conflict and the Christian mission became confused even in the most sober Protestant minds. The military system, its officers and fighting men, its methods and mind, became the temporary idol which organized Protestantism sought to emulate. This phenomenon, at its height when the war came to an early end, did not suddenly disappear. The wartime spirit remained intact throughout the year 1919 as churchmen prepared to complete the Allied military victory for world-wide Christian democracy by occupying the fields with missionary forces. In their words, "War drives for world freedom [were] passing into Christian drives for world redemption." But for this operation, "the Church must get on a war basis or give up her battle hymns." Five days after the signing of the Armistice, *The Standard* (Northern Baptist) announced that "Christian churches mobilize when armies demobilize."[24]

This statement was meant to be an historical observation. American Protestant leaders strained their interpretative judgments of events in church history in order to buttress their hopes for a Christian post-war world. Compensating for the necessity of recognizing obvious damage to Christian missions caused by the war, they sought to prove that historically war conditions had been favorable to missionary expansion. They noted that the fall of Jerusalem in 70 A.D. led to the scattering of the disciples and hence the spread of Christianity; that the Roman Imperial conquests paved the way for the rapid growth of the church; that barbarian invasions opened the doors to Europe into which marched a stream of great missionaries (Ulfilas, Patrick, Columba, Columban, Boniface, Ansgar, Vladimir); that the relative quiet by the ninth century was also a period of general missionary inactivity until the Crusades stimulated new missionary conquests. More frequent were references to the rise of England's modern missionary movement coincident with the Napoleonic wars and the extension of British colonial power; to the rise of American Protestant foreign missions during and after the War of 1812, and the great expansion of those missions after the Civil War and especially after the Spanish-American War. It seemed natural in

1919 to move directly from historical analysis to prophetic proclamation that the greatest of all wars, a world war, would usher
in the greatest era of world-wide Christian missionary expansions.[25]

Hence in the spirit of war the churches mobilized their
forces through the Interchurch World Movement, "a new Gideon's
army wherein picked men, each fighting under his own banners and
following his chosen leaders [denominational forward movements],
are moving forward in a single campaign under a unified command."[26]
If, as Frederick Lewis Allen later claimed, "the country was not
in the mood to think twice," the churches had abandoned the principle of "safety first" for the "same sacrificial and daring
spirit" which they believed had "characterized the work of our
men in the war."[27] Churchmen were ready to spring for their
ecclesiastical trenches with reckless abandon in a crusade to
carry Christianity into every corner of the earth.

In the spirit of "marching as to war," the official Interchurch World Movement hymn sheet contained such martial songs as
"Soldiers of Christ Arise," "The Battle Hymn of the Republic,"
and as a theme song, "Onward Christian Soldiers" with the opening
line of verse two used as a slogan:

> Like a mighty army
> Moves the Church of God;
> Brothers, we are treading
> Where the saints have trod;
> We are not divided,
> All one body we . . . .

The "picked men" of this "new Gideon's army," the Generals
and Lieutenants of the church militant, were widely considered
America's best. The list of officers and departmental directors
of the Interchurch World Movement reads like an honor roll of the
most capable, reputable lay and ordained leaders of American Protestantism of the day. It is an honor roll which must not be for-
gotten in the annals of American religious history. Seldom has
there been a greater supply of popular charismatic leaders on a
national level in American Protestantism, especially among lay-
men--inspirers of enthusiasm for great causes, men of the platform
and pulpit who through the spoken word convinced masses of church
people of all ages to give time and money for religious enterprises. They were men of high idealism, indefatigable optimism,
and extraordinary piety, yet down-to-earth comprehension of the
necessity for practical organization. They might be described
as "spiritual pragmatists," but also as Christian statesmen of the
first rank. Their primary concern was not doctrinal particulari-
ties but getting on with the business of evangelizing the world.

They planned large programs and inspired people to put them over. Action before theory, movement without second thought: this philosophy guided their religious ambitions and concretized their idealistic visions. Coming from many denominations, they were the leaders of progressive evangelical Protestantism reaching its apex in the Interchurch World Movement.

A few of these outstanding officers of the Interchurch organization require special mention. Two laymen, John R. Mott (Methodist) and Robert E. Speer (Presbyterian), stand alone as the preeminent "apostles of the world mission."[28] As ecumenical statesmen of the American Protestant world enterprise, they brought their wisdom to bear on the Executive Committee (Mott as chairman). Practically along side them stood General Committee Vice-Chairman Fred B. Smith (Disciples of Christ), another layman of great promotional ability, "heralded over the nation and the world as one of the most effective speakers to men of his genera- tion." During his world tour for the Men and Religion Forward Movement in 1913, Smith had expressed perfectly the spirit which led to the Interchurch World Movement:

> I believe in "Movements" more than ever. I am grateful to God that Moody led out in that great evangelistic movement. I am thankful for the Men and Religion Forward Movement. . . . I am happy in the anticipation of the Movements yet to be born. Anything but a calm![29]

The real "animating spirit and director" of the movement, however, the "first to see the far-flung sweep of the idea" was S. Earl Taylor--"the General Pershing of the Methodist Episcopal 'expeditionary forces.'" Taylor was a born promoter, described by a contemporary as "one hundred per cent pragmatist" who thrust himself into grandiose enterprises with extreme confidence that whatever he did would succeed. Another called him "that explo- sive dynamo. . . The seer who can make the hearers see with him, until the Movement grows and glows and almost awes one with its well-nigh infinite possibilities for the future of the churches and the ushering in of the Kingdom, with Christ on his throne."[30] He more than anyone else staked his whole reputation and career as a Protestant lay-leader on the success or failure of the Inter- church World Movement, of which he was General Secretary and chief in command.

Taylor had many excellent lieutenants. A cursory glance at some members of the Cabinet of Associate Secretaries will demonstrate the calibre of leaders holding the Interchurch reins.

John Y. Aitchison was General Director of the Northern Baptists'
New World Movement and first General Director of the new Baptist
Board of Promotion. Abram E. Corey, a fifteen-year veteran
missionary in China, Secretary of the Disciples Foreign Christian
Missionary Society and leader in the Men and Millions Movement,
became Director of the Interchurch World Movement Field Department. William E. Doughty, from 1910 to 1918 Educational Secretary of the Laymen's Missionary Movement, headed the Interchurch
World Movement's Department of Spiritual Resources, a position
similar to that which he held in the Methodist Centenary Movement. Methodist Bishop Fred B. Fisher was appointed Director of
the Industrial Relations Department of the Interchurch World
Movement. William H. Foulkes, delegate to the 1910 World Missionary Conference in Edinburgh, General Secretary of the Northern
Presbyterian New Era Movement, was elected Vice-Chairman of the
Interchurch World Movement Executive Committee.

Chief executive of all Interchurch surveys was Fred P.
Haggard, seven years a missionary in Assam, India (1893-1899),
Home Secretary of the American Baptist Foreign Mission Society
from 1905 to 1915, leader in the Y.M.C.A. and the Laymen's
Missionary Movement (Secretary, editor of *Men and Missions*),
charter member of the Missionary Education Movement, General
Director of the National Committee of Northern Baptist Laymen
Campaigns of 1918 and 1919. William B. Millar, Methodist, Secre-
tary of the International Committee of the Y.M.C.A. (1896-1910),
General Secretary of the Laymen's Missionary Movement since 1910,
was elected Secretary of the General and Executive Committees of
the Interchurch World Movement. Daniel A. Poling of the United
Evangelical Church, long-time leader in the temperance movement
(Vice-President of the Anti-Saloon League, and President of the
Federation of Temperance Organizations), was appointed Director
of the Laymen's Activities Department of the Interchurch World
Movement and Vice-Chairman of the Commission of Inquiry. Finally,
J. Campbell White, United Presbyterian, President of the College
of Wooster, who had been one of the most outstanding leaders in
the Student Volunteer Movement and the Laymen's Missionary Movement, was appropriately appointed Director of the Life Work
Department of the Interchurch World Movement. Expressing the
common mind of his colleagues, White claimed that he was "willing
to stake everything on my conviction that God is moving now in
His Church in a mighty way."[31]

These were the men of the hour.   (Leadership was dominated by men, women being consigned to the lower ranks.)[32]   Fascinated by the spectacular success of war drives, enamored of the notion that organized effort and dedicated promotion could accomplish all things, obsessed with the belief that some regenerating work had been done by the war itself, they appropriated for the churches the mechanism of war-work organization and plunged optimistically into their own "great crusade."   Immediately they became deeply involved in a broad spectrum of matters related to Protestant church life in America.   The problems of religious unity and diversity, of religious organization, and of religious involvement in social issues assumed priority.

NOTES TO CHAPTER III

1. "Minutes of the Conference of the Representatives of the Home and Foreign Mission Boards of North America and affiliated Interdenominational Movements," IWM Documents, I, pp. 1-5.

2. Quoted in "Foreign Missions Conference of North America, Report of the Boards, 1919" (henceforth referred to as "Foreign Missions Conference Reports"), p. 172.

3. W. A. Brown, *The Church in America* (New York, 1922), p. 119.

4. The resolutions and committee membership are printed in IWM Documents, I, pp. 4-5. For the 1919 interdenominational mission agencies' meetings, see *World Call*, I (March, 1919), p. 49.

5. For the full "Report of the Committee of Twenty," see IWM Documents, I, pp. 6-8.

6. For accounts of these approvals, see the following: "Foreign Mission Conference Reports of 1919," pp. 171-81; "Proceedings, Twelfth Annual Meeting of the Home Missions Council, 1919," pp. 32-33; "Minutes and Reports of Federation of Woman's Boards of Foreign Missions of North America, Fourteenth Conference, 1919," p. 6; and IWM Documents, I, p. 9.

7. See IWM Documents, I, pp. 27-30; *The Christian Advocate*, April 10, 1919, pp. 463-64; *World Call*, I (April, 1919), p. 55.

8. *The Missionary Review of the World*, LXII (February, 1919), p. 82.

9. See, for example, Cornelius H. Patton, *Christian America in the New World: an Interpretation of the Interchurch World Movement* (New York, 1920), p. 23; and the Interchurch "Program for Regional Conference," Cincinnati, Ohio, May 13, 1919.

10. See conference reports and Executive Committee minutes in IWM Documents, I, pp. 30-43, and V, pp. 1-2.

11. For a list of conference personnel, see *Pastors Conference, Report-Addresses* (New York, 1919), p. 41.

66

12.   Tyler Dennett, "The Interchurch World Movement," *The
        World's Work*, XXXIX (April, 1920), p. 569; and *Findings
        of the Cleveland Interboard Conference April 30-May 1* (New
        York, 1919).

13.   Lyman P. Powell, "Real Cooperation of the Churches," *The
        American Review of Reviews*, LIX (June, 1919), p. 633.
        See also *World Call*, I (June, 1919), p. 51.

14.   *The Standard*, October 4, 1919, p. 105.

15.   See *World Outlook*, V (September, 1919), pp. 18-19; and
        Interchurch Newsletter, October 2, 1919, p. 1.

16.   *The Christian Advocate*, January 23, 1919, p. 100. See
        also in the same issue, Brenton T. Bradley, "The 'Cen-
        tenary' Leads to an 'Interchurch World Movement,'" p. 91.

17.   *Annual Report of the Board of Home Missions and Church
        Extension of the Methodist Episcopal Church, 1919*, p. 113;
        and *Seventy-Third Annual Year Book Board of Missions,
        Methodist Episcopal Church, South, 1919*, p. 91.

18.   Conference programs and reports are contained in IWM Docu-
        ments, V, pp. 16-21, 25-33.

19.   An account of the meeting, including portions of Mott's
        speech, appear in IWM Documents, V, pp. 38-40.

20.   See *The Missionary Review of the World*, XLIII (February,
        1920), pp. 81-82; *Federal Council Bulletin*, III (February,
        1920), p. 26; and *Watchman-Examiner*, January 15, 1920, p.
        73.

21.   *Federal Council Bulletin*, III (February, 1920), p. 25.
        See also *World Call*, II (February, 1920), p. 15.

22.   These figures, later altered, were commonly advertised,
        for example, in *New York Times*, January 10, 1920, p. 11:1.

23.   Such language was common. For statements quoted, see the
        following: *Interchurch Newsletter*, October 2, 1919, p. 1
        and November 13, 1919, p. 2; *New Era Magazine*, I (March,
        1919), p. 120; *Watchman-Examiner*, October 9, 1919, p. 1422;
        The Christian Advocate, January 23, 1919, p. 98; Robert
        Speer, *Prayer and Missions* (New York, 1919), p. 1; and
        "Report of the Committee on the Financial Ingathering,"
        IWM Documents, V, p. 52.

24.   Milton G. Evans, "Why Christian Enlistment Now," *The
        Standard*, November 16, 1918, p. 262. See also J. Lovell
        Murray, *The Call of a World Task in War Time* (New York,
        1918), pp. 166-67.

25. See especially Murray, *The Call of a World Task in War Time*, pp. 132-36; and William I. Chamberlain, "The Effect of War on Missionary Activity: An Historical Study," in *The Missionary Outlook in the Light of the War* (New York, 1920), pp. 199-209.

26. *Interchurch Newsletter*, November 27, 1919, p. 4.

27. F. L. Allen, *Only Yesterday* (New York, 1931), p. 21; and an extract from the findings of the Chicago Regional Conference in February, 1919, in IWM Documents, I, p. 31.

28. Few would have argued with this judgment, made by G. M. Fisher, *John R. Mott, Architect of Co-operation and Unity* (New York, 1952), p. 11.

29. Extracts of letters from Mr. Fred B. Smith Relating to the World Tour of the *"Men and Religion Forward Movement" Team* (n.p., 1913), p. 148. See also A. G. Knebel, *Four Decades with Men and Boys* (New York, 1936), pp. 104, 155-57.

30. Quotations from *The American Review of Reviews*, LIX (June, 1919), p. 633; *World Outlook*, V (September, 1919), pp. 18-19; Howard B. Grose, "The Interchurch World Movement Conference," *Missions*, XI (March, 1920), p. 141; and from conversations with Mr. Samuel McCrea Cavert who in 1919 was Associate General Secretary of the Federal Council of the Churches of Christ in America.

31. From an unpublished galley printing of speeches delivered at the Interboard Conference in Cleveland, April 30-May 1, 1919 (henceforth referred to as galley printing of speeches April 30-May 1, 1919).

32. Unpublished lists of membership in the various committees and councils of the Interchurch World Movement indicate that women were well-represented everywhere except in positions of official leadership. Moreover, the military atmosphere of the movement frequently was manifested in the use of the expression "masculine Christianity."

CHAPTER IV

TO FURTHER UNITY: THE WHOLE NATION, THE WHOLE
CHURCH, THE WHOLE WORLD TASK

Uniting religious forces for the common enterprise was
priority number one. On the morning of April 30, 1919, J. Campbell White told five hundred representatives of various denominational boards and societies gathered at Cleveland that "a real
united Protestantism, filled with the spirit of God, may undertake anything and a divided Protestantism with all our communions
in separate compartments must stand alone with its hands palsied
in the presence of the needs of the world today."[1]

His words would not fall on unsympathetic ears, for American Protestants had emerged from the Great War engrossed in the
virtues of pragmatic unity. Not only were they impressed with the
effectiveness of wartime cooperation among diverse religious
bodies; they were awestruck by the fact of their nation joining
forces with other nations to accomplish military victory. "The
war threw the nations into a veritable furnace of fire," said
W. E. Doughty at the first Interchurch General Committee meeting
in February, 1919, "and out of it came cooperation and action
under a unified command on a scale never before seen." Here was
an example for the churches to follow: "denominations [could] be
likened to nations and churches to armies." Leaders of the
Interchurch World Movement thus announced that "the American
Protestant Armies have united under an allied command," to
accomplish with divine aid the humanly impossible."[2]

Such language was not mere religious rhetoric in 1919.
It expressed the mushrooming aspirations among churchmen since
the turn of the century to bring unity to the many religious
bodies and the increasingly heterogeneous twentieth century
American religious population. It reflected a profound desire
by Protestant Americans that the national unity they had experienced during the war be preserved with a religious core and
thereby manifest a new stage in what they understood to be
America's Christian democratic mission at home and throughout

the world. Leaders of the Interchurch World Movement identified their efforts with religious unity at all levels both nationally and internationally. Their visions and actions, moreover, helped build the bridge between the missionary thrust of nineteenth century American Christianity and the twentieth century ecumenical movement.

The world war brought a sense of priority and of emergency to the largest dimension of Christian unity envisaged--the whole world. Begin with the greatest task, the final goal; plan and organize accordingly without delay, and all intermediate and lesser problems of disunity would solve themselves or be swept aside in the tide of ultimate concerns. Do not become bogged down in the minute details, for the Christianization of the world is at hand.

The war had intensified what long had been developing within American Protestantism. The indivisibility of the churches' mission to the whole world and its universal oneness (ecumenism) had been the widespread maxim of American churchmen for a century. The home and foreign mission tasks, persistently intermingled with a popular feeling of American religious manifest destiny, tended to provide a spirit and purpose often transcending denominational divisions. A generally common cultural-religious heritage of the large majority of nineteenth century American Christians--white, Anglo-European, Calvinistic-rooted Protestants in the main--had implanted in them a sense of bearing the burden of America's role in the Christian world mission. For these Protestant Americans, therefore, who had been and would continue to be deeply involved in the Faith and Order and Life and Work movements germinal to the World Council of Churches, missions was the essence of ecumenical Christianity. As missionary ecumenists they visualized their post-war task: to facilitate America's participation in the ecumenical movement, to represent the uniting religious force in American cultural development, and to provide an instrument of American church unity.

To begin with, the Interchurch World Movement would thrive on the rejuvenated American Protestant fascination with organized Christianity in the old world. The war had thrust Americans into close contacts with Europeans--on European soil for a change. For a century, to be sure, American divinity students had studied theology and Bible in the great European schools, mainly in Germany. But World War I directly engaged American churchmen in

common activity with European Protestants, not only in conferences with top national leaders, but also in local churches,
especially in France and Belgium. The work mainly entailed providing material relief and helping to rebuild destroyed churches;
but in the process the American and European churches rediscovered
one another, and their mutual relationships continued during the
post-war reconstruction period.

In 1918, for example, the Federal Council of Churches
formed a Committee for Christian Relief in France and Belgium,
and the French followed suit with a *Comité d'Union Protestante*.
These two organizations maintained a variety of relationships
transcending mere monetary exchange. Continental churches began
sending representatives to America for fraternal exchange, while
the Americans sent delegations of "friendly visitors" to Europe.
Plans were made to exchange students and professors, and even
ministers. At the Third Quadrennial Meeting of the Federal
Council of Churches in Boston, December 1-6, 1920, delegates were
welcomed from Great Britain, France, Belgium, Holland, Hungary,
Transylvania, Italy, Japan, Mexico, Switzerland, and China. Most
of these countries had already entertained visitors from the
American churches. The *Federal Council Bulletin* (and other Protestant periodicals to a somewhat lesser degree) during the years
1918 through 1921 was filled with articles and photos of the
European churches and leaders, noting the new American awareness
of religion across the seas. French Protestant history became
especially popular in America, with the Huguenots romantically
portrayed as suffering pioneers in the cause of democracy and
justice and general goodness. Hence in a new way American Protestant eyes had been turned to the history, the faith, and the
life of churches on the other side of the Atlantic. As reported
in the *Federal Council Bulletin*: "The new ties of friendship
and new plans for cooperation which the war has brought about
between the churches of America and Europe are omens of the new
day which is arising out of the darkness of that struggle."[3]

Visions of "the new day" in which not only American and
European Christians but Christians around the world would join
hands in common cause energized the heartbeat of the Interchurch
World Movement. The Movement was conceived in the American brand
of ecumenical spirit with a world missionary vision. Its leaders
desired no absolute or permanent national limitations to the
Movement, even insuring its legal right to move beyond American
shores.[4] *The Christian Advocate* captured their ecumenical mood:

72

"It is not too much to expect that this step taken now by American Protestantism will lead ultimately to a federation of the Protestant churches of all nations under a common leadership for the conquest of the world for Christ."[5] That actual plans for such a world federation were being considered by Interchurch World Movement leaders is apparent from statements made at the World Survey Conference in January, 1920, asking that the Movement's plans and activities be communicated to missionary organizations in Great Britain, in Europe, in Asia and Africa.[6]

Moreover, with something like an international federation of denominations in mind, the Interchurch World Movement was modeled conceptually after the proposed League of Nations: "While the League of Nations is based on international laws and is to hold governments in check, the League of Denominations is based on loyalty to Jesus Christ and is intended to promote His Kingdom on earth."[7] This identification with the League of Nations, made by both Interchurch supporters and critics, secured the ecumenical image of the Movement.

This ecumenical vision was complemented, or balanced, by a determination to make America's participation in international Christianity a clearly identifiable Protestant national thrust. Aside from ecclesiastical factors engaging American Protestants in early twentieth century ecumenism, the overarching forces of cultural unity and disunity played a significant role in interchurch relations during this time. The dominant Protestant cultural heritage which informed the United States' popular interpretation of her role in World War I as defender of Christian democracy at home and abroad tended to enhance the churches' consciousness of bearing together the inspiration and ethical meaning of military victory. Wholehearted endorsement by Protestant leaders of America's claim to magnanimity in entering the war had crossed nearly all confessional barriers. The wartime experience seemed to demonstrate that the churches' programs remained essential to the health of the nation, that the well-being of mankind continued to depend upon the Christian influence of America, and that the diverse churches could join forces in a forward march. To Americans the war had presented a supreme challenge to Christian civilization, and, the military conflict won, it now remained for a full cultural thrust (with Protestantism at its core) to seal the overall moral victory.

Churchmen quite naturally expected encouragement for their post-war programs from the general public and their elected public leaders, and at first these expectations were met. Denominational gatherings to plan forward movements received messages of sympathy and appreciation from public figures. The Presbyterian New Era Movement Conference at Lake Geneva, Wisconsin, for example, heard from President Woodrow Wilson, Vice-President Thomas B. Marshall, Secretary of State Lansing, and Secretary of Interior Franklin K. Lane--Presbyterian Elders all. Wilson commended the church for its vitality as an "instrument of high public service in the nation." Marshall acknowledged the historic virtue of church-state separation in America but warned that "it would be a distinctly evil thing to separate state and Christianity." Lansing called for "a living, aggressive Christianity" to win the "supreme conflict" between good and evil in the world as the new era emerged. The *New Era Magazine* editors, believing that "these words of wisdom from leaders of the nation [carried] a resistless challenge to the mind and heart of every thinking man and woman," were confident that their denomination, at least, was moving forward in rapport with the national powers that be.[8] Other denominations thought the same of themselves; and their involvement in the grandiose programs of the Interchurch World Movement meant, in part, that they would insure their place in the vanguard of American cultural Protestantism.

The Interchurch World Movement represented, potentially, the formalization and institutionalization of a quasi-Protestant establishment in the United States. The thirty denominations participating in the joint budget represented about sixty percent of Protestant church membership in America, and it was expected that more denominations would join in subsequent years. Of the approximately one hundred million population of America in 1920, twenty-five million were recorded Protestant church members and another twenty-five million were considered "of Protestant root, or Protestant training." This made "a Protestant constituency in America, conservatively, of fifty million."[9] The Interchurch World Movement thus sought to identify with, and seek the financial support of, at least half the American population, to which it attributed an amorphous evangelical religiosity nearly indistinguishable from the traditionally dominant characteristics of American culture, ideals, and political-social-economic policies. It intended to become the central organizational representative of American Protestantism *in toto*. If successful, it could have become the most powerful organized religious force in the nation's history. That Secretary of State Robert Lansing became chairman

of the Interchurch General Committee and an active promoter of the
movement gave it political prestige. But Lansing was not alone,
for Vice-President Marshall, House Speaker Gillett, Senators
Spencer of Missouri and Harding of Ohio, Secretary of Treasury
McAdoo, Navy Secretary Daniels, General John J. Pershing, Mrs.
Woodrow Wilson, and a host of other persons closely related to
top government power publically and actively promoted the Interchurch World Movement.[10] The largest segment of American religion,
it seemed, not only was becoming officially identified with a
single organization but was promoted by top political forces.

On the assumption that America still was not only essentially Christian but essentially Protestant, and believing that
Protestant Americans had proven by their wartime performance
their true unified Christian spirit, Interchurch World Movement
leaders planned to raise the joint budget and finance their movement from the support of the general public. Not only had
America's military goals and the Christian mission become confused, but practically all traditional distinctions between church
members and non-church members in defining the word "Christian"
had been discarded.

Interchurch leaders thus coined a new category of "friendly citizen" to denote non-church members who made no public pro-
fession of faith yet called themselves "Protestant" or "Christian."
These "unattached Christians," explained the *Christian Advocate*,
"were persons of business mentality and virtue who, "in obedience
to their best impulse," often gave to hospitals, schools, etc.,
organizations "which embody and express the humanitarian side of
Christ's gospel." Moreover, since they had given generously to
the war cause, they could be expected to give liberally to the
Interchurch World Movement. They therefore would "be visited
and invited to give proof of their friendliness by subscribing
to the Fund." In this vein a *Saturday Evening Post* advertisement
called on "each person who loves and believes in America" to contribute; while a *New York Times* ad asked, "will you do your share
for a better America and a better world" (by contributing).[11]
The friendly citizens canvass was meant to build up the Interchurch central treasury, which would be used to finance the
Interchurch programs and pay off all denominational underwritings.
Ironically, therefore, the central organizational force of unitive
American Protestantism was to be supported financially by non-
church members. In essence, it was to be a public supported
religious organization, albeit voluntary. On this voluntary

basis, therefore, a nation becoming united religiously would pave
the way to the Christianization and democratization of the world.

It became apparent, however, that the grand vision of
national religious unity could not begin to be fulfilled until
divisions among American churches were considered at the funda-
mental ecclesiastical (if not theological) levels. The denominational bodies were agonizingly slow in committing themselves
legally and financially to the Interchurch World Movement, and
then as commitments finally did emerge, other interdenominational
groups became confused about their own existence. Care had to be
taken to prevent the Interchurch World Movement from becoming
more divisive than unitive, an accomplishment soon to seem impossible. The entire process displayed for all to see the various
facets and the conflicting forces at play in unitive American
Protestantism.

The Interchurch World Movement arose within a century-old
American Protestant tradition of voluntaryism--non-ecclesiastical
(extra-ecclesiastical) cooperation of persons from various denominations in forming societies for well-defined religious oriented
tasks. Without any formal or ecclesiastical authority, the origi-
nators of the Interchurch World Movement entered into a covenant
and developed an organization to facilitate cooperative church
work. Only after the movement was well under way did its leaders
begin to secure formal participation and support of ecclesiastical
bodies. And then they sought, at first, only endorsements and
cooperation rather than organic ecclesiastical ties.

Even after the Movement by necessity became organically
related to denominational bodies it retained the air of an extra-
ecclesiastical, voluntary association intent upon being not a
permanent union of churches or denominations, but only a temporary
"instrumentality of cooperation and coordination of administrative
agencies designed to serve and not to supplant them."[12] The terms
most often used to describe its role in unitive Protestantism were
arouse, stimulate, instigate, facilitate, coordinate, supervise,
and promote. But the Interchurch World Movement, unlike all
previous voluntary societies, tried to accomplish these functions
by combining all aspects of Protestant endeavor.

Whereas cooperation on an extra-ecclesiastical, voluntary
basis inspired the formation of the Interchurch World Movement,
a second, more churchly-oriented movement for unity developing
within the denominational structures of American Protestantism
presented an alternative approach. It already had assumed the

pattern of interchurch, interboard, and interdenominational counciliar federations.[13] The federative movement, therefore, arose in the context of an increasing denominational self-awareness, denominational strength, and denominational unification in American Protestantism during the late nineteenth and early twentieth centuries. First came the formation of denominational boards and commissions to do the kind of work already begun by nondenominational movements and agencies, such as social service, student and laymen missionary promotion, Sunday schools and youth fellowships. Then followed the coordination and unification of these various boards and commissions within the denominational machinery. The total result was a strengthening of denominations at the same time that cross-denominational activity was flourishing. Many churchmen were becoming convinced that federation was the most feasible means of maintaining and furthering unity without countering denominationalism.

The successful wartime military alliances convinced many American Protestants that denominations could be federated without losing their autonomy or individuality. Diverse nations like Russia, England, Serbia, Belgium, Japan, Italy, and the United States had become "progressively and unconquerably one" in war without sacrificing their autonomy or sovereignty or nationality. Since "the doughboy was no less an American, the *poilu* no less a Frenchman, and Tommy Atkins no less British because they had clasped hands," could not Presbyterians, Baptists, and Methodists clasp hands without losing their peculiar identities? Many thought that they could and should.[14]

Leaders of the Federal Council of Churches had from its start in 1908 affirmed the principle of a close cooperation of fully autonomous church bodies by limiting the Council's constitutional powers accordingly. In 1919 the General Secretary reaffirmed this principle in his annual report to the Executive Committee, recognizing that the various denominations were "real entities . . . grounded in history . . . built upon foundations of principles . . . effectively organized in well-ordered administrative machinery . . . . Each [making] its distinct contribution to the whole life of the church."[15] Hence the Federal Council did not seek organic union of churches or denominations, but simply the consultation and cooperation of churches and denominations through accredited ecclesiastical delegations. The Council itself held no superior ecclesiastical authority, but acted only in an advisory capacity.

Organic union, however, is not necessarily incompatible
with federation, the obvious example being a political state such
as the United States of America in which each State surrenders
part of its sovereignty to the central body.   Proposals actually
were made in 1920 for a federal union of churches to be known as
"The United Churches of Christ in America," in which certain
powers would be delegated to the central agency.   But this movement, which began in 1918 with a Conference on Organic Union in
Philadelphia called by the Northern Presbyterian Church, was distinguished from the Federal Council of Churches not so much by
its explicit proposals ("The Philadelphia Plan") as by its impli-
cit goal of ultimate organic church union.[16]   The plan never
materialized, being criticized both by those who thought it too
similar to the Federal Council to merit existence, and by those
who believed that it leaned too heavily toward organic union.

The Philadelphia Plan, advertised as a first step toward
organic church union, caused some to suspect all unitive movements of the day.   Especially did the Interchurch World Movement,
with its massive organization and comprehensive scope, loom large
as a potential threat to denominational autonomy.   Moreover,
organic union could be read into some of the public statements
about the Movement's goals.   For example, S. Earl Taylor told the
Foreign Missions Conference in January of 1919 that the Interchurch World Movement was not striving toward "organic union
immediately."   Likewise, *The Christian Advocate* reported that
"the question of organic union is not involved in it, though no
one can tell what the ultimate reach of this unprecedented movement may be."   But *New Era Magazine* frankly called it the "practical precursor" of organic union.[17]

The Interchurch World Movement meant many things to many
people; but it made no serious official claim to be furthering
the organic union of the churches.   Like the Federal Council of
Churches, it took the framework of denominational organization
as it found it.   Moreover, from the very beginning its formal
statements explicitly disavowed any intentions to usurp denominational authority or autonomy.   The World Survey Conference in
January, 1920, declared that "the authority of the Movement rests
solely in the challenge of the facts it is able to present."[18]
Hence the Interchurch World Movement sought to exert an authority
over American Protestantism based on wisdom and knowledge and
spiritual fuel--not binding, but profoundly influential.   It con-
templated no Christian union in which it would have legal ecclesiastical authority.

Despite their insistence that the Interchurch World Movement not be in itself an ecclesiastical union of any kind, but merely an instrumentality of cooperation, leaders of the Movement soon found it necessary to seek the "closest possible ecclesiastical affiliation." In the process, the Interchurch World Movement became transformed into an interboard, interdenominational federation.[19]

The Interchurch leaders, themselves representatives of denominational organizations, had always desired the support and cooperation of the missionary and benevolent boards. That was basic to the Movement's whole purpose--to facilitate cooperation. Moreover, the Movement began with the specific intention of combining the efforts of denominational forward movements. But it soon became apparent that in many cases no more than cordial approval or endorsement could be secured from these organizations. Denominations generally had for a decade or more been progressively unifying their various organizations to the point that individual boards could not or would not commit themselves--their programs and resources--without official denominational authority. Furthermore, because forward movements comprised all of the boards and societies of their respective denominations acting as a unit, any alteration in their plans would require denominational rulings. Consequently, only by securing official denominational endorsement and, finally, affiliation could the Interchurch leaders expect concrete support for their large, highly organized, and many-faceted Movement.

Concrete financial support soon became an urgent necessity, and it was this fact which finally changed the nature of the Interchurch World Movement. Its leaders had hoped immediately to set the Movement on an independent financial basis by means of borrowed capital from banks. In addition to borrowing on their own credit (which was insufficient) they intended to ask the various boards and societies to underwrite bank loans on behalf of the Interchurch World Movement with the expectation that subsequent donations in the united financial campaign would cover the underwritings. But by the time the General Committee met in September, 1919, although over seventy denominational and interdenominational agencies had endorsed the Movement, only its bare expenses up to that time had been borrowed through underwritings. The greatest expense was yet to come! It was then that the Executive Committee decided to seek the "closest possible affiliation" with ecclesiastical bodies, through their official

representation on the General Committee, and systematically to
solicit financial support for the large and expensive Interchurch
campaigns ahead.[20]

At this juncture a new category of legal financial affiliation began to transform the Interchurch World Movement into an
ecclesiastical federation. In virtually every case a denomination's decision to underwrite meant uniting its forward movement,
including its campaign budget, with the Interchurch World Movement. As this happened, the Movement became a denominationally
financed and controlled agency, resembling the Federal Council
of Churches.[21]

In many ways denominational control of the Interchurch
World Movement brought it into conflict with other unitive Protestant organizations, especially with the Federal Council of
Churches. The problems focused on duplication of work and compe-
tition for financial support. When the Interchurch World Movement became generously underwritten and bound closely to the
large denominational financial campaigns of 1920, the Federal
Council of Churches and other federated agencies were left to
fend for themselves against difficult odds.

The Interchurch World Movement and the Federal Council of
Churches were natural competitors in the cooperative religious
enterprise. Both operated in the whole scope of Protestant endeavor, thus sharing common concerns in many areas. The Federal
Council had gained the confidence of the churches during the war
and secured its place as their official representative in matters
of common interest. But the Interchurch World Movement caught
the imagination of many Protestant leaders who considered it *the
new unitive force* in American Protestantism. Some of the Federal
Council leaders themselves--especially those also holding Interchurch positions--were prepared either to merge the Council with
the Interchurch World Movement or see the Council die.[22] Against
them remained a core of stalwart defenders of the Federal Council
led by its General Secretary Charles S. Macfarland.

Feeling the need for a common understanding of the relationship between the two organizations, the Federal Council's
Administrative Committee arranged for a conference with the
Interchurch Executive Committee for April 28, 1919. At this conference, Fred B. Smith (an advocate of merging the two organizations) and Macfarland presented papers for a basis of discussion.[23]
Smith, who was chairman both of the Federal Council's Commission
on Interchurch Federations and of the Convention Committee of the

Interchurch World Movement, suggested that the Interchurch World
Movement utilize existing local federations of churches, and that
the Federal Council in turn insure the adequacy and cooperation
of these federations. Macfarland differentiated between the
Federal Council as the one "permanent organization, ecclesiastically constituted," providing a foundation of all other unity
movements, and the Interchurch World Movement as a temporary,
non-ecclesiastical voluntary movement with limited objectives.
The two organizations thus should remain mutually independent,
he reasoned, and care must be taken to avoid duplication of work.
Yet the two organizations may be of mutual benefit, and "the
Interchurch World Movement will necessarily have special relationships with certain Commissions of the Federal Council." Finally,
Macfarland considered it important that "in its financial campaign the Interchurch World Movement should take into account
its effect on the financial support of the Federal Council, and
arrangement should be made whereby the Federal Council shall be
protected."

After long discussion, these papers were accepted by both
Committees (which together became a Joint Committee on Cooperation) as an informal agreement regarding their mutual relationships. Almost immediately Federal Council Commissions and
Departments of the Interchurch World Movement began cooperating
in joint programs, sharing personnel and resources, until the
two organizations became entangled in a complex web of inter-
relationships.[24] Meanwhile, the Federal Council, at a special
meeting in Cleveland on May 6-8, 1919, saw fit to endorse the
Interchurch World Movement formally and publically with a carefully worded statement clarifying the differences in nature and
function between the two organizations.

During the next few months, however, as the Interchurch
program expanded beyond all expectations, it became apparent to
Federal Council leaders that distinctions of function and field
between the two organizations were increasingly blurred, especially after the September concordat between the Interchurch
General Committee and the denominations. On November 14, 1919,
therefore, the Federal Council Administrative Committee asked
Macfarland to meet privately with S. Earl Taylor to consider
further the matter of relationships. On November 25, the two
General Secretaries met in Taylor's office, where Macfarland
presented a series of questions and asked that the Interchurch
Cabinet reply. The questions pertained mainly to the April 28

agreement (Was it being kept?) and to the Interchurch leaders'
present conception of their Movement's role in the whole program
of cooperative Protestantism. In a lengthy written reply[25] the
Cabinet stated its intention to respect the earlier agreement,
then explained "that the rapid enlargement of the staff of the
Interchurch World Movement and the unprecedented expansion of its
whole enterprise may have conspired to prevent the agreement being
lived up to fully in all of its provisions." Some adjustments of
Interchurch policy had been necessary, requiring modifications of
its agreement with the Federal Council. The Cabinet reaffirmed
the unique role of the Interchurch World Movement in "the con-
ceiving and carrying out of plans and programs so much faster
than any that have yet been proposed, that they may well terrify
any but resolute and courageous souls." Christian unity on a
lesser basis would be inadequate. Finally, the Cabinet encouraged
more extensive and intimate cooperation between the Interchurch
World Movement and the Federal Council.

For the Federal Council, these rather vague statements
did not solve the problems, especially financial ones. Beginning
on December 16, 1919, there began an extensive correspondence
between Macfarland and Taylor about the financial difficulties
of the Federal Council due to the relationship of the Interchurch
World Movement to the denominations. Unintentionally the Interchurch World Movement was encroaching on the Federal Council's
main source of income--individual contributions. Many former
contributors failed to understand the distinction between the
Federal Council and the Interchurch World Movement, thinking that
by giving to their denomination's forward movement (which pastors
and denominational leaders urged them to do) they were supporting
both the Interchurch World Movement and the Fedearl Council. The
Interchurch leaders, who regretted not being able to include the
Federal Council in the joint budget, asked the denominations to
include in their budgets appropriations for the Federal Council.[26]
But the denominations, already burdened with greatly increased
budgets, did not respond; and Macfarland found it nearly impossible to keep the Federal Council afloat financially.

It was increasingly clear to Federal Council leaders that
the Interchurch World Movement threatened to become a representative organization similar to the Federal Council, yet with a
more adequate budget. In April of 1920 the *Federal Council Bulletin* carried an article explaining that "the Interchurch World

Movement is only carrying forward, in an aggressive way, the
interests of the missionary agencies of the churches whose normal
activities of a more general sort have been so successfully provided by the Federal Council."[27] It soon would be apparent which
one would emerge as the strongest, most useful and enduring unitive force in American Protestantism.

Actually this rather dramatic contest between the Interchurch World Movement and the Federal Council of Churches had
become less a battle of principles than a power struggle for
organizational control of unitive American Protestantism. The
nature and purpose of the "real united Protestantism" (to repeat
J. Campbell White's words of April 30, 1919) was understood
similarly by advocates of both organizations and resembled more
the Life and Work aspect of the rising ecumenical movement than
the Faith and Order aspect.

By historical precedent and conviction, American Protestants conceived of church unity as a practical matter requiring
operational, corporate discipleship--the Christian life being
lived together in common activity. Not unity per se, as an end
in itself, but unity in and for action was their goal. Their
utilitarian argument for unity raised the question: "How can we,
in our diversity, combine our forces for more efficient, more
effective life and work in the world?"

The Federal Council of Churches operated on a utilitarian
premise, seeking to determine the will of its component bodies,
to interpret their will in terms of common policy, and to effect
the policy through the united action of its component bodies.
It spent no effort on matters of theology and polity. In 1916,
the Report of the Council's Executive Commission declared that in
Faith and Order "perfect agreement in opinion, placid uniformity
in expression and method, do not appear. It is a waste of energy
to seek for either." In 1917, R. B. Guild, Executive Secretary
of the Commission on Interchurch Federations of the Federal
Council of Churches, expressed the "work-together" spirit which
dominated the Council's interpretation of its *raison d'être* in
his book appropriately entitled *Practicing Christian Unity*.[28]

The Interchurch World Movement likewise expressed the
notion of pragmatic unity for life and work. The Movement's
literature spills over with statements to that effect. The
"Report of the Committee of Twenty" called for "a united program
of Christian service . . . . to unite the Protestant churches

in the performance of their common task." A widely distributed
pamphlet noted the deepening conviction "that since the churches
can do so much more by working together than they can do by working without intelligent regard to each other, it is their clear
duty to cooperate to the fullest possible extent." A special
Committee on World Survey Program and Budget reporting to the
World Survey Conference in January, 1920, stated that "we believe
the time is fully ripe for such unity of action on the part of
united Protestantism, that, without attempting to solve the problems arising from divergent and conscientiously held points of
view in matters of doctrines and policy, the churches are ready
for a common program of activity.[29]

At an earlier national conference, Executive Committee
member Hubert C. Herring (General Secretary of the National
Council of Congregational Churches) left no doubt about the Movement's disinterest in Faith and Order: "It involves no ecclesiastical question . . . . It does not demand that we become
sponsor for one another's theology . . . . It demands simply
that we be sponsors of one another's Christianity." James I.
Vance, with a touch of sarcasm, pressed the same point, calling
the Interchurch World Movement "not a scheme for a rosewater
creed." Rather was it a magnificent plan, in the words of W. E.
Doughty, to "lay aside our differences, while retaining our
identity, yet in obedience to the call of God, under a unified
command face our whole common task together." But it was Shailer
Mathews who, after carefully observing the Interchurch World Movement from his Dean's chair at the University of Chicago, best
described its true nature and purpose with the kind of lavish
phraseology common to its advocates:

> The Interchurch World Movement is the greatest
> piece of cooperative activity Protestantism has
> ever undertaken. It is outstanding evidence that
> denominationalism is not sectarianism. In a sing-
> ularly happy way the movement as now organized
> maintains the integrity of denominations, yet
> unites millions in a common effort to further the
> kingdom of God. . . . It raises no question of
> organic church unity, and beyond the great evan-
> gelical truths does not demand a common platform
> of theology. It is an outstanding exhibition of
> the practical as over against the theoretical.
> And what theory ever ventured to dream what it
> is really doing?[30]

In summary, the Interchurch World Movement originated as
an independent voluntary association of individuals to promote
and coordinate ambitious post-World War I missionary-benevolent

programs of American Protestantism. But whereas its primary function as servant of the churches via promotion and coordination never basically changed, organizationally the Movement was gradually transformed into an interboard-interdenominational federation through (in most cases) their own forward movements. Never did the Interchurch World Movement intend or attempt to usurp ecclesiastical authority or autonomy, nor did it seek to unite organically churches or denominations. With an ecumenical vision on the basis of Life and Work, the Interchurch World Movement sought to transcend all Protestant divisions as a great, overarching unitive force. The attempt was made to organize accordingly, in a manner befitting religion in a business civilization.

1. Galley printing of speeches April 30-May 1, 1919, p. 3.

2. *The Christian Advocate*, February 27, 1919, p. 266; R. B. Guild, *Practicing Christian Unity* (New York, 1919), p. 60; and *World Outlook*, V (September, 1919), pp. 18-19.

3. *Federal Council Bulletin*, III (April, 1920), p. 76; also II (April, 1919), p. 66; IV (January, 1921), pp. 14-15; and the General Secretary's *Report to the Executive Committee of the Churches of Christ in America for the Year 1919* (New York, 1919), pp. 11-16.

4. See the "Certificate of Incorporation of Interchurch World Movement," in IWM Documents, VII, p. 41.

5. *The Christian Advocate*, January 23, 1919, p. 98.

6. IWM Documents, III, p. 90.

7. *The Missionary Review of the World*, XLII (June, 1919), p. 403.

8. *New Era Magazine*, I (October, 1919), pp. 558-60.

9. A. E. Cory, "Field Program of the Interchurch Movement," galley printing of speeches, April 30-May 1, 1919, p. 19. See also *World Call*, II (April, 1920), p. 57. *The Year Book of Churches*, 1920 (New York, 1920), p. 196, states Protestant church membership in America at 25,980,456, adding that "the whole number of those who could call themselves Protestant is of course much larger."

10. See *New York Times*, January 22, 1920, p. 17:3; March 29, 1920, p. 6:3; and April 21, 1920, p. 17:6.

11. *Saturday Evening Post*, April 24, 1920, pp. 122-23; and *New York Times*, April 8, 1920, p. 32.

12. "Findings of the Cleveland Interboard Conference, April 30-May 1, 1919," IWM Documents, I, pp. 33-35, which also states that the Interchurch is "not an ecclesiastical movement" and "has a definite and temporary mission."

13. The term *counciliar* refers to the function of an assembly (discussion, advice, administration, etc.); whereas *federation* refers to the structure of an assembly, namely a

central organization formed by a number of separate
agencies, each retaining control of its own internal
affairs.

14. For example, Charles Edward Jefferson, *What the War has
Taught Us* (New York, 1919), p. 119; *The Interchurch World
Movement of North America: What It Is* (New York, 1919);
World Outlook, V (September, 1919), pp. 18-19; *The Chris-
tian Advocate*, February 27, 1919, p. 266; and *The American
Review of Reviews*, LIX (June, 1919), p. 635.

15. *Federal Council Bulletin*, II (June, 1919), p. 106. A clear
statement of the federative principle held by the Federal
Council was R. B. Guild, *The Manual of Inter-Church Work*
(New York, 1917), pp. 195-206. Organic union, in contrast,
generally meant the outward and internal oneness of churches
under a single structure, forming one body (though perhaps
with many congregations), and the implication of finality.
See W. A. Brown, *Introduction to Christian Unity: Its
Principles and Possibilities* (New York, 1921), pp. 11-12.

16. On the Philadelphia Plan, see *World Call*, I (February,
1919), pp. 27-28; (March, 1919), pp. 23-24; II (January,
1920), p. 42; (April, 1920), pp. 24-25; *New Era Magazine*,
I (January, 1919), pp. 13-14; and II (July, 1920), pp.
512-13.

17. *Foreign Missions Conference of North America, Report of
the Boards*, 1919, p. 175; *The Christian Advocate*, January
23, 1919, p. 98; and *New Era Magazine*, I (March, 1919),
p. 120.

18. "Report of the Committee on World Survey Program and Budget," in IWM Documents, III, p. 91.

19. This decision was made formally by the Executive Committee,
September 29, 1919, recorded in the minutes, IWM Documents,
II, p. 17. A distinction sometimes was made between federation and administrative union or bureau, the latter
bringing denominational agencies into union through their
supreme judicatories specifically. The distinction was
slight but valid, yet the separate terms sometimes confus-
ing. Federation was the more comprehensive term and
applicable to the Interchurch World Movement's final
organization. See, for example, C. R. Athearn, *Interchurch Government* (New York, 1925), pp. 175-230.

20. For accounts of this development, see minutes of Executive
Committee and minutes of Cabinet, IWM Documents, VI, pp.

111-113; "Report of Special Committee on Underwritings to Cabinet, September 18, 1919," and "Report on Budget and Underwriting to General Committee," September 24-26, 1919, in *ibid.*, VI, pp. 112-119.

21. The Interchurch World Movement's loss of independence was admitted by S. Earl Taylor in *Federal Council Bulletin*, III (April, 1920), p. 67.

22. Federal Council General Secretary Charles S. Macfarland recalled the pressure from within his organization in his *Christian Unity in Practice and Prophecy* (New York, 1933), p. 69, and *Across the Years* (New York, 1936), p. 190.

23. See "Minutes of April 28, 1919, Meeting between Federal Council Administrative Committee and Executive Committee of Interchurch World Movement," IWM Documents, II, p. 24. The statements presented by Smith and Macfarland were published in several places, such as the *Federal Council Bulletin*, III (January, 1920), p. 15.

24. Correspondence between Federal Council and Interchurch leaders, on file at the Research Library of the National Council of Churches in New York City, reveals the intricacies of these varying relationships (henceforth referred to as FCC-IWM papers).

25. Letter from Taylor to Macfarland, December 12, 1919, including the full text of the reply. The text also appears in IWM Documents, II, pp. 29-32. See also Macfarland's "Report to the Executive Committee of the Federal Council . . . 1919," p. 22, and correspondence between Macfarland and Taylor on November 17, 1919, and November 26, 1919, in FCC-IWM papers.

26. Macfarland to Taylor, December 24, 1919, and January 27, 1920; W. H. Foulkes to Macfarland, April 2, 1920; and Macfarland to F. B. Smith, April 7, 1920, in FCC-IWM papers.

27. *Federal Council Bulletin*, III (April, 1920), pp. 63-64.

28. Guild, *Practicing Christian Unity*, p. 46. For another discussion, see Mode, "Aims and Methods of Contemporary Church Movements in America," *The American Journal of Theology*, XIV (April, 1920), pp. 224-230.

29. The report is in IWM Documents, III, p. 85. The pamphlet entitled *The Interchurch World Movement of North America: What It Is.*

30.   Mathews' statement in *Watchman-Examiner*, VIII (January,
       1920), p. 20.   Other quotations are H. C. Herring, "The
       Historical Development of the Interchurch World Movement,"
       galley printing of speeches April 30-May 1, p. 6; and J.
       I. Vance, a speech at the Tennessee Training Conference,
       December 8, 1919, in IWM Documents, I, p. 45.

CHAPTER V

THE BUSINESS OF RELIGION: EFFICIENT PIETY
AND SACRED PROMOTION

On the eve of a united Protestant evangelistic campaign in
April of 1920, a bulletin was sent to churchmen across the nation
from Interchurch Headquarters in New York City concerning "the
biggest business of the biggest man in the world."

> Christ was big, was He not? None ever bigger.
> Christ was busy, was He not? None ever busier.
> He was always about His Father's business.

Evangelism, declared the bulletin, is big business; and "Christ
needs big men for big business."[1]

By the end of World War I "our business civilization" had
come of age, and during the following decade it promised to fulfill the American dream. The potential of business in helping
to create a rich and efficient economy--mass production, mass
consumption, high profits and high wages--apparently had been
proved during the national wartime crisis. The old progressive
opposition to big business seemed to have died. Americans accepted
business almost religiously as a way of life, attributing to it
values usually reserved for religion or the church.[2]

The churches did not escape the cult of business, nor did
they want to. Churchmen affirmed the principles and patterns of
business with sincerity; they too were believers. Big business
had demonstrated how large programs could be accomplished without
waste of energy or resources. Pragmatically the many denominations could only benefit from this example in carrying through
their common tasks. "There is just as great need of business in
religion as of religion in business," stated *New Era Magazine*,
"and both together are to be transformed into the service of men
and the glory of God."[3]

The marriage of business and religion already was well on
its way. In August of 1920, *The Baptist* carried an article stating that "the church is an immense business enterprise, acquiring
and managing property, employing and paying men, building and
running great houses and sending its representatives around the

world." A few months earlier, a *New Era Magazine* editorial
pointed to the "notable fact that the church is rather wide awake
to the importance of employing approved business methods in sys-
tematizing and administering its work."[4] Now the Interchurch
World Movement was not meant to be *a church* either in structure
or function (congregation, ministry, sacraments), but an agency
of the churches helping them to function together more efficiently.
Nevertheless, the Interchurch World Movement did intend to represent organized Protestantism; and if not a church in a traditional
sense, it was a religious business enterprise with much "new
machinery" and employing all "approved business methods."

If in the pre-war movements (such as the Men and Religion
Forward Movement) business and religion became partners, in the
Interchurch World Movement the two were wedded. With its complex
structure--its hierarchy of committees, its core of executives
and staff covering the nation yet centralized in a New York City
headquarters, and its gigantic budget--the Interchurch World
Movement self-consciously exemplified most of the characteristics
of big business bureaucracy. All of this was geared to promote
and coordinate, but not control, organized Protestant work in
America from the national level down to each of approximately
two hundred thousand local churches. Considering the haste in
which this large, complex structure was assembled, it seemed, at
the end of the first year, "well balanced and so related as to
insure coordination in all of its parts with a minimum of fric-
tion and duplication."[5] Interchurch Headquarters in New York
City started the engine and furnished the fuel, but the whole
nation was its field of operation.

In order fully to appreciate the business-like character
of the Interchurch World Movement, one must recognize both the
actual organization in New York City and the plans envisaged for
the future. The Movement had been launched as a five-year program, but its leaders anticipated such success that the churches
finally would demand its continued, perhaps permanent, establishment.[6] These anticipations were set in concrete form with the
creation of a large central headquarters having many features of
a permanent business house.

During the first year, the Interchurch organization rented
office space in various New York City buildings, until finally
the booming enterprise was housed in parts of ten different
buildings scattered about the city. This was both inefficient
and costly--$1,200,000 per year. By the summer of 1919, the

Interchurch leaders had begun looking for some building large
enough to house all central activities. Numerous proposals were
made concerning an Interchurch Headquarters, proposals both to
rent and to build. Of the latter proposals, the most ambitious
was an offer by a finance agency to erect a forty-story Interchurch Tower at Madison Square Garden costing around twenty-five
million dollars. The building would house all American Protestant
organizations and within thirty years become property of the Interchurch World Movement free of debt. The Interchurch leaders, after
careful thought, rejected the offer temporarily. They could not
see their way to engage the denominations in such a long-range
Interchurch expense, despite such "a splendid business opportunity," until the success of their working together on a large-scale
basis had been proved.[7] But they were thinking in terms of thirty
years or more.

Meanwhile, the search for an adequate Interchurch Headquarters continued through the remainder of the year. Office
rental was high, but early in 1920 an excellent negotiation was
made. The Greenhut Building at 45 West 18th Street, a five-story
ex-department store used by the Government during the War as a
debarkation hospital, was secured on a ten-year lease for the low
sum of $441,111 per year. This building was larger than the
Interchurch World Movement needed at the time; but it was expected
that through expanding the Interchurch activities, providing space
for denominational forward movements, and sub-leasing the remaining space, the building soon would become fully occupied.[8]

It was not long before the Interchurch work itself made
good use of the building. A growing volume of business required
the purchase of four trucks which were kept in constant employment. By May of 1920, the Interchurch World Movement had staffed
its massive bureaucracy with a total of 2,612 employees, a majority of them working in the Greenhut Building. Like many big
businesses after World War I, the Interchurch World Movement
organized its large staff of employees into a cohesive social
unit, assuming the functions of a variety of social organizations.
The Personnel Department, trying to keep the employees "efficient
and happy at their work. . . . organized a choral society, orchestra, baseball club, hiking club and an employees' publication. It [kept] nurses in constant attendance for the care of
those ill or injured in the building, or for visiting the homes."[9]

The Interchurch leaders, however, had in mind a larger,
permanent consolidation of Protestant enterprises under one great

92

roof. According to George M. Fowles, Treasurer of the Movement,
"The Interchurch had more than enough applications from religious,
philanthropic and educational organizations, to use every foot of
the Greenhut Building that was not needed by the Interchurch. . . .
on the condition that the building would become a religious headquarters." Moreover, the vision of a great, forty-story Protestant headquarters in New York City--an Interchurch Tower--had not
been lost. "In due time," it was confidently said, "the churches
will desire to establish a church headquarters for the purpose of
housing the seventy-five or more international, national, metropolitan and civic religious agencies now inadequately located in
almost as many different offices in widely scattered buidings."

> In addition to the ordinary office facilities,
> this building would provide large and small
> assembly, conference and committee rooms, a
> restaurant, hospital, first-aid, rest-room and
> other social facilities for the hundreds of
> employees. A reference library of Christian
> literature, joint transportation, purchasing
> and shipping service, map, chart, and lantern-
> slide departments and every practical facility
> for promoting efficiency and economy in the
> great advance program of the Protestant churches
> of the entire country as well as those of the
> New York metropolitan area.

Here was the most magnificent of all American Protestant conceptions of pragmatic unity on the basis of efficiency and economy--
a building "to stand before the world as a great object lesson
of Protestant unity."[10]

Surely the world would marvel at such a demonstration.
"The principles of the Interchurch World Movement should appeal
to every businessman," wrote John D. Rockefeller, Jr. in 1920,
"because it aims to develop the maximum of efficiency in doing
the Lord's business." Rockefeller, a businessman of philanthropy
administering the distribution of his father's oil fortune, was
also a devoted Baptist churchman with a particular concern for
practical Christian unity. He became the most active of a large
number of prominent businessmen enthusiastically supporting the
Interchurch World Movement. His membership on the Interchurch
Executive Committee enhanced the Movement's prestige and added
business savvy to its leadership. Men like Rockefeller helped
define the specific functions and methods of the Interchurch
enterprise, making it an instrument through which the production
line of America's religious industry could operate with efficiency and economy.

American Protestants had begun to interpret their world
Christianization goals as a huge business venture. They intended
to establish local churches virtually everywhere on the globe
which would infiltrate and transform the social order. Reporting
as chairman of the Special Committee on Survey to the Northern
Baptist Convention in 1919, F. W. Padelford noted a revolutionary
new conception of the church's mission which had been developing
over the past quarter-century--"to create a Christian civilization." "Our business," he continued, "is to establish a civilization that is Christian in spirit and in passion, the world around,
in Borneo as much as in Boston." A year later, *New Era Magazine*
reported that, "Today foreign missions is by all odds the largest
business carried on by the people of the United States outside
the bounds of the land itself"--where the home missions enterprise
was also booming.[12]

The function of the Interchurch World Movement was to put
the business of religion on as efficient and economical a basis
as possible by acting as a clearing-house, a fact-finding and
data-processing firm, and a promotion agency. The aims of the
Training Division of the Life Work Department suggest one way in
which the Interchurch World Movement acted as a clearing-house of
information:

> To list the young men and women of character,
> capacity, and training, throughout the nation,
> and rate them so as to have available a classi-
> fied list of suitable persons to approach in
> order to meet emergency or specific needs for
> any kind of employed Christian service, as well
> as to rate those who are definite candidates for
> Christian callings. . . . To create a clearing
> house for workers seeking suitable fields, and
> agencies seeking workers.[13]

In other ways the Interchurch World Movement sought to improve
the communication among diverse groups and persons doing similar
work by providing occasions for face-to-face sharing of information and ideas. In January of 1920, for example, Interchurch
leaders brought together representatives of the Council of Church
Boards of Education, the Association of American Colleges, the
National Association of State Universities, the Association of
Theological Seminary Presidents, and the Association of American
Universities to discuss possible future plans for expanding the
nation's higher education facilities. In March, a similar conference was held in New York with editors of religious periodicals
and Sunday School publications throughout the country.[14] Hence
the Interchurch World Movement sought to facilitate a smooth,
coordinated operation of all American Protestant activities.

The Interchurch World Movement also acted as a fact-finding and data-processing firm by making a survey of "the home and foreign fields of the world" for the purpose of securing accurate and complete data relevant to the churches' Christianization operations. The surveys were very much a part of the business orientation of the Interchurch World Movement. "This great survey," Rockefeller told a New York gathering of twelve hundred clergymen in March of 1920, "is prophetic of a new era in Christian work. It is just such a survey as the conservative businessman makes of any field which he is proposing to enter." A few days earlier, *The Outlook* carried an article stating that "to the businessman the most impressive feature of these surveys and plans is their precision and definiteness and their effectiveness in contrasting what *has* been done with what *can* be done to forward the cause of Christianity throughout the world." In a publicity advertisement entitled "Now the Church Has Taken a Leaf from Successful Business," the Interchurch World Movement portrayed the surveys in a business image:

> Do you know why nine out of every ten business ventures fail? . . . They lacked the facts! Business cannot succeed without facts. The Church cannot prosper without facts. The Church today has the facts.[15]

With the facts, it was thought, the business of religion would prosper. The surveys were more than business tools; but the important point to note here is that gathering and processing data pertinent to the work of the churches became one of the main functions of the Interchurch World Movement.

As a promotion agency of the churches, the Interchurch World Movement did its most extensive and creative work. By reshaping and perfecting old techniques, experimenting with new ones, and formulating rationales for using them, the Interchurch World Movement helped usher the churches into the modern era. Promotion, essentially a kind of persuasive public education intended to garner support for religion, was done primarily through literature, publicity and advertising, exhibits and dramatics, conferences and public lectures.

Keeping pace with the rapidly growing business of mass media literature in twentieth century America, the Interchurch World Movement created Literature, Editorial, Periodical, Graphics, Statistical, Sales, and Research and Library Departments, as well as an Interchurch Press. Its various kinds of publications included bulletins, leaflets, pamphlets, periodicals, and books.

A Graphics Department handled map making, charts and illustration work. The Literature Department supervised the preparation, production, and distribution of all printed matter.

By the end of 1919, the Interchurch leaders had formed a Periodical Department producing four promotional-educational periodicals, each suited to a different clientele. *Everyland*, a magazine for teenagers, came with the Missionary Education Movement. For work in Latin America and among Spanish-speaking Americans, the Periodical Department created *La Nueva Democracia*. Beginning on October 2, 1919, an eight- to ten-page weekly *Interchurch Newsletter* was published which ran until December 25, 1919, at which time a larger newspaper was formed called the *Interchurch Bulletin*. The *Bulletin* actually reached a circulation high of over five hundred thousand--mainly pastors and other religious workers involved in Interchurch activities.[16]

The most spectacular publication of the Interchurch World Movement, and the one most suited to its promotional aims, was *World Outlook*. As early as February of 1919, the Executive Committee had begun thinking about entering the popular magazine business by consolidating some of the leading missionary magazines into an attractive monthly under the Interchurch name. Most overtures were politely turned down (such as one made to *The Missionary Review of the World*). But the Methodists already were publishing *World Outlook*, which was much like what the Interchurch leaders had in mind. Moreover, *World Outlook*, with a circulation of only thirty-four thousand, was running at an annual deficit of thirty thousand dollars. The Interchurch leaders not only succeeded in purchasing the magazine for one dollar per subscription (thirty-four thousand dollars), but also combined with it the monthly *Men and Missions* of the Laymen's Missionary Movement.

The first issue of *World Outlook* as an organ of the Interchurch World Movement appeared in November of 1919. The magazine's editorship remained the same. Willard Price, a world traveler who in 1918 had worked in the War Reconstruction Service in France and Italy, not only continued as editor of *World Outlook*, but became Director of the new Interchurch Periodical Department. He set about to make *World Outlook* the most effective missionary publication of the church. This meant, on the one hand, that the broad, progressive conception of the church's mission remained at the core of editorial policy. "It is the purpose of *World Outlook*," wrote Price, "to hold and enlarge its place as an authoritative magazine on world events viewed from

the Christian standpoint."[17] On the other hand, under Interchurch
auspices *World Outlook* became competitive in the class of large
national magazines with huge circulations appealing to the general
public interested in a variety of subjects. Here was a religious
magazine trying to be as attractive to the general reader as any
other magazine of sport, travel, science, art, or letters. Its
glossy pages presented fancy advertisements for all kinds of products, excellent photography and striking illustrations, even
serial short stories combining religion with sentimental romances--
a popular literary prelude to the 'twenties! Such popularizing
paid off, as the magazine nearly doubled its circulation within
six months (over sixty-three thousand). *World Outlook* thus became a very important means by which the Interchurch World Movement, utilizing the most modern literary methods, promoted American religion.

There were other means of promotion for Interchurch leaders
to utilize. By the second decade of the twentieth century, organized religion in America had begun to experiment, along with
business and industry, in the art of mass publicity and advertising. While promotion of religion through the written word was
hardly new, "scientific" advertising was an innovation. A big
step was taken when the Men and Religion Forward Movement formed
a Publicity Commission which made an exhaustive study of the
church and the secular press. Due partly to the Commission's
recommendation that the churches have a central agency through
which religious news might be fed to the newspapers, the Federal
Council of Churches formed a Religious Publicity Service. "Religious publicity is a science," explained R. B. Guild, Executive
Secretary of the Federal Council's Commission on Interchurch
Federation. "It is founded upon the laws of psychology, sociology, theology, and all the laws which apply to ordinary advertising." Furthermore, continued Guild, "the same painstaking efforts
are required in religious publicity that are demanded in commercial
advertising."[18]

The success of promotional techniques used by the Government to sell Bonds during the War further aroused churchmen to a
consideration of the possibilities of applying the new practice
to religion. "The moral of any money-raising drive," stated an
article in *World Outlook*, "seems to be that there's nothing you
can't get if you have good publicity. It's easier to raise a
well-advertised million dollars than a badly advertised hundred."
In addition to raising money, moreover, some thought that church

advertising might become a new means of evangelism. Early in 1919, *New Era Magazine* urged its readers to utilize the daily press in order to reach the public: "Information will reach the people in smaller, more frequent and more digestible doses, and after awhile it, and the spirit and purpose back of it, will get into their systems without conscious effort on their part.[19]

Church advertising became commonplace during the 'twenties, but in 1919 and 1920 the practice itself had to be promoted and sold to the churches. Its strongest advocates--at least the most outspoken--were the Northern Presbyterians, who in 1918 formed a Department of Publicity. James B. Wootan, Editor of *New Era Magazine*, wrote a pamphlet which circulated among Presbyterian clergymen in 1919, stating that were Jesus alive "He would use the great channels of advertising to extend His Gospel." The following year *New Era Magazine* claimed that "advertising actually solves church problems" by raising attendance and contributions. "The cash value of advertising" made it a "good business invest-ment," claimed another article. "If all the pews are not occupied every Sunday, the church plant is to that extent running at a loss." In April, 1920, *New Era Magazine* began publishing the church "ad of the month." But the Presbyterians only led the way, and other denominations followed close behind. The Baptists, for example, had their new General Board of Promotion, the Dis-ciples their Joint Committee on Promotion; and *The Christian Advocate*, not to be outdone, announced that "the Methodists who were once known as 'shouters' are not today afraid to advertise"--and they were not. The Federal Council of Churches also helped make advertising orthodox. At a special Federal Council meeting on February 12, 1920, advertising executive Bruce Barton, later to publish a nonfiction best seller entitled *The Man Nobody Knows* (1925) in which Jesus was portrayed as a master salesman always "about [his] father's business," advised the church leaders on how, through advertising, "to put across to the public the goods which the Church has to sell."[20] The business of religion was about to enter its merchandising stage.

But it was the Interchurch World Movement that really embarked American Protestantism in the Madison Avenue-type promo-tional enterprise, not only by advertising the church in general as "a sound business proposition," but also through an intensive publicity campaign for Interchurch programs. Interchurch Publi-city, Advertising, and Distribution Departments were formed with salaried publicity agents in each state. Tyler Dennett, head of

publicity for the Methodist Centenary Movement, became Director
of the Interchurch Publicity Department with headquarters in New
York, Boston, and Chicago. On November 9, 1919, Dennett announced
to the press that the Interchurch World Movement planned a tremendous advertising campaign--"the greatest paid campaign ever
undertaken by a religious organization or group of religious organizations which will compare in size with the largest of the
Government's advertising campaigns during the war." The Interchurch leaders reasoned that "if the cooperating churches were
to work on a business basis, they must necessarily adopt business
means. What advertising had done for commercial houses, certainly
it could do for the House of God."[21]

Tyler Dennett and his colleagues made good their promise.
During the next six months, they advertised through lapel buttons,
window flags, posters, street car cards, window display material,
windshield posters, stamps, trade and technical and other class
papers, newspapers, magazines, religious papers, agricultural
papers, fraternal order papers, mail-order magazines, business
men's magazines, foreign language press, and bill boards. They
produced sixty different pieces of ad copy for fourteen monthly
magazines, four weeklies, 268 religious publications, fifteen
hundred daily newspapers, ten thousand weekly newspapers, fifty
legal papers, 129 labor papers; and they produced 2,500,000 posters and several million pamphlets.[22]

To help in this work, two New York firms, the Joseph
Richards Company, Inc., and Barton Durstine and Osborn, Inc.,
were hired to act together as an advertising agency of the Interchurch World Movement. Appealing to the business virtues of
"results, success, money, hustle," the Interchurch ads declared,
for example, that "Jesus gave the Church its advertising instruc-
tions and program: 'Go ye into all the world.'" "Have you ever
stopped to think what business owes to Christ?" asked another ad;
while church-going readers learned that they were "stockholders
in the greatest business in the world."[23] God's business advertised in a business-like way.

The Interchurch World Movement also engaged in the promotion of religion through public exhibits and live drama. An
Exhibits Department was formed to handle all details relating to
displays at Interchurch conferences and to begin planning a possible future Interchurch exposition. They planned no large exposition for 1919 or 1920, however, mainly because the Methodist
Centenary celebration featured a great exposition of Methodist

world missions at the State Fair Grounds in Columbus, Ohio from
June 20 to July 13 in 1919. Because of the sheer magnitude and
uniqueness of this Methodist undertaking, but also because it fit
the spirit and aims of the Interchurch World Movement as the most
spectacular piece of religious promotion in connection with the
post-war forward movements, the Centenary exposition deserves
special analysis.[24]

In some ways the Columbus exposition was both "the most
remarkable meeting in Methodist history" (according to S. Earl
Taylor) and the supreme public display of the American Protestant
mind at the close of World War I. It had every element of a Protestant World's Fair. Great exhibit halls representing thirty-five
nations in addition to two huge buildings containing exhibits
depicting American life, plus a fifty thousand-seat amphitheater
were scattered about the 114-acre grounds. In the amphitheater
stood a giant picture screen 105 feet high and 115 feet wide
(equivalent to an eight-story building) upon which were shown
slides from the world's largest stereopticon machine requiring
an eight man operating crew. In addition to nightly pageants,
daily concerts were performed by a large Centenary chorus and a
one hundred piece trombone choir, plus a Centenary orchestra
comprising musicians from the Boston, Chicago, and Cincinnati
orchestras. Speaking appearances were made by such notables as
ex-President Taft, William Jennings Bryan, and many top government and military officials. In the tradition of Wesley's and
Whitefield's open-air preaching in the eighteenth century and
continued through nineteenth century revival preaching, hourly
addresses were made in a large open field by notable Methodist
pulpit orators. There were athletic contests featuring famous
athletes, and bucking bronco contests. History was also made
from a blimp hovering two thousand feet overhead equipped with a
wireless telephone and megaphone making audible "the first of all
aeroplane sermons."

All of this was meant to promote Christianity-in-general,
and Christian missions in particular, by means of educating the
public in a clever, spectacular fashion. The Centenary exposition "was a thoroughly organized educational propaganda, a University of Methodist Missions . . . to so present the facts of
missions as to communicate knowledge, produce conviction and
secure cooperation." Some called it "the most daring venture
in missionary education ever inaugurated." To keep it serious,
each noon a siren stopped everything for a minute of silent

prayer on behalf of missions. Yet even more striking than the
mixture of post-war gaiety with evangelical piety was the exposition's demonstration of the marriage of religion with the entre-
preneurial mentality; and this in turn bore the imprint of a
church still efficiently at war.

The Methodist Centenary exposition illustrated the militaristic, optimistic idealism which had captured American Protestantism during World War I. It portrayed "a great and growing
army of the militant Christ." The Methodists even formed an army
of Centenary Cadets, one thousand young men in their late teens
"of intelligence and soldierly bearing" ("the best product of
Methodism") carefully selected from across the nation to act as
police guards and guides and to parade before the grandstand.
They went through "hard drilling and severe military discipline,"
were regimented into battalions, companies, platoons, and squads,
with regular army officers acting as field officers, and Major
General Leonard Wood as Honorary Colonel. Associating soldiers
with missionaries the Methodists tried to enlist young men, who
had been too young to fight in the Great War, into missionary
service by offering them this "religion, manly, muscular and
attractive to boy life." Protestant America had not yet had
enough war. At Columbus they watched the Lowell Thomas Trave-
logues--a pictorial record of the war which had just been so
successful in New York theaters. To explain it all, the American
life exhibits spoke a single message:

> The eyes of the world are upon America. Here we
> have the purest form of democracy known to the
> world, contrasted with the other nations of the
> earth. Here the open Bible, the free school and
> the Christian home have builded a civilization
> which now must steady the world in the upheavals
> of many races and nations of men.

It seemed as though the best nation, led by its best Protestant
citizens, was about to mold the world in the image of American
goodness.

The mixture of religion with business and militarism at
the Columbus exposition fully suited the Interchurch World Movement. The Exhibits Department secured one hundred thousand dollars worth of materials used at the exposition, much of which
was displayed at Interchurch conferences. Moreover, what turned
out to be the biggest single attraction at the exposition, a
musical-dramatic pageant entitled *The Wayfarer*, became a promotional instrument of the Interchurch World Movement. Written by
Rev. James E. Crowther, a Methodist minister in Seattle,

57024

Washington, *The Wayfarer* was an attempt to sermonize through the
stage. At the Columbus State Fair Grounds, 350 actors and one
thousand singers dramatized the American gospel of optimism and
idealism amid the ruins of war, as reviewed in the *New York
Times*:

> The ringing keynote in the pageant, "The Way-
> farer," is the similarity of our conditions
> with conditions in the various progressive
> states of civilization. The conclusion indi-
> cated is that it is but a matter of time before
> things will settle down to their true levels.
> The opening scene is laid in Flanders Field,
> after a battle has been fought. The ground is
> strewn with figures of the slain and wounded.
> It is then that the Wayfarer, who typifies any
> man, begins his plaint against the injustice
> and inhumanity of the world. He rails against
> the powers that be, human and superhuman, and
> demands to know the reason for all the suffer-
> ing and misery of the world. He is encompassed
> by the influence of Despair, who fills him with
> the hopelessness and injustice of life. Under-
> standing, however, comes to him through his
> traveling back into the centuries where the
> various incidents of human struggle are depicted
> to him. He sees that the aftermath of war is
> always unrest, but that after unrest there is
> peace. The Jews in Babylon form one episode
> in the pageant. The climax is the story of
> Christ and the Passion. Then the Wayfarer is
> brought back into the present with new appre-
> ciation and new understanding of the forces that
> control human progress.[25]

The Interchurch leaders saw in *The Wayfarer* "a piece of
great inspirational and educational religious propaganda," and
they decided to bring it to New York.[26] In so doing, they put
the Interchurch World Movement into the big entertainment business. Henry Hadley, an American musician, composer, and conduc-
tor of world fame, was engaged to compose a series of composi-
tions supplementing exerpts from great oratorios. (Thus Hadley's
"Moonlight by the Rivers of Babylon" preceded portions of Handel's
Messiah!) To perform this music, under Hadley's baton, were members of the Metropolitan Opera House Chorus and Richard Bodanzky's
Symphony Orchestra. The Methodist cast was tripled to one thousand actors and three thousand singers. On December 15, 1919,
the pageant began a five-week stand at Madison Square Garden.[27]

The *Wayfarer* met with success in New York, although the
New York Times review did not lavish praise; spectacular, impressive, and dazzling were the descriptive terms.[28] Financially
the pageant stayed in the black, with a six thousand plus audience
every night. Praise abounded in the religious press. *The Baptist*

for example, stated that "nothing save the Passion Play at
Oberammergau approaches this spectacle."[29] That judgment is
debatable; but it may be said that no religious stage production
of such magnitude had ever before, and perhaps has not since, been
seen in America. In the realm of religious promotion, the Interchurch World Movement had struck a new note.

In the last analysis, however, the most important promotional method used in the Interchurch World Movement was the
spoken word. Three centuries of preaching "for decisions" and
persuasive oratory for support of various causes, from the solemn
New England meeting house to the frontier camp meeting to large
urban platforms, provided a rich tradition from which twentieth
century promoters of religion could not help but draw. Once
again the spoken word sounded in all corners of the nation in the
cause of religion, this time through the highly organized program
of Interchurch conferences and public lectures.

The Field Department took overall charge of public assemblies through its Conference and Convention Division. The object,
according to A. E. Cory, was "to carry down the results of the
surveys, the stewardship message, the life work message [enlist-
ment into Christian service], the message of intercession and
evangelism, the educational message, to the last man in the last
church."[30] Moreover, the discovery, enlistment, and training of
lay workers to utilize their talents of vocal persuasion in promoting the Interchurch ideals was an important element in the
whole program.

Intensive preparation for the campaign conferences of 1920
began in Atlantic City at a National Leaders' Training Conference
on November 5-7, 1919. About one hundred outstanding denominational leaders were schooled in the fundamentals of conference
promotion. This "faculty" then divided into twelve teams taking
divergent routes across the country to conduct a series of sixty-
four State Leaders' Training Conferences during the month of
November 17 to December 19. By this process over twelve thousand
churchmen (sixty percent pastors) were trained to lead a standardized conference program on the state level, which included, in
turn, the training of many others to lead similar conferences on
the county, city, community and local church level.[31]

No stones were left unturned in the training process.
All of the minute details of conference organization were gone
over, in order that uniform assemblies might be ticked off across
the nation with clock-work efficiency. Themes were suggested for

each series of speeches as well as the order in which speeches
should be given to fit an overall conceptual framework. Even the
types of persons to give particular addresses were described, such
as a pastor "who is powerful in his prayer life and who has the
devotional note without being a mere mystic" to make an appeal to
pious instincts. The art of modern salesmanship was thoroughly
taught--"pick out a few salient points and put them across with
great vigor."[32] Each conference team was to have its portable
exhibit and collection of literature, and each would have its
lantern slide crew to project visual aids in conjunction with
speeches. Everything was geared to applying the power of the
spoken word to raising men and money for Protestant work.

The Field Department also formed a Speakers' Bureau to
enlist and train speakers and teams of speakers to promote the
Interchurch World Movement "at every important commercial or lay
gathering" across the nation. The number of speakers reached
several thousand. In addition, the Speakers' Bureau copied the
wartime program of promoting the Allied cause through short,
patriotic speeches by local citizens. Approximately five hundred
thousand lay "minute men" formed an army of speakers to promote
the Interchurch World Movement in local churches and everywhere
they could gain a hearing. The Lantern Slide Department not only
produced over two hundred thousand slides and 150,000 prints to
assist speakers, but even composed one thousand full-length lectures to go with various slide assortments.[33]

Hence through various kinds of literature, advertisements,
exhibits and dramatics, but especially through the spoken word,
the Interchurch World Movement sought to promote the work of
American Protestantism with big-business efficiency.

The degree to which the cult of business penetrated
American Protestantism may be seen even more clearly in the
accommodation of traditional piety to the principles of bureau-
cratic organization and the revelry in material prosperity that
followed the World War. Prayer, always a central element in
Christian piety, became a structured form of personal and social
energy exploited for the promotion of religious enterprises.
Furthermore, the post-war financial campaigns for the forward
movement of Protestant work forced evangelicals to reaffirm their
peace with money, which they did in the doctrine of stewardship.
With prayer as fuel and stewardship as policy, therefore, the
Interchurch World Movement "sounded the spiritual note" in the
mobilization of men and money to do the church's business.

The Interchurch World Movement used prayer as a promotive instrument. To devout, business-oriented Protestants prayer represented the transcendent spiritual power brought to bear on Christian work. It meant human transmission of other-worldly energy to this-worldly endeavor--"the kinetic energy of the soul applied to the highest tasks of the Kingdom." Interchurch litera- ture portrayed "the man who prays [as] a man of power" mediating "wave currents of spiritual energy." If successful business depended on good communications and wise dealings with suppliers of necessary materials, how important that businessmen of religion "link up with the infinite" through conscientious prayers, "where important interviews with God take place and where great trans- actions are undertaken and performed." A well-ordered piety could be validated as an asset to the goals of modern business society. "If you get the prayer straight, and practice it, really pray as a habit, things will happen. Prayer is really turning the spirit- current of power out on the spot you are driving at. And as the current is turned out, things get done."[34]

Prayer, thus, became frankly pragmatic--practiced for its results. "The putting forth of prayer energy," wrote W. E. Doughty, "releases forces which God can and does use to accom- plish definite and practical ends." Especially could interces- sion (prayer for, or on behalf of others) be used to "release money for the spread of the Kingdom," since "it goes in through stone walls, past locked doors, into the inner room, and touches the heart of the man there, changes his decision and bends or unbends his will." As a promotional tool, therefore, prayer was thought invaluable--"the greatest human influence in raising money."[35]

The cultivation of prayer-centered piety became an import- ant aspect of the Interchurch program. Like everything else, prayer was structured according to the principles of a big busi- ness operation. "Just as the laws of nature are God's orderly ways of expressing Himself," explained Doughty, "so methods and organization are essential to the manifestation of God's power." As Director of the Spiritual Resources Department, with ten Divisions, Doughty organized prayer on a grand scale. The Department published a total of thirty-nine different pamphlets with a circulation of 1,728,973 copies, published special prayers in over five hundred thousand newspapers, advertised prayer, held conferences of prayer and prayer meetings, promoted family wor- ship and church prayer services, for every Interchurch Conference planned "devotional hours, periods of intercession, addresses on prayer," and generally undergirded the Movement with prayer and permeated its activities "with spiritual motives and power."[36]

By April of 1919, Doughty was organizing a Fellowship of Intercession comprised of selected names from each denomination "to whom requests for prayer may be sent quickly as occasion may require." Eventually one thousand persons enlisted into this standing army of veteran prayers, for whose direction an Inter-church Fellowship of Intercession Division of the Spiritual Resources Department was organized. They received "prayer cycles" for regular duty, special bulletins for emergency praying, and on January 29, 1920 they received notification of all important events for which to pray during the following months. Doughty also organized a "tremendous prayer power" of missionaries and native churches on mission fields.[37] Perhaps never before or since has Protestant America been so rigorously organized on a national scale to pray efficiently for specific goals.

The Interchurch leaders consistently promoted their enterprise as "primarily a great spiritual movement" rather than simply "a money movement." Yet money remained at the heart of the matter, the apparent contradiction being overcome by a spiritualization of money in the doctrine of stewardship. The doctrine itself was not new, but with the flowering of big business it received a peculiar emphasis in Christian ethical thought.

Doing good with money had become a Christian apologetic for securing it. Steelmaster Andrew Carnegie, for example, espoused and practiced the "gospel of wealth" as a program of social betterment through constructive philanthropy. Within the church, Carnegie's use of money resembled the age-old doctrine of stewardship. The early nineteenth century voluntary societies to promote Protestant work had existed on contributions by laymen practicing stewardship. Later in the century, as America's industrial revolution brought increasing prosperity, home missions advocate Josiah Strong called for the Christianization of wealth on the basis of a radical practice of stewardship. "Money is power in the concrete," wrote Strong, "it is the modern miracle worker." But it must be used sacrificially to further God's Kingdom. Christians are "not proprietors, apportioning their own, but simply trustees or managers of God's property," reasoned Strong, hence "of our possessions, every dollar, every cent, is to be employed in the way that will best honor God."[38] The

crusading missionary movements which arose and prospered during
the thirty years prior to World War I promoted systematic stewardship among laymen as the concrete expression of spiritual devotion
to God's advancing kingdom. Interest in stewardship consequently
grew after the turn of the century. Literature on the subject
abounded, and stewardship societies were formed such as the United
Society of Christian Endeavor and the Twentieth Century Tither's
Association of America.

The gospel of wealth, however, even when expressed philan-
thropically on the principle of stewardship, had been sharply
criticized by social gospel spokesmen who considered wealth ac-
quired through the evils of unrestricted capitalism to be
"tainted." Yet critics were a minority fighting a losing cause.
The Laymen's Missionary Movement and the Men and Religion Forward
Movement campaigned for money from whatever source it might be
forthcoming, and it was the churches' "good use" of money which
alone mattered. It was the good use of money during World War I
which finally convinced church leaders of the potential power of
money. Wartime campaigns showed that money could be raised in
unprecedented amounts from the general populace, while business
and industry showed how capital could be used to accomplish great
ends. "In a sense, money won the war," rang out a *New Era Magazine* editorial, "and in the same sense, money will win the world
for Christ."[39] If the social gospel had become orthodox during
the progressive era, during World War I and after the gospel of
money became orthodox.

In 1919, progressive churchmen believed that America had
the financial resources and that the combination of sound business methods with religious values could exploit prosperity for
the Christian mission. But in order to accomplish this end, the
great body of American churchmen would have to be thoroughly
convinced that money and religion were entirely compatible, and
religion itself would have to be organized financially according
to accepted principles of business. The Interchurch World Movement tried to do both.

As for the relation of money to religion, the Interchurch
apologetic took two slightly different lines. First, the goodness of money, according to its use, was made clear: "Capital
may be as much considered the gift of God as any other of His
gifts, and may be used for Him. According to *New Era Magazine*,
"money is only a means to the spiritual fruit of the church."

> Even Jesus, when he was going around with only
> a little band of disciples, had to have a
> Treasurer who carried a bag of money . . . .
> Money is religious. Money is our time and
> labor, our very life-blood, minted into coin
> which lubricates and energizes all the activi-
> ties of the church. Money is one way by which
> we consecrate our very selves and souls to the
> Lord. And so Paul followed up his splendid
> chapter on the resurrection with the immediate
> application, "now concerning the collection."

Money, in itself morally neutral, could thus become a spiritual
blessing if consecrated by Christian stewardship. "If men are
right with God on the money question," wrote Fred B. Smith, "the
chances are good that they will be right all around." Consequently money might be "a means of worship . . . just as religious
as praise and prayer;" and some Episcopalians even spoke of "money
as a Sacrament . . . an outward and visible sign of inward and
spiritual grace."[40]

Closely related, the second apologetic simply pointed out
that Christian ethics provided the solid ground upon which wealth
grows. "The Church has better bread than that of earth," noted
New Era Magazine, "but it is not unmindful of the body, and in
all fields it promotes prosperity," and readers of *The Baptist*
were cautioned that "only a revival of religion can make our good
times continue." With money correctly related to the concerns
and practices of the church, it could finally be argued, "business
and all methods of money acquisition are sanctified."[41]

Heirs of a tradition of positive thinking about money, and
having made a quasi-theological case for the church's dealing
with money, the Interchurch leaders now set about placing American Protestantism on a sound financial basis. This entailed, in
the first place, forming a budget commensurate with the giving
potential of Christian American in relation to the needs of the
world. Moreover, the method of formulating a joint budget according to the data of a world-wide survey appealed to the big business instinct. William B. Hollinshead, an Interchurch statisti-
cian, noted that "formerly we [church leaders] asked for what we
thought the Church would or could give, based on what the Church
had given. Now for the first time in our history, we ask on the
basis of what the world needs. This is the most complete change
in the attitude toward benevolences the church has ever known.
All former standards of giving are going to smash." Interchurch
propaganda sounded this same optimism on the basis that "never
before has America had so much money as it has today. Every

deserving cause can get all it needs. If the Church underwrites
its appeal with hard facts and a forward program based on actual,
ascertained need, money will flow into its treasury."[42]

The budget matched all ambitions. By March 2, 1920, it
could be announced that thirty denominations had approved their
respective shares in a total campaign budget of $336,777,572 to
be pledged in 1920, and of that amount $175,446,349 to be col-
lected during 1920. The latter sum alone equalled well over five
times the amount given by the same boards in 1919 and called for
an increase in per capita giving from ninety-four cents in 1919
to $4.20 in 1920. According to the *New York Times* this was "by
far the largest sum that a religious organization ever started
out to raise." *The Christian Advocate* called it "the greatest
public asking in the history of the world." Yet it was not
thought extravagant, but simply realistic and even conservative
in light of world needs and American ability to give. Its
defenders never tired of pointing out that in 1919 Americans
spent, for example, $174,000,000 on perfumes and cosmetics,
$275,000,000 on jewelry, and $507,000,000 on theater entertainment. Surely $175,000,000 could be raised for the total work of
thirty denominations. S. Earl Taylor felt certain that it could
be raised because this was "the first scientific cooperative budget ever seen, a budget which will stand analysis by the most
business-like as well as the most devout."[43]

The second aspect of the task of placing Protestantism on
a sound financial basis was helping to raise the budget through
the promotion of stewardship. Once again the Interchurch World
Movement set up an intricate nation-wide organization, this time
through a Department of Stewardship. To head this work the Movement employed Ralph Spaulding Cushman, one of the nation's outstanding authorities on stewardship promotion. An ambitious program of stewardship education through conferences, classes, and
reading courses was set in motion, as well as the publication of
fifteen pamphlets which circulated in about 1,500,000 copies,
and intensive promotional advertising in newspapers and magazines.
A Ten Million League of Christian Stewards was formed with the
intention of enlisting a huge army of dedicated givers, each
carrying a card bearing the following principles:

> (1) God is the owner of all things; (2) Every
> man is a Steward and must give account for all
> that is entrusted to him; (3) God's ownership
> and men's stewardship ought to be acknowledged;
> (4) This acknowledgement requires, as part of

its expression, the setting apart for the extension of the Kingdom of Christ, such a portion of
income as is recognized by the individual to be
the will of God; (5) The separated portion ought
to be administered for the Kingdom of God and
the remainder be recognized as no less a trust.[44]

In order to make their giving as efficient and business
like as possible, League members were advised to make "some kind
of ledger account, where we may put down what we receive and spend
for Christ, that there may be no embezzlement, however inadvert-
ent, of that which is not ours." The Puritan conscience persisted
as card-holding stewards were told to examine their ways of living
so as to make certain that they spent their money mainly on life's
necessities, only partly on conveniences, less on comforts, and
almost never on luxuries. Money, the "vehicle of love," thus
became a center of pious attention while the Interchurch World
Movement promoted stewardship as "really being in step with the
Infinite as he marches on to victory."[45]

The Interchurch World Movement was an enterprise whose
expenditures were congruous with its large-scale programs. By
the end of 1919, nearly two million dollars had already been
spent. But after that the Movement began spending about one
million dollars per month for the next five months, until by May
total expenditures amounted to well over seven million dollars
and had not stopped rising. Yet its leaders were confident that
not only efficiency but economy had been gained through uniting
thirty denominations in a joint campaign--perhaps as much as two
million dollars to be saved in total cost.[46] Thinking in terms
of war practices, they believed that money must be spent lavishly
to get big results. At the World Survey Conference in January,
a special Board of Review, comprised of several respected business leaders with J. D. Rockefeller, Jr., as spokesman, made a
favorable report on the total program and expenses of the Interchurch World Movement. "The plans are wisely and conservatively
drawn," declared Rockefeller, "and not more extensive than necessary in view of the stupendous and unparalleled undertaining con-
templated."[47]

With the blessing of big business, therefore, leaders of
the Interchurch World Movement forged ahead, though they were
becoming aware that the blessing was mixed.

NOTES TO CHAPTER V

1.   The bulletin is on file at the National Council of Churches
        Research Library in New York City.

2.   See Edward Earl Purinton, "Big Ideas from Big Business,"
        The Independent, April 16, 1921, p. 395.

3.   *New Era Magazine*, II (May, 1920), p. 325.

4.   *New Era Magazine*, II (February, 1920), p. 112; and *The
        Baptist*, August 21, 1920, p. 1036.

5.   Detailed outlines of the organizational structure appear
        in *IWM Documents*, VIII, pp. 4-14, 45-49; and V, pp. 3-11.

6.   "Report to the Churches, May, 1920," *IWM Documents*, VII,
        pp. 6-7.

7.   In a letter to Charles S. Macfarland, July 18, 1919, S.
        Earl Taylor noted offers to take over the car barns
        opposite the Park Avenue Hotel, to erect a building on
        the 34th Street side of the Pennsylvania Station, and
        others. Correspondence, National Council of Churches
        Research Library.

8.   *New York Times*, March 31, 1920, p. 25:4; *IWM Documents*,
        VII, pp. 38-39.

9.   "Report to the Churches, May, 1920," *IWM Documents*, VII,
        p. 35.

10.   *World Survey by the Interchurch World Movement*, Vol. I,
        p. 56; and letter by Fowles to *The Christian Advocate*,
        April 14, 1921, p. 488.

11.   "Efficiency in the Lord's Business," *New Era Magazine*, II
        (June, 1920), pp. 418-19.

12.   *New Era Magazine*, II (August, 1920), p. 586; and *The
        Standard*, June 14, 1919, p. 1054.

13.   See outline of the Life Work Department in *IWM Documents*,
        IV, p. 52.

14.   *New York Times*, January 26, 1920, p. 28:3; and March 9,
        1920, p. 10:7.

15.   This advertisement appeared in several places, for example,
        World Call, II (April, 1920), p. 63. See Rockefeller's

112

statement in *New York Times*, March 16, 1920, p. 4:2. See also "The Economic Value of Religion and the Interchurch World Movement," *The Outlook*, March 3, 1920, p. 371.

16. For the promotional organization and publication data, see *IWM Documents*, IV, pp. 33ff, and IX, p. 4ff.

17. *World Outlook*, V (November, 1919), p. 2.

18. See R. B. Guild, *The Manual of Interchurch Work* (New York, 1917), pp. 151, 158-59.

19. *New Era Magazine*, I (January, 1919), pp. 28-29; and Phyllis Duganne, "Adventures in Raising Millions," *World Outlook*, V (February, 1919), pp. 3-5.

20. Quotations from *New Era Magazine*, II (February, 1920), pp. 110-111, (March, 1920), pp. 188-89, (April, 1920), pp. 151, 270-71; *The Christian Advocate*, February 6, 1919, p. 174; and *Federal Council Bulletin*, III (March, 1920), p. 42.

21. *Federal Council Bulletin*, III (April, 1920), p. 70; *The York Times*, November 10, 1919, p. 12:7.

22. "Report to the Churches," May, 1920, *IWM Documents*, VII, pp. 32-33.

23. *The Nation*, June 5, 1920, pp. 746-47.

24. For material on the Centenary exposition, see issues of *The Christian Advocate* during the period of March through July of 1919; *World Outlook*, V (August, 1919), pp. 19-23; and *Handbook of Information for Centenary Celebration of American Methodist Missions*, an official exposition souvenir.

25. "Sermons Supplemented by Pageantry," *New York Times*, November 30, 1919, IV, p. 5.

26. *Interchurch Newsletter*, October 23, 1919, p. 5; and *IWM Documents*, VII, pp. 37 A-D.

27. *New York Times*, October 26, 1919, p. 6:8; November 30, 1919, IV, p. 5; and December 14, 1919, VIII, p. 6:1.

28. *Ibid.*, December 16, 1919, p. 13:1.

29. *The Baptist*, January 31, 1920, p. 20.

30. A. E. Cory, Director of the Field Department in *The Missionary Review of the World*, XLIII (March, 1920), p. 218.

31. *New York Times*, November 7, 1919, p. 18:3; *Federal Council Bulletin*, II (December, 1919), p. 190; and *IWM Documents*, V, p. 32.

32. Outline of the National Leaders' Training Conference, and Executive Committee minutes for January 20, 1920, in *IWM Documents*, V, pp. 16-21, 63-65.

33. *Federal Council Bulletin*, II (December, 1919), p. 190; and "Report to the Churches, May, 1920," in *IWM Documents*, VII, p. 24.

34. Quotations from the following pamphlets: S. D. Gordon, *Prayer Gets Things Done* (New York, 1919, p. 2; W. E. Doughty, *Intercession* (New York, 1919), p. 7; J. M. Campbell, *The Place of Prayer in God's Plan of World Conquest* (New York, 1919), p. 13; and H. W. Frost, *The Meaning of Intercession* (New York, 1919), p. 1.

35. Quotations from the following pamphlets: W. E. Doughty, *If Millions Prayed* (New York, 1919), p. 15, and *Intercession*, p. 7; and Gordon, *Prayer Gets Things Done*, p. 7.

36. Documents related to the Spiritual Resources Department, and "Report to the Churches, May, 1920," in *IWM Documents*, IV, pp. 1-8, VII, pp. 27-28; and *Interchurch Newsletter*, October 2, 1919, p. 4.

37. Doughty's Letter to Intercessors of January 29, 1920, appeared in a pamphlet entitled *New Ventures of Faith* (New York, 1919), p. 6. See also "Report of Special Committee on Spiritual Resources," September 25, 1919, in *IWM Documents*, IV, p. 8.

38. Josiah Strong, *Our Country: Its Possible Future and Its Present Crisis*, ed. Jurgen Herbst (Cambridge, Mass., 1963), pp. 219-35.

39. *New Era Magazine*, I (May, 1919), p. 223.

40. *Speakers' Manual, Nation-Wide Campaign*, Episcopal (New York, 1919), pp. 21-23; *World Call*, II (May, 1920), p. 10; *New Era Magazine*, II (June, 1920), p. 408; and *The Stewardship of Money* (New York, 1919), p. 7.

41. *The Baptist*, February 14, 1920, p. 86; *New Era Magazine*, I (November, 1919), p. 627; and Roger Babson, "Business and the Church," *The Baptist*, September 4, 1920, p. 1089.

42. *Interchurch World Movement Speakers' Manual*, p. 58. See also *The Missionary Review of the World*, XLIII (March, 1920), p. 216; *World Call*, II (April, 1920), p. 9; *World Outlook*, VI (April, 1920), p. 17; and *Federal Council Bulletin*, III (April, 1920), p. 75.

43. *Federal Council Bulletin*, III (April, 1920), p. 67. See also *World Outlook*, VI (April, 1920), pp. 15-16; *New York*

114

Times, March 8, 1920, p. 9:3; *The Christian Advocate*, May 13, 1920, p. 668; *World Call*, II (April, 1920), p. 57. For a breakdown of the budget according to denominations and designations, see *World Survey by the Interchurch World Movement*, Vol. II, p. 313.

44. Cushman's program is outlined in *IWM Documents*, IV, p. 97. According to the Interchurch pamphlet entitled *Sunday School Stewardship Programs* (New York, 1919), p. 31, the Ten Million League of Christian Stewards was "a league of all persons in every communion, who, in loving loyalty to their Lord, purpose to set apart a definite first proportion of income as an acknowledgment of God's ownership and their stewardship." See also "Advertising Stewardship Proves Itself," *Federal Council Bulletin*, III (April, 1920), pp. 69-70.

45. *Sunday School Stewardship Programs*, p. 14; and David McConaughy, *Money, the Acid Test* (New York, 1919), p. 65.

46. Total expenses were $10,633,943. For analysis, see *IWM Documents*, VI, pp. 114-39, X, p. 18; "Report to the Churches, May, 1920," p. 9; *Federal Council Bulletin*, III (April, 1920), p. 64; and *World Outlook*, VI (June, 1920), pp. 10-11.

47. The report is included in *IWM Documents*, III, p. 115.

CHAPTER VI

THE SOCIAL QUESTION: CONTROVERSIAL DIMENSIONS
OF THE CHURCHES' MISSION

Not all big business blessed organized religion after
World War I, and some churchmen found that their ideals could
clash soundly with business interests. When on March 24, 1920,
a news release announced that the "kings of American finance and
industry" had thrown "the wealth of Wall Street" behind the Interchurch World Movement in order to combat "a rapid spread of Bolshevism from infected areas overseas," the Interchurch Cabinet
immediately replied that the statements were unauthorized and
misleading.[1]

True, the Interchurch World Movement had capitalized on
the increasing power and popularity of big business in post-World
War I America. Moreover, the movement contained within its ranks
at least as many supporters as opponents of the anti-Bolshevik
hysteria of 1919 and 1920. But the movement also expressed the
profound social involvement of religious leaders who did not lose
sight of the plight of the underprivileged as well as the power
of moneyed interests. Here was embodied climactically, in the
midst of social upheaval and popular conservative response, the
kind of progressive social reformism that had swept America for
nearly two decades. As a last great thrust of social gospel
progressivism before its temporary decline in popularity in the
1920's, the precarious Interchurch World Movement activities
illustrated a changing attitude of the churches and of the general public toward "the social question."

Before World War I, divergent social views were partially
submerged in the reformist frenzy. Official ecclesiastical
acceptance of social gospel idealism and programs after the turn
of the century, for example, tended to blur the difference between traditional moral reformism against "sin" (alcohol, gamb-
ling, prostitution, sabbath desecration, etc.) and more radical
social gospel critiques of the social-economic order. Moreover,
there had developed much popular support for "democratic reforms"

of obvious corruptions within the free enterprise democracy.
The social order, it seemed especially to native rural-oriented
Yankees, was afflicted with disease at the points of rapid social
and cultural change--urban centers. Most reformers found no great
fault with the inherited social order in basic principle or structure. But the symptoms of disease needed treatment: urban slum
dwellers needed relief, business and politics needed cleansing,
and labor conditions needed improvement. The "alien element"
also required attention. Progressive reformers believed that the
immigrant masses who inhabited the slums, who suffered politically
and economically, who made up the labor force, and whose social
and cultural ways differed, must be Americanized, "lifted up,"
molded into the traditional pattern.

Some liberal politicians, economists, social scientists,
social gospelers, and others went further, seeking to improve
the social system itself by making it more democratic and Christian at its economic core. They dealt with the deeper questions
of balancing individual freedom and justice, private gain and
public good. Furthermore, while New Nationalism Republicans, New
Freedom Democrats, religious liberals and conservatives often
differed in philosophical-theological diagnosis of the social
ailments and disagreed on specific remedial policies, all could
progress together in the cause of social betterment regardless
of variations of thought--all taking for granted traditional
American values and goals. Common ideals thus bound progressive
reformers; they led an aroused democracy.

The "American way" entailed reform. Revolt against old
world conditions to gain spiritual and material freedoms and justice in new world democracy was native to the American character.
Moreover, the ideal of a civic-minded, enlightened public, confident of the inherent goodness and invulnerability of the Christian democracy, formed an essential plank in the progressive
platform. The merit of American tradition, progressives assumed,
would speak convincingly for itself; but "foreigners" must be
taught the tradition and be educated in American ideals; and
natives must be informed about corruptions of the tradition. An
enlightened public would be the greatest reforming force. Hence
progressives concentrated on enlightening the public in the belief
that when evil and good are revealed, the people will choose the
good.

This premise helped spur the muckraking vogue, which produced the sensational works of Tarbell, Lawson, Steffens, Phillips,

Henrick, and Sinclair.[2] Journalism became revolutionized as the "major organs of respectable reform" felt the challenge of more sensationalist muckraking magazines. Social-minded clergymen participated strongly in the movement. Indeed, one of the earliest muckraking ventures had been the exposure of Tammany Hall in 1892 by Rev. Charles H. Parkhurst of the Madison Square Presbyterian Church in New York City. Social gospel literature was full of "conditions revealed" which demanded reform. Even the social gospel novels such as Rev. Charles M. Sheldon's best seller, *In His Steps: What Would Jesus Do?*, appealed to the public conscience by exposing social maladies.

In 1910, a slightly new turn was taken within the general muckraking tradition when the Commission on the Church and Social Service of the Federal Council of the Churches of Christ in America investigated the steel strike at South Bethlehem, Pennsylvania. The investigation produced a twenty-one page report giving the long-range and immediate causes of the strike, discussing all aspects of the problem within the community context, condemning the twelve-hour day and the seven-day week as "a disgrace to civilization," and recommending action by the government and the churches to oppose industrial injustices. With this report, the business of exposure became official and institutionalized in organized Protestantism.

Delving into industrial disputes was bound to be controversial even in the age of reform. But the churches also exhibited their increasing social consciousness in less controversial and less dramatic ways. They began to study their mission fields in order better to understand the nature and scope of their task, and to awaken slumbering consciences with impressive data. The way had been paved by Josiah Strong's social analysis of *Our Country* in 1886 which suggested the possibilities of applying the methods and tools of social science to analysis of the on-going missionary enterprise. Soon local churches began to make crude socio-religious surveys of their neighborhood parishes. This developed into more systematic and "scientific" survey programs carried on by federations of churches, covering a wide range of sociological data about city conditions.

The Men and Religion Forward Movement of 1911-1912, as part of its social-evangelism crusades, surveyed seventy cities with a combined population of twenty million, providing data concerning population, government, social influences, industrial life, the saloon, social-service agencies, public schools,

118

libraries, recreation, juvenile delinquency, and religious conditions. From this information, specific programs for local
churches were outlined. Shortly after, the Disciples of Christ
published a brief general survey of its world missions fields as
part of the promotion of the Men and Millions Movement. In 1918,
the Methodists published an elaborate *Centenary Survey* as a basis
for its financial campaign for missions in the spring of 1919.
Surveying the world became standard practice in the denominational
forward movements immediately following World War I.[3] As a
methodology preparatory to social mission, it received great im-
petus in the Interchurch World Movement.

By the time of the Interchurch World Movement, however,
conditions had changed drastically in America, altering the public
attitude toward "the social question." The Progressive impulse
had begun to fade even before World War I, but America's military
involvement in Europe diverted the progressives' attention from
domestic reform to the new cause of protecting national ideals
and goals from contesting outside forces. During the war, the
national mood shifted from a positive liberalism, tolerant of
freely-expressed divergent social philosophies which were not
greatly feared as harmful to the American Christian democratic
tradition, to a conservative defense of social uniformity as
Christian democracy itself appeared threatened with violent
destruction.

Americans, in fact, were taking a reactionary turn,
despite the lofty idealism in which they fought in the war.
German autocracy presented a non-democratic force to be crushed
at all cost. As it turned out, part of the cost was the limita-
tion of democratic freedom in America and strong pressures for
unquestioned support of national policy. Civil liberties were
grossly violated and diversity of social philosophies practically
silenced. Many clergymen preached a one hundred per cent Americanism which virtually prohibited criticism of the national
policies. All viewpoints became automatically categorized as
either pro- or anti-American--either Christian democracy or
atheistic autocracy, with no allowance for diversity or qualifi-
cation.

Nor did the reactionary impulse end with the armistice,
for it seemed that a new enemy had appeared preaching dictator-
ship of the masses. The Bolshevik Revolution in Russia during
November of 1917 represented a social radicalism which repelled
even the most progressive-minded Americans. When in March of

1918 the Russian Bolsheviki made a separate peace with Germany, many Americans became convinced that "Reds" and "Huns" were of a kind. After the war, Bolshevik aggression increased in Europe. In March of 1919 the Third International was formed to facilitate the global thrust of the revolution, which apparently was making large gains in Germany, Poland, Italy, and especially Hungary.

Americans not only looked warily at this movement in Europe, but they soon began to watch for "Reds" infiltrating the homeland. During the great Red scare of 1919-1920, any signs of social radicalism (or even liberalism) became suspect; and there was much social excitement during those years to fan the flames of fear. In 1919 alone there were 3,600 labor strikes involving four million workers, the most sensational being the Seattle shipyard-general strike, the Boston police strike, the steel strike, and the coal mine workers strike. Because organized labor had always been associated in the public mind with socially leftish tendencies, and because there was in fact some radical socialism involved in the vigorous post-war strikes, the general public became convinced in 1919 that labor uprisings were part of an organized conspiracy to take control of the Government by violence. Bomb explosions during the spring of 1919 directed toward public figures, and social agitations that at times broke out in riots transformed fear into public hysteria. More inno-cent persons than guilty ones suffered during the raids of Attorney General A. Mitchell Palmer, the deportation of aliens, and the many other forms of local hostility against foreigners and laborers. American civil liberties were greatly violated. Yet the "inescapable conclusion" of the most thorough study of the phenomenon is that "at no time either before, during, or after the Red scare did the radical movement in the country ever approach anything remotely near revolutionary proportions."[4] It was a phantom threat that gripped the war-minded nation.

The fear was real, however, and based on deep convictions rooted in progressive religious tradition, as *The Christian Advo-cate* made clear: "America is God's final reservation for the moral schooling and training of civilization. To have her mis-sion miscarry would be a measureless misfortune to universal humanity. For the sake of the entire world, America owes every-thing to the preservation of her own best ideals."[5]

Leaders of the Interchurch World Movement embodied this popular American feeling and acted accordingly. "The church must not simply survive the storm that shakes the world," Interchurch leaders declared, "she must take her place as leader among the constructive forces of society."[6] But upon what principles, and by what methods ought the church to act? The Interchurch World Movement, seeking to unite all elements of American Protestantism in a general forward movement, planned its program on the broadest possible foundation--the traditional ideals and goals of "old white stock" America. As for technique, there was strong precedent in the gathering of social-religious data objectively demonstrating needs to be met. An enlightened church--an enlightened public--could best solve difficult social problems.

The Interchurch World Movement stood on the premise that "to be great, a nation does not need to be of one blood, but it must be of one mind." In 1919, Americans were struggling to protect their claim to greatness. They fought disruptions of the common mind, supposing that spiritual and cultural uniformity could be enforced in a pluralistic democratic society. By 1920, the urban-industrial population, comprised largely of foreign-born and their offspring, finally became the nation's majority, a situation which Interchurch leaders considered "the great turning-point in American history." They viewed the "aliens" as a "dangerous foe. . . . not generally in sympathy with American religious ideals." Immigrants brought into warfare "old-world prepossessions and prejudices--political, social, economic, and religious--with new world ideals and standards [reconcilable] only through the spirit of Jesus." Therefore Christian Americanization became a central task of evangelism, and the field of labor became increasingly urban.[7]

Strengthening American Protestantism at its weakest point, the city, did not mean neglect of the country towns. Rather it meant maintaining a strong rural Protestantism in order to mold the more diversified cities into its image. Progressives and social gospelers were still entrenched in the American myth of agrarian purity, and if they concentrated on urban problems it was partly because here they perceived the threat to American cultural and ideological unity--a threat to traditional Christian democracy. An article interpreting "the Interchurch Rural Survey," appearing in the Presbyterian *New Era Magazine*, so clearly expressed the rural-oriented, middle class, native white Protestant American mind which dominated the Interchurch World Movement, that it merits lengthy quotation:

> If the United States is to be one nation, with
> common feeling, language, habits, customs and
> moral and spiritual attitude, the Americanization
> must center around the largest racial group, the
> old white stock. Without touching the contentious
> question whether this stock is the best in the
> country, even the largest of the other groups is
> so small compared with the whole that an attempt
> at ethnic unity about it could only result in
> failure and permanent disunity. This principle
> underlies the crucial importance to the nation
> of the great rural survey of the Interchurch World
> Movement of North America. The rural people, the
> agriculturists, have the least admixture of for-
> eign blood of any portion of the population. The
> native whites of foreign and mixed parentage and
> the foreign-born whites--the foreign and the
> semi-foreign--make up only 25.4 percent of all
> white persons having occupations in agriculture,
> as compared with 35.3 per cent in the professional
> group, 49.2 per cent in the building and hand
> trades, 72.9 per cent in the liquor and beverage
> industries (prior to prohibition), 77.2 per cent
> in the woolen and worsted mills and 80.3 per
> cent in the clothing industry. The only group
> with less of a foreign element than the agri-
> culturalists is the comparatively small class of
> workers about salt works, oil wells and gas wells,
> and this group is also largely rural. The leader-
> ship in American activities still comes from the
> rural districts. It must be so for some time.
> If American life is to have a tone, this tone must
> come not from the cities with their varied and
> heterogeneous racial groups, but from the villages
> and country districts. It is the task of the
> churches to see that this tone continues one of
> godliness and patriotism, high ideals and clean
> living.[8]

Protecting the "tone" of American life from social and
cultural disunity thus became an underlying purpose of the Interchurch World Movement, which during the tensions of 1919 and
1920 meant involvement in the anti-Bolshevik campaign. A considerable number of churchmen, many within the respectable ranks
of denominational officialdom, succumbed to the hysterical extremes; while at the same time others who also opposed social
radicalism nevertheless deplored wholesale violations of civil
liberties and indiscriminate hostility toward all foreigners.
The latter sought more constructive measures. "Arrest and deportation are but temporary expedients," cautioned *The Baptist*,
"and must be supplemented by an intelligent effort to educate
those most susceptible to Bolshevistic propaganda."[9]

The Interchurch World Movement furthered Americanization
through Christian education. Like most of the religious press,
World Outlook, the Movement's official organ, presented

Protestantism as the chief bulwark against Bolshevism. The same theme was expressed in live drama when *The Wayfarer*, a pageant showing how religion alone could end social unrest, was staged in Madison Square Garden in New York City during the height of the Red Scare. The pageant was promoted as a sermon "aimed at agitators and Bolsheviki throughout America," conveying the message that whereas "Red leaders" were "unwelcome guests in this Country," the "great mass of American people [would] be ready to fall into step in the march of progress and prosperity that is surely ahead of us."[10]

No Interchurch gathering, moreover, escaped involvement in the Bolshevik mania. At least once (on May 2, 1920, at the Belasco Theater in New York City), a mass meeting was held in the interest of the Interchurch World Movement specifically to stir churches to oppose radicalism in defense of democracy. But the most important method by which the Interchurch World Movement endeavored to enlighten the public was the finding and processing of social-religious facts, both through general surveys and through investigations into specific social conflicts.

In light of prevailing social tensions, a missionary survey seemed innocent enough. What patriotic American could balk at the churches doing "a national spiritual stock-taking" by studying their own resources in relation to the world's needs? The church must know its field of labor: "Know--then do" was the Interchurch motto. Moreover, while the social gospel was by no means unanimously accepted by American Protestants, few doubted the church's responsibility as a moral force in society. "The church," argued Interchurch leaders, "must recognize that all social and community problems are in their very essence spiritual problems." Hence a broad, liberal interpretation of the church's mission, including social and educational activities, guided the Interchurch surveys from the start.[11]

As an agency (ideally) of all the churches, the Interchurch World Movement strove to be neutral on controversial issues in its surveys, avoiding interpretative commitments by holding scrupulously to the function of securing facts scientifically and objectively. "At the outset it is 'taking stock' of the Whole Church in all the world," explained the *Federal Council Bulletin*, in order that the churches might "plan intelligently for winning the whole world to the Saviour--to plan without guesswork, hesitation or uncertainty."[12]

The survey was divided into the two primary categories of home and foreign missions; but in conjunction with the American survey, special studies were made of American education, religious education, hospitals and homes, and ministerial salaries, pensions, and relief. Both the foreign and home surveys dealt extensively with "the social question" simply by describing conditions. The foreign survey dealt with the geography, population, and government of each nation in the world as well as conditions of food, health, education, literature, status of women and children, and finally religion. The home survey likewise described practically all conceivable social conditions, from logging camps in mountain regions, to metropolitan slums, as well as the condition of various ethnic and racial groups.

As published in the spring of 1920 in two volumes entitled *World Survey, Revised Preliminary Edition*, the survey was frankly promotional. According to Fred P. Haggard, who administered the whole survey program, "the heart and conscience of the Church should be aroused by the survey so that adequate support to the work will be given."[13] Consequently the published material was calculated to attract and hold the attention and support of the average middle class citizen. The text was limited to concise, startling (but not sensationalistic) statements of fact presenting the problems and needs of America and the world in light of traditional American values and goals--somewhat akin to Josiah Strong's *Our Country* written thirty-five years earlier. But in place of Strong's prose presentation, the *World Survey* featured many charts and graphs, protographs and attractive illustrations, and a wealth of statistics. Also unlike *Our Country*, and unlike the comprehensive examination of "the state of religion" in the post-war world made by the Committee on the War and the Religious Outlook over a five-year period (1918-1922), the Interchurch *World Survey* was almost void of analytical treatment. The survey's goal remained objective reporting, free of all controversial interpretation.

In one aspect of the social question, however, no American Protestant organization could remain objective. Hardly a Protestant voice was raised in 1920 against the Prohibition Amendment, for nearly all considered it a great victory for the church in its traditional role as the nation's moral conscience. But neither did they believe the battle to be over against social vices, of which alcohol was but the worst. The Interchurch World Movement joined the attack by inaugurating a survey Department on

Temperance and Moral Welfare, confident of the solid support of
the vast majority of Protestant Americans during a period of
grave social crisis.

Not all Protestant leaders were convinced, moreover, that
the Interchurch World Movement, as the publicly acknowledged
representative of American Protestantism, could or should remain
aloof from the deeper social issues confronting the nation.
Those who embraced the social gospel recognized the difficulty,
yet necessity, of speaking in the cause of justice at a time when
justice prevailed. Shailer Mathews, past president of the Federal
Council of Churches and a long-time social gospel spokesman,
praised the Interchurch World Movement for its factual presentation of social problems facing the churches. "Hereafter," he
declared, "no Protestant body has any excuse for ignorance as to
the multiplicity and magnitude of the task which Christian people
must face if our present social order is to embody the ideals of
Jesus." But social amelioration was only part of the task, cautioned Mathews, for the economic order itself must be Christianized. The church had a responsibility, he thought, to take an
impartial stand for the Christian principles of love and justice
in the raging conflicts between capital and labor. "Pronounce-
ment is a delicate and difficult duty," concluded Mathews, "but
it is imperative."[14]

The distinction between traditional Protestant moral
reform and the social gospel could no longer be glossed over by
1919, nor could the social gospel enjoy general public approval.
The lines of specific loyalty and principle were too sharply
and rigidly drawn. The social gospel had always opposed social
radicalism while defending the rights of organized labor against
oppressive big business. But in 1919 and 1920, public opinion
almost hysterically associated social radicalism with organized
labor, while championing big business for its stringent opposition to both. Interchurch leaders knew that the identification
of their movement with the business world and its dealings in
large sums of money threatened to alienate the laboring masses
and play into the hands of the anti-Red fanatics. On the other
hand, the churchmen realized that endorsement of organized labor,
or even criticism of the business interests, would bring accusa-
tions of social-radicalism upon the Interchurch World Movement,
and the financial consequences would be deadly. The alternatives
were clear: they could remain silent on the controversial issues
involving freedom and justice in order to hold the support of the

great middle class (and its money); or they could become involved
in the issues in order to know the truth, striving more for social
justice than for popularity. There was no middle way.

The necessity for decision on the social question came home
to Protestant leaders on the afternoon of May 1, 1919, as five
hundred delegates to the Cleveland interboard Conference of the
Interchurch World Movement recessed for lunch. During the noon
intermission, a parading demonstration of socialists and laborers
turned into a bloody riot in downtown Cleveland, a city with a
high percentage of foreign-born and a comparatively strong social-
ist party. Many of the delegates witnessed the riot, which continued into early evening, and the conference was electrified by
the reports of violence. After several impassioned speeches
calling for the development of some kind of organization through
which the churches might combine their efforts in helping to solve
pressing industrial problems, a committee was formed to analyze
the situation and make recommendations. In its report the next
day (May 2) recommending the formation of an Interchurch Department of Industrial Relations, the Committee sounded the classic
social gospel theme.

> The test of democracy lies, not chiefly in the
> organization, but in the heart of society. Our
> nation helped to win the war against autocracy
> and to make possible the application of democracy
> among the peoples of the world. It now remains
> for Christian America to apply completely these
> principles in the realm of industry. The sharp-
> est challenge for the Church today is to make
> religion and democracy real in the common life
> of mankind. The current disorders and disasters
> cannot be cured without recognizing the essential
> partnership of capital and labor and the inter-
> dependence of social and industrial groups and
> their mutual obligations.[15]

The Interchurch Industrial Relations Department would tread
in the thick of controversy. But entering controversy did not
mean embracing one particular social philosophy or policy against
another. The social gospel critique had been intended to be primarily an impartial judgment of injustice, which could be made
from a liberal or conservative social ethical position. Therefore Worth M. Tippy, former pastor of Epworth Methodist Church
in Cleveland, who had become head of the Federal Council of
Churches' Department of Social Science, recommended "that the
Department of Industrial Relations base itself squarely on the
teaching and the spirit of Christ, taking no positive position in
favor of any one general plan for the reconstruction of society."

Tippy sought to create "a religious fellowship which shall be broad enough to allow for conservative, liberal and radical thinkers."[16]

By the end of September, 1909, the Industrial Relations Department had formulated a working policy broad enough in basic principle to command the support of most social-minded churchmen, yet specific enough in application to involve them in the issues and conflicts of the day. The policy affirmed "the principles as taught and lived by Jesus Christ . . . [as] the dominating force in the proper adjustment of industrial relations. But the application of these principles (love, justice, brotherhood, cooperation) must be applied equally to all parties in dispute. Upon this policy the Industrial Relations Department set about to study industrial disputes, including their social consequences, in order to determine the ethical issues involved and hence the demands of justice. Investigations were undertaken, for example, into the coal-mining situation, railway problems, agricultural difficulties, migratory labor, immigration and deportation activities, and the steel strike of 1919-1920.

The great steel strike of 1919-1920, one of the most significant labor conflicts in American history, drew the attention of the Interchurch Industrial Relations Department almost immediately and became the *cause célèbre* and chief point of religious controversy during the time of its duration.

The steel industry, the keystone of modern mass-production industry, had successfully countered attempts by organized labor to unionize steelworkers, so that by the start of World War I, led by U. S. Steel Corporation president, Judge Elbert Gary, management controlled labor and the open shop prevailed. Production needs and the demand for labor during the war, however, resulted in increased government control of the industry. The National War Labor Board guaranteed the workers' right to organize, forced management to sit at the conference table with labor leaders, and brought about wage increases and a shorter working day. After the war, however, conditions quickly began returning to normal. Wages did not rise with the cost of living, and the old twelve-hour day and seven-day week returned. Management resumed its opposition to organized labor; Gary reasserted his paternalistic control of labor, refusing even to talk with union representatives. Labor, seizing upon wartime idealism, proclaimed war on industrial autocracy at home. A National Committee for

Organizing Iron and Steel Workers was organized, with A. F. L.
leader Samuel Gompers as chairman. In August of 1919, the steel-
workers voted to strike, and on September 22 an unprecedented
250,000 men (about half the industry's work force) walked off
their jobs.

The cry of social radicalism soon fell hard upon the
strikers. One of the master-minds behind their drive to organize
was William Z. Foster, secretary-treasurer of the National Committee for Organizing Iron and Steel Workers, whose radical past
(an I. W. W. syndicalist) allowed labor's opponents to point to
him as proof that outside agitators had infiltrated the unions
and were using the strike as a means to instigate revolution.
Moreover, the accusers fell upon a choice piece of ammunition by
discovering a pamphlet entitled *Syndacalism* written by Foster
several years earlier. *Syndacalism* violently denounced capitalism
and called for its overthrow. The press seized upon this pamphlet,
referring to it constantly in coverage of the strike. On October
3, Foster was called before the Senate Committee on Education and
Labor investigating the strike. The "Red book" (as Senator
McKellar called Foster's pamphlet) dominated the line of inquiry.
When Foster became vague and evasive in his replies to questions
about how and when his views might have changed since the pamphlet
was published, arguing that his personal ideas were irrelevant to
the issues involved in the strike, the case against him tightened.
Guilt by association took over. The Senate Committee eventually
concluded that the steel strike involved "a considerable element
of IWW's, anarchists, revolutionists, and Russian Soviets."[19]

Meanwhile, just as the Senate investigation was getting
under way late in September, Methodist Bishop Fred B. Fisher,
Director of the Interchurch Department of Industrial Relations,
spent several days in Washington interviewing government, labor,
and business leaders in order to discover their attitudes toward
the Interchurch involvement in industrial problems. Probably
partly in response to Fisher's questioning, Senator Kenyon,
Chairman of the Senate Committee on Education and Labor, Labor
Secretary Wilson, officials of the A. F. L., and the Chamber of
Commerce of the United States expressed their desire that Protestant churches aid in solving labor problems. Soon after, representatives of several denominational social service commissions
joined the Federal Council Commission on Social Service in recommending that the Interchurch Industrial Relations Department call

a conference of prominent church leaders to consider industrial problems. On October 2-3, therefore, the National Industrial Relations Conference of Christian Representatives was held in New York City's Hotel Pennsylvania.[20]

The conference, presided over by Methodist Bishop Francis J. McConnell, long-time social gospel leader, did not intend to make judgmental statements about specific industrial conflicts. It rather sought "to point out the moral principles involved in all industrial relations and to suggest some methods applicable to the present situation. . . . to indicate the Christian bases upon which these problems can be solved."[21] The conference issued just such a statement. It was similar to the Federal Council of Churches document, "The Church and Social Reconstruction," formulated five months earlier, and the (American Catholic) "Bishops Program of Social Reconstruction" adopted in 1919, calling for the application of Christian love to industrial relations, supporting the right of collective bargaining, and advocating equal opportunity for women, Negroes, and foreign-born in industry.

The conference, however, did not feel that the churches had gone their limit with simply another statement of general principles. Glenn H. Plumb, counsel for the four railroad brotherhoods who was observing the conference, cautioned against "glittering generalities in the resolutions endorsed by the conference which are not going to carry much comfort to those men beneath who look to the church organization for succor."[22] Discussion turned repeatedly to the steel strike, the facts of which were concealed by the uproar of anti-Red hysteria. How could justice be secured if the public remained ignorant of the issues? According to McConnell, "sentiment grew in the assembly to ask the Industrial Relations Department of the Interchurch World Movement to investigate the strike and report," and a motion to that effect was carried "without a dissenting vote."[23]

On October 5, 1919, the Interchurch Industrial Relations Department formed a special Commission of Inquiry to investigate the steel strike and appointed Francis J. McConnell chairman. Daniel A. Poling of the United Evangelical Church, a member of the Interchurch Cabinet, was appointed vice-chairman. In all, nine persons formed the Commission. The Commission employed a staff of qualified investigators, headed by Heber Blankenhorn of the Bureau of Industrial Research in New York. In addition, technical assistance was provided by such agencies as the

Bureau of Industrial Research, New York, and the Bureau of
Applied Economics, Washington, D.C. But the Commission of Inquiry took complete charge of the investigation, having been
given full control by the Interchurch Executive Committee with
the sole stipulation that final decision as to publication of the
findings would remain with the Executive Committee.[24] Thus began
an intensive investigation of the steel strike which ultimately
produced two significant volumes--a primary *Report on the Steel
Strike of 1919*, and supplementary reports on *Public Opinion and
the Steel Strike*.

Because the Commission of Inquiry was seeking to uncover
the inside facts about a notorious situation pertaining to social
order and justice in order to enlighten and stimulate the public
to action, the Interchurch steel strike investigation may be
placed within the general muckraking tradition. The investigation was undertaken because a group of Protestant churchmen were
convinced that the public was uninformed of the basic facts of
the strike, which allowed the real issues to be side-tracked and
public attention to be diverted to knocking down "straw-man
explanations." Ignorance had bred "a public fear akin to panic."
The press had sided with steel and through selectivity of news,
suppression of facts, and deliberate "coloring" of news events,
had successfully molded public opinion sharply against the
strikers. Hence "the failure of the press was one of the reasons
for an Interchurch investigation of the steel strike." The investigation not only substantiated the failure of the press,
however, but also the failure of government and labor to inform
the public. "Analysis of the data collected proved that neither
the United States Steel Corporation, nor organized labor, nor
governmental agencies have considered it their normal business to
ascertain the current facts regarding conditions of employment,
etc., in the steel industry and to take the public constantly
into their confidence on such facts."[25]

Assuming, therefore, that industrial relations was part
of the church's social mission field (a social gospel assumption
not shared by all), that moral judgment could be made only on
the basis of facts, and that the facts were not forthcoming from
secular sources, the Commission on Inquiry justified its investigation. The Commission wisely chose to do its work as quietly
as possible, avoiding all publicity, in order to minimize outside pressure on the investigators and to protect the Interchurch

World Movement as a whole from the hostilities of the public.
The Commission knew that many powerful leaders in industry would
resent the church's meddling in their affairs (they had already
opposed the right of organized labor to be involved in labor disputes), and that even a fair consideration of the strikers'
grievances would counter the public mood. Better to wait until
all the facts were in before meeting the public.

The Commission, however, fully intended to meet the public
with facts--facts secured in the strictest possible objectivity
and neutrality. Fred Fisher announced at the outset that the
investigationwould "take all the records available, visit each
center, and through personal contact, interview, and direct observation strive to arrive at the truth. We will unflinchingly
tell the truth as we see it," Fisher continued, "and are ready
to take all consequences of telling that truth, and our report
will receive the widest publicity."[26]

On January 8, 1920, the second day of the Interchurch
World Survey Conference in Atlantic City, the steel strike ended
in crushing defeat for steelworkers and organized labor. Along
with the general public, Protestant churchmen gave a sigh of
relief, since few of them had sympathized with the strikers'
cause. Silently the Commission of Inquiry completed its investigation and began preparing a report. At a two-day session,
March 29-30, 1920, the Commission unanimously adopted the report
and submitted it for examination by the Interchurch Executive
Committee, with whom the decision to publish rested. But the
Executive Committee, being preoccupied with the simultaneous
financial campaign, put off consideration of the report until
after the money drive. No doubt the Interchurch leaders preferred
to minimize the potential financial consequences of publicizing
the facts. Word (or rumors) had quickly spread that the report
was critical of steel and favorable to the workers' cause, which
alarmed some of the Interchurch leaders.

The investigation had in fact drawn some startling conclusions. A large proportion of steel workers worked twelve
hours a day, seven days a week. Yet the large majority of all
workers received earnings "below the level set by government
experts as the minimum of comfort level for families of five,"
and many of them earned less than "the minimum subsistence standard." Moreover, working conditions and wages were applied dis-
criminately against immigrant workers and resulted in race divisions within the working community. The corporation arbitrarily

and impersonally controlled hours and wages of the labor force,
providing no means by which workers' grievances might be communicated to management. Company control extended beyond the plants:
"The steel industry was under the domination of a policy whose
aim was to keep out labor unions. In pursuit of this policy,
blacklists were used, workmen were discharged for union affiliation, and 'undercover men' and 'labor detectives' were employed
and efforts were made to influence the local press, pulpit and
police authorities." In many communities, "the civil rights of
free speech and assembly were abrogated without just cause."
The press, local police authorities, company management, and many
church pulpits contributed to the charge of Bolshevism; yet the
investigation found no evidence that radical leadership controlled
the strikers. All of these forces of opposition, plus the unsatis-
factory organizationof the combined unions conducting the strike,
contributed to the downfall of the workers' cause. In conclusion,
the Commission stated that "the causes of the strike lay in grie-
ances which gave the workers just cause for complaint and for
action. These unredressed grievances still exist in the steel
industry."[27]

On May 10, 1920, the Interchurch Executive Committee,
meeting in Cleveland, heard a presentation of the steel strike
report by Bishop McConnell. Upon a statement of appreciation
"for the painstaking work of the Commission," the Executive
Committee voted to accept the report. But the question of publication required a more thorough study of the findings. Therefore
a small committee was formed to scrutinize the report and bring
it again before the Executive Committee at a future, unhurried
session for its careful examination. Before long, rumors began
to spread that the Executive Committee, fearful of hostile public
reaction to the report's conclusions, had decided to suppress the
findings and prevent publication. These rumors, vigorously denied
by Interchurch leaders, were unfounded.[28] Actually the Executive
Committee, recognizing the seriousness of the report's findings,
was taking every precaution that the truth had indeed been
recorded before releasing the report for publication.

Once convinced of the soundness of the report, the Interchurch Executive Committee did not waver in deciding to make it
public. On June 28, 1920, the special committee to examine the
report told the Interchurch leaders that it was "impressed with
the thoroughness of the work done, the completeness with which
all factors of the case have been recognized and the fairness of

spirit with which the report has been compiled." Then the special committee made a bold, yet realistic statement (realistic according to the Commission of Inquiry's principles of operation) of the Interchurch duty in light of the facts:

> Taken as a whole, the Commission's report consti-
> tutes a serious indictment of the steel corpora-
> tion and of the public authorities in many places.
> On the other hand, it deals frankly with certain
> delinquencies and the weaknesses of the labor
> organizations. There can be no doubt that it will
> be regarded by the public as strongly favoring
> the laboring man's side of the case. So far as
> your committee can see such impression corresponds
> wholly to the facts discovered. It feels that
> however distasteful may be the duty of pointing
> out what appear to be grievous wrongs, we have
> no option in the matter. The Church of Christ
> has not only the privilege but the duty of wit-
> nessing against injustice, not matter by whom it
> may be done.[29]

The Executive Committee promptly voted unanimously to authorize the report's publication. On July 27, the final manuscript was sent to President Wilson in Washington, and the following day copies were sent to newspapers. Shortly after, *Report on the Steel Strike of 1919* was published in book form. Within a few months the gist of its contents, having been given the widest publicity, was common knowledge across the nation.

The steel strike report caused a sensation, for it countered the most widely held view of the strike and disclosed working conditions and wages below American standards. In the main, editorial opinion endorsed the report and reversed its previous condemnation of the strikers to support their grievances. Even the "militant minority, led by trade journals, financial organs and spokesmen of great corporations," attacked not the findings so much as the "radicalism" of the investigators.[30] During the next year, members of the Commission of Inquiry helped keep the report in the lime-light by means of public speeches and "open letters" supporting the report and answering critics. In May, 1921, the supplementary volume, *Public Opinion and the Steel Strike*, was published. It added weight to the original report's conclusion. Public pressure on steel to improve workers' hours and wages steadily mounted, until by the end of 1922, U. S. Steel had largely ended the twelve-hour work day, seven-day week and had raised the wage scale. It is fair to conclude that the Interchurch steel report helped bring about this partial redress of steel-workers' grievances.

Can it be said, then, that the steel strike investigation
marked a social gospel victory in the Interchurch World Movement's
confrontation with a social problem? There may be room for question, of course, whether or not the report was essentially a
social gospel document. Recent scholarly opinion, while praising
the quality of the report, has concluded that the essential social
gospel concern for justice in the social-economic system itself
made little headway in 1920 by virtue of the Interchurch report.[31]
But the more important consideration at this point is whether or
not the social gospel, insofar as it was represented in the
Department of Industrial Relations, finally determined the Interchurch response to the social tensions of the day. There can be
no precise verdict because the Interchurch World Movement as a
whole participated in the increasingly conservative attitude of
the churches (and the nation as a whole) toward social questions
and included within its ranks a diversity of social thought.

Due to the extreme post-war tensions, it was unusually
difficult, if not impossible, for a church program tolerating
liberal and conservative social thought to function smoothly or
unitedly. Worth Tippy himself, who advocated a broad, inclusive
social policy in the Industrial Relations Department, discovered
the hazards of such a policy during a time of social unrest, when
he ran into conflict with his more liberal Methodist colleague,
Harry F. Ward. Ward had been in the public eye throughout 1919
for his willingness to analyze the Russian Bolshevik "experiment"
objectively without firmly condemning it. As a member of its
Executive Committee, Ward became deeply involved and quite influential in the Interchurch Industrial Relations Department. He
arranged, for example, to make his liberal Social Service Bulletin
also an organ of the Interchurch World Movement. Tippy, also on
the Executive Committee, believed that Ward's socially leftest
views fed "straight into the revolutionary movement" and could
bring the Interchurch World Movement into disrepute.[32] Nevertheless, men whose social views clashed, as did Ward's and Tippy's,
were able to work together in the Industrial Relations Department
on the basis of their common concern for justice in labor-manage-
ment relations.

The concerns of the Department of Industrial Relations,
however, were never more than an undercurrent within the Interchurch mainstream. But this fact only adds to the significance
of the courageous endorsement of the steel strike report by the
movement's top executive body. The Interchurch leaders had been

forced to decide whether or not the movement would embrace the
social gospel, which was rapidly losing the popularity it had
enjoyed during the progressive era. It was no easy decision, for
to voice the social gospel in the post-World War I period required
something of the courage which had characterized the prophets of
social Christianity during the 1880's and 1890's.

The conclusion must be that the Interchurch World Movement's involvement in nation-wide industrial affairs marks a high
point in the history of American social Christianity and progressive reform. The steel strike report, dealing with an event embodying many of the post-war social fears and conflicts, was so
responsibly carried out that it altered public opinion on a most
controversial issue. The complex combination of hostile criticisms of the effort and of positive responses to its accomplishments forecast a new day of uncertain, often controversial but
never-ceasing religious involvement in modern urban-industrial
society. Meanwhile, the Interchurch World Movement's involvement
in the steel strike had reflected and contributed to the problematic forces with which crusading Protestants were beginning to
contend as they brought their post-war campaign to its climactic
moment.

1. *IWM Documents*, IV, p. 140.

2. Ida M. Tarbell, *History of the Standard Oil Company*; Thomas
    W. Lawson, *Frenzied Finance*; Lincoln Steffenas, *The Shame
    of the Cities*; David Graham Phillips, *The Treason of the
    Senate*; Burton J. Henrick, *The Story of Life Insurance*;
    Upton Sinclair, *The Jungle*.

3. The Disciples' survey was entitled *The Whole Church Lift-
    ing the Whole Task* (Cincinnati, 1914); The Methodists' was
    Centenary Survey (New York, 1918).

4. See Robert K. Murray, *Red Scare: A Study in National
    Hysteria, 1919-1920* (Minneapolis, 1955), p. 278.

5. *The Christian Advocate*, July 31, 1919, p. 966.

6. *Interchurch World Movement Speakers' Manual*, p. 9.

7. Quotations from *World Survey*, Vol. I, pp. 40, 74, 80.

8. *New Era Magazine*, I (September, 1919), p. 522.

9. *The Baptist*, January 31, 1920, p. 6.

10. "Putting the Bible on the Stage to Combat Unrest," *New
    York Times*, November 30, 1919, IV, p. 5.

11. See *World Survey*, Vol. I, pp. 7, 43-44; II, p. 11; Tyler
    Dennett, "The Enlarging Definition of Missions," *The Mis-
    sionary Review of the World*, XLIII (March, 1920), pp. 182-
    184; and Robert L. Kelly, "The Relation of Christian Edu-
    cation to the Interchurch World Movement," *Religious Edu-
    cation*, IV (August, 1919), pp. 279-83.

12. *Federal Council Bulletin*, II (September, 1919), p. 159.

13. "Surveying the Foreign Fields," *The Missionary Review of
    the World*, XLIII (March, 1920), p. 185.

14. *The Independent*, May 1, 1920, pp. 167-68.

15. *IWM Documents*, IV, p. 109.

16. *Ibid.*, IV, p. 112.

17. *Ibid.*, IV, pp. 19-20.

18. See "Industrial Relations and the Churches," unpublished
    document issued by the Interchurch World Movement, on file
    at the National Council Research Library in New York City.

19.   An account of the interrogation appeared in *New York Times*, October 4, 1919, p. 1.

20.   See Henry H. Lewis, "The Facts in the Case of the Interchurch World Movement," *Industry*, 2 (July 15, 1920), pp. 2-5; *Federal Council Bulletin*, 11 (December, 1919), p. 193; and *New York Times*, September 30, 1919, p. 14:5, and October 1, 1919, p. 2:4.

21.   "Report of the Findings Committee, National Industrial Conference of Christian Representatives," *Interchurch Newsletter*, October 2, 1919, p. 3.

22.   *Interchurch Newsletter*, October 9, 1919, p. 7.

23.   McConnell, *By the Way* (New York, 1952), p. 214. See also *IWM Documents*, IV, p. 25.

24.   The Executive Committee voted its approval of the investigation on October 14, 1919, as recorded in *IWM Documents*, IV, p. 125.

25.   Quotations from *Report on the Steel Strike of 1919* (New York, 1920), pp. 21, 31; and *Public Opinion and the Steel Strike* (New York, 1920), p. 87.

26.   *New York Times*, October 4, 1919, p. 2:7. See also Fisher's report to the Interchurch Cabinet on October 9, 1919, in *IWM Documents*, IV, pp. 123-24.

27.   Quotations from *Report on the Steel Strike of 1919*, pp. 11-16.

28.   For denials of suppression, see *New York Times*, July 2, 1920, p. 16:4; and July 3, 1920, p. 14:8. See also Executive Committee minutes, in *IWM Documents*, IV, pp. 134-35.

29.   *IWM Documents*, IV, p. 138.

30.   See *Public Opinion and the Steel Strike*, pp. 71-85, 308.

31.   See D. B. Meyer, *The Protestant Search for Political Realism 1919-1941* (Berkeley, Calif., 1961) pp. 60-62.

32.   The Tippy-Ward dispute is preserved in a lengthy memorandum sent on February 7, 1920, by Tippy to S. Earl Taylor and to John R. Mott.

CHAPTER VII

PROTESTANT CRUSADE, 1920:   THE BATTLE WAGED,
THE MOVEMENT DEAD

During the early months of 1920, as Interchurch World
Movement leaders enthusiastically prepared for the final state of
their great campaign, a discordant note increasingly interrupted
the harmony of their optimism.   The editor of *Missions* (a Baptist
magazine) had echoed the growing dismay of American churchmen
over the state of the nation and the world in December of 1919.

> The world was never in sorer need of multitudes of
> men and women of good will. Many had hoped that
> the severe lessons of the world war would be
> learned, and that old bitternesses and prejudices
> and hatreds would speedily be submerged in a tidal
> wave of good will. The dream of a world brother-
> hood, the ideal of a permanent league of peace,
> the ushering in of a new day of peace, fraternity
> and altruism--these were visions that often found
> expression in words. But how soon and sadly have
> the splendid visions vanished and the old greed,
> selfishness and hatefulness appeared. The nations
> are not at peace with one another nor within them-
> selves. Grasping unrest is seen at work in nearly
> all lands.[1]

The dawning era seemed more a violent onslaught upon the
forces of progress than the expected blossoming of a golden age.
If the Interchurch World Movement was originally projected as a
victory crusade of the churches to complete the evangelization of
the world which had been made safe for Christian democracy, by
the start of its campaigns of 1920 the Movement was being interpreted as the churches' great effort to preserve American idealism
and to secure peace in the world.

The contrast between expectation and reality accounts for
the shock experienced by American Protestant leaders during the
course of the year 1919. Looking back over the preceding twelve
months, delegates to the Foreign Missions Conference of North
America in January, 1920, recalled having "pictured 1918 as the
high tide of Christian idealism, when the world, after its bap-
tism in blood, seemed to be touched with light never seen on sea
or land, and everywhere paeans of hope were being sung." At that

earlier gathering they had thrilled at "the unanimity and enthusiasm with which the Interchurch program was adopted." The gate
to earthly paradise had seemed open, the road straight and true,
with America leading the way "as the torch bearer, the Sir
Galahad of the race."[2]

Even in early 1919, however, only the most naive had failed
to anticipate a struggle in efforts to Christianize a war-torn
world. But churchmen took the burden as confidently as they did
seriously, convinced that the secular powers--the government and
military, business and labor, the American people in general--had
become the church's allies. Sacred and secular, religion and culture, church and state had become mixed in a compound of patriotic
religious idealism which had given the appearance of a unified
nation engaged in the final battle before the Christian millennium.
Indeed it was not uncommon in 1919 for promoters of Protestant
campaigns to ask, "shall the Christian Church lag behind the state
in its defense of Christian principles?"[3]

As the year wore on, however, churchmen became disillusioned
with the secular powers and appalled at the breakdown of unifying
idealism. The nation was racked with social, economic, and political dissension; the people's ability to rise above partisan concerns for the good of the whole seemed lost. "If, under the
stress of those trying [wartime] days, the best in them came to
the top," wrote *The Baptist* editor early in 1920, "the best seems
to have sunk out of sight now that peace has come." Speaking
before the General Conference of the Methodist Episcopal Church
three months later, Bishop William F. McDowell described the
world as "war-torn, debt-ridden, in social ferment, economic
revolution, governmental storm."[4]

Nothing upset Protestant leaders more than the bitter
political bickering that finally prevented the United States from
ratifying the Versailles Peace Treaty and entering the League of
Nations. They abhorred the thought that the supreme goal for
which Americans had fought--permanent world peace--might be lost
sight of by American politicians at the crucial hour of international peace-making. When by March, 1919, the Republican block
led by Henry Cabot Lodge began to attack Wilson's peace policies,
the religious press protested that "as politics were largely sub-
ordinated to winning the war, so they should be sternly relegated
to the rear at this time."[5] During the summer and fall the
churches stood solidly with the vast majority of Americans in
favoring America's entry into the League of Nations. The

National Committee on the churches and the Moral Aims of the War
formulated a petition, signed by 14,450 clergymen representing
nearly every denomination, urging the United States Senate "to
ratify the Paris Peace Treaty, embodying the League of Nations
Covenant, at the earliest possible date without amendments on
such reservations as would require resubmission of the treaty to
the Peace Conference and Germany." The Church Peace Union blasted
the Senate for its "shameful and inexcusable" political partisan-
ship which threatened to bring Americans into "the deep disgrace
of abandoning the ideals for which we fought and the shame of
putting safety first in this hour of the world's deep and dread-
ful need."[6] When on November 19, 1919, the treaty failed to pass
a senate vote, S. Earl Taylor, General Secretary of the Interchurch World Movement, voiced the feelings of many Protestant
leaders:

> I am humiliated and sore at heart. If there ever
> was a time when men needed to be big and broad-
> minded, and generous and sympathetic, as well as
> statesmanlike, that time is now. It is unthink-
> able that America will throw away her unique
> opportunity for moral and spiritual world leader-
> ship. If America was justified in entering the
> war to help in the accomplishment of great works
> of destruction, she surely is justified in enter-
> ing whole-heartedly and unselfishly in bringing
> about an era of peace and good will for the whole
> world. Any men who subordinate the world interests
> of our time to partisanship or to a narrow spirit
> of nationalism will ultimately be swept away by a
> rising tide of public condemnation.[7]

On March 19, 1920, the Senate again voted on the treaty
for the last time, and to the chagrin of church leaders it was
defeated. "On one side," wrote a Presbyterian editor, "stood
Woodrow Wilson, idealistic and firm; on the other side stood
Henry Cabot Lodge, patriotic and firm. . . . As between Christian men it does seem that some adjustment might have been made."[8]

Others, too, had begun to question whether or not the
government could any longer be considered an ally of the evangelical mission. "The Government at Washington," wrote *The Baptist*
editor, "by which we mean Congress and all, has made forward-
looking men sick at heart. It has been fiddling the old tune of
partisan politics while the world has been on fire." "It seems
that God won the war and the devil won the peace," former Secretary of the Treasury William G. McAdoo told an Interchurch gathering on April 20, 1920.[9] In this disillusionment with the secular
powers in 1920 may be detected one of the early cracks in the
mortar cementing Protestant churches and the secular order.

Protestant leaders began to look for their churches' peculiar
identity in the cause for human betterment.

If churchmen had begun to lose faith in secular powers,
they maintained confidence in the ability of the church to succeed
where others had failed. John R. Mott reaffirmed his contagious
optimism before an Interchurch dinner on March 22, 1920. "My
friends," said Mott, "if you and I didn't have tasks that we
honestly know are too great for us, we would not have become
acquainted with the living God. Let us count it all joy that we
have got possible impossibilities--things that will deepen our
acquaintance with the great fountain of vitality."[10] The pain of
a delinquent state was offset by signs of an obedient church.
The Interchurch World Movement was being promoted as "America's
chance to make good before a disappointed world."

> No matter how much our political leaders have
> failed us in this supreme hour of duty and honor,
> the Christian people of America still have a chance.
> The challenge comes to the church all the stronger
> because it is being refused by the state. How else
> shall we bear our humiliation before the world?
> America, which went into the war placarding her
> passion for service, her devotion to the good of
> all mankind, America, whose idealism was the
> strength of the armies of the Allies, the solace
> and hope of the crushed and bleeding nations
> throughout the world--American to fail them in
> the end![11]

The Interchurch answer was no! By the strength of united
Protestantism, America would not fail the world. In January of
1920, Charles L. Thompson, President of the Home Missions Council, declared that the church "has marched as if sometimes she
intended to fight. Has not the time come?"[12] By then the Interchurch World Movement had emerged from its great Atlantic City
World Survey Conference prepared to go to battle.

To battle they went. "This is war!" declared a Disciples
of Christ editor during the climactic moment of the great Interchurch campaign of 1920. "The supreme issues of the military war
were not settled; the way was merely cleared for their settlement.
It is the Christian war that must permanently save the world from
greed and lust and tyranny."[13] Protestant leaders had not lost
faith in the holy crusade they perceived in World War I; nor did
they cast off the spirit of war when hostilities ceased. Instead,
as the nation at peace failed to maintain its zealous wartime
idealism, the churches vowed to fulfill the military goals by
shrouding their forward movements with the elements of war. So

militant had American Protestantism become, that its very life
seemed to depend upon the constancy of its battle spirit.

Beginning in January with the Atlantic City World Survey
Conference, the Interchurch World Movement entered its "intensive
period" of battle preparedness. For four solid months the churches
bombarded the nation with propaganda to raise their spiritual weapons, their men, and their money. Conferences provided the main
line of attack, beginning with two- to three-day State Pastors'
Conferences, followed by large city and county conferences, and
culminating in community and local church conferences. Inter-
spersed were special national and regional conferences for laymen,
women, and young people, as well as roving teams of Interchurch
leaders speaking before various businessmen's and other assemblies,
and countless special rallies for the Interchurch cause. Interchurch leaders pulled out all stops in their one hundred or so
days of cross-country crusading with advertising and literature,
audio-visuals and exhibits, and a careful mixture of reverent
"devotional exercises" and enthusiastic, revival-type oratory.
Long before the conferences began, their warlike conceptual framework had been fixed:

>   First--a study of the enemy and his strategy, viz.
> the human need as disclosed by the surveys.
> Second--the outlining of the plan of our allied
> campaign against the enemy, including its goals
> and objectives. Third--the marshaling of the
> allied forces of Protestantism to accomplish its
> objectives. Fourth--marching orders.[14]

An army marching to battle needed weapons, soldiers, and
financial backing. During January of 1920, spiritual resources
(prayer) received special attention by the Interchurch World
Movement, and February was devoted to the stewardship theme. In
March, the Interchurch focused on life work--the enlistment of
persons for "full-time Christian vocations." The World War had
drained off many potential young recruits for Christian missions,
but Protestant leaders were convinced that returning American
soldiers had been so inspired in battle by a "new conception of
helpfulness to the whole world . . . that they will long for a
self-forgetful service in the place of greatest need." Soldiers,
it was thought, were "the ambassadors of God," ready to enlist
in an even bigger war for Christian advancement. Missionary
leaders also believed that many young persons, unable to participate self-sacrificially in the World War, would readily fulfill
their desires in Protestant missions.[15] With this in mind, the
Interchurch World Movement waged an intensive campus recruiting

142

campaign in cooperation with the Student Volunteer Movement, not
only for missionaries, but for all types of church-related work.

Througout the four-month intensive period, evangelistic
meetings were held in cities and local communities across the
nation, culminating in a week-long simultaneous evangelistic campaign from Palm Sunday, March 28, through Easter, April 4, 1920.
At a time when mass revivalism was fading from the scene as the
dominant method of popular evangelism, special evangelistic campaigns required justification by church leaders. While Christian
evangelism is "a continuous battle and attains some objective
every hour," explained a Presbyterian editor, "this warfare also,
like a military campaign, has its culminating points where there
is a climax of aim and effort and a special victory is achieved.
It encourages and inspires any army to reach its objectives, and
we gain heart and increased energy and efficiency as we move forward in the good fight of faith."[16]

The Interchurch World Movement thus stressed evangelism
"not as a spasm, but as the normal function of the churches."
But a great forward thrust also called for a special campaign to
conserve past victories and prepare for advance. Bishop Theodore
S. Henderson, Methodist Centenary evangelism leader who became
Director of the Interchurch simultaneous evangelism campaign,
spoke of "the primary importance of the evangelistic emphasis at
this particular hour in the history of American Protestantism.
Issues of kingdom and conquest are in the balance."[17] During the
campaign week, daily meetings were held in churches across the
country, plus noon meetings in theaters and shops, with church
bells ringing as a call to prayer. Special three-hour Good Fri-
day meetings were held as merchants closed their shops. The
campaign culminated on Easter ("join-the-church Sunday") with an
ingathering of "decisions for Christ" to increase the ranks of
American Protestant forces.[18] The final stage was thus set for
the greatest campaign of all--the Interchurch simultaneous
financial campaign to raise the budget set forth on the basis of
the world survey.

At a meeting of denominational forward movement leaders
in New York City on January 20, 1920, basic details of the Interchurch financial campaign were ironed out. It was announced that
Lyman L. Pierce, one of the masterminds of wartime Y.M.C.A.
drives, had been appointed Director of the United Simultaneous
Campaign. With a goal of $176,000,000 to be paid during the
first year, forty million dollars of which was to be subscribed

by "friendly citizens," the drive was set for the week of April 25 through May 2, 1920. "We are expected to accomplish in about ten weeks the normal work of several months," General Secretary S. Earl Taylor told the Interchurch Executive Committee.[19] By the first of April, after the evangelistic campaign, all efforts had turned to this final battle.

On April 5, John D. Rockefeller, Jr. began a sixteen-day tour of fourteen major cities with several other Interchurch leaders, speaking before meetings of businessmen on behalf of the financial campaign. A quiet, unpublicized pre-campaign canvass of wealthy Christian persons--perhaps with no church affiliation but with "Christian sympathies"--had already begun for "really notable gifts" later to be advertised as examples of generous giving. The campaign itself was to be based on personal interviews through house-to-house visitation by local church and community teams, made up partly of "outstanding men and women of the community who are independent of denominational connections" (the better to reach "friendly citizens"). Planned for maximum efficiency--"based on elimination of lost motion"--the campaign was expected to reach nearly every Protestant home in the country.[20]

Meanwhile, Interchurch "minute men," supplemented by denominational corps of the same, prepared at a moment's notice to speak on behalf of the financial campaign, began "laying down barrage after barrage, and shell after shell into the field to be attacked," to be followed by the campaign teams who formed "the infantry of the drive." As "zero hour" approached, the religious press called the churches and the nation back to war. "The 'great war' is over," warned *The Baptist*, "but a greater war still goes on."

> Those who follow the great Captain know that
> ultimate victory is certain. Jesus Christ cannot
> be defeated. Sometimes the enemy seems to make
> appalling gains, and the hearts of his followers
> are filled with dismay. Ever and again we see
> "right upon the scaffold, wrong upon the throne,"
> but surely, even if slowly, the kingdoms of this
> world are becoming the kingdom of our Lord and
> of his Christ. . . . We are facing a great hour
> in the spiritual world war. The Christian hosts
> of America are in the trenches ready for a great
> advance. For weeks and months they have been
> preparing for this zero hour.

William E. Doughty, Director of the Interchurch Department of Spiritual Resources which for months had been mobilizing an army of "intercessors," sent out a special bulletin calling for

144

increased prayer power. On Sunday, April 25, at 2 p.m., Protestants the nation over and in many foreign lands joined in five minutes of silent prayer, after which the great campaign began.[21]

Just as the Interchurch army of five thousand began its canvass of the nation, announcements were made of large gifts already given. The largest single donations came from the Rockefeller fortune--nearly five million dollars to Interchurch World Movement related budgets. Then, beginning at a luncheon in the McAlpin Hotel in New York City on April 26, Interchurch Headquarters released to the press daily progress reports of the campaign. By April 30, the one hundred million dollar mark had been surpassed; and by May 2, the end of the formal campaign week, reported subscriptions totaled over $124,000,000.[22] But the campaign organization pushed forward as daily totals continued to rise. The sheer size of the task demanded more time; the nation could not be canvassed in a few days, and it might take weeks to know the final results.

Nevertheless, when the Interchurch Cabinet met on May 4, 1920, there was no doubt that the financial campaign had fallen short of highest hopes. Denominational subscriptions, though many were below the goals set, were already unprecedented; but the friendly citizens fund, needed to finance the Interchurch World Movement itself, was failing miserably. The Cabinet voted to reorganize the campaign for its continuation, and on May 7, William E. Doughty sent another bulletin to the Fellowship of Intercessors calling for increased prayer power. On May 10, the Interchurch General Committee, meeting in Cleveland, issued the following statement:

> Christian men and women of America, the Interchurch World Movement with a program of brotherly cooperation hangs in the balance. Upon the degree of your conviction and response to its call depends the success of this program. It is upon these hearts which Christ had entered and transformed that the burden of this great forward movement must rightfully rest. It is to all such that we specially appeal, not as to representatives of denominations, but as to individuals who would sacrifice and serve rather than see this great cooperative Movement fail. . . . If, with the gratifying degree of success which promises to crown the denominational efforts, we can now all move forward together for the general fund of the Movement, we will experience the joy of seeing our venture of faith in God and in the spirit of cooperation justified and the kingdom of our Lord advanced.[23]

On May 17 and 18, the General Committee of the Interchurch
World Movement together with denominational board representatives
met in Assembly Hall of the Foreign Missions Conference of North
America in New York City--the same "upper room" where on December
17, 1918, many of them had gathered for the first meeting to plan
the Interchurch World Movement. At that earlier meeting, the
question had been whether or not a united forward movement should
be undertaken. Now, exactly seventeen months later, the question
was whether the Interchurch World Movement should continue to
function or go out of business.

Had the financial campaign been a complete success, the
question probably would not have arisen. The denominational campaigns were approaching the two hundred million dollar mark, which
by all former standards could be considered "a magnificent success." But of the forty million dollar goal for the "friendly
citizen" fund, only three million dollars had been subscribed!
This meant more than a great disappointment; it was a financial
crisis. Over the past sixteen months (up to May 15), the Interchurch World Movement had spent nearly eight million dollars, all
of which was borrowed money underwritten by the participating
denominations. Whereas leaders of these denominations had from
the start been fully aware of their legal responsibility should
the Interchurch World Movement fail to raise its own expenses,
they seem to have been almost completely certain that the Movement would succeed. Interchurch leaders expected a large enough
contribution to the central treasury by "friendly citizens" to
pay the Movement's debts, finance it for the future, with a sur-
plus left over to divide among the denominations.[24] Instead, to
the dismay of all concerned, the failure even to raise eight
million dollars for the central treasury created a large financial
burden that hit the denominations like a bomb. No matter what
amount the churches might raise, failure to raise the large Interchurch expense budget would cast a shadow of defeat over the whole
enterprise.[25]

It was thus in the shadow of defeat, while on the verge of
victory, that the General Committee met on May 17 and 18. Denominational victory at the cost of Interdenominational defeat seemed
unthinkable; the Interchurch World Movement had visions far greater
than just financial success. Dr. William Chalmers Covert, Pastor
of the First Presbyterian Church in Chicago, expressed the dominant
feeling of the General Committee: "I can think of no greater
spiritual tragedy to the modern Christian, coming out of a period

of unparalleled confusion, than to have the great Pentecostal
vision of the Interchurch World Movement sidetracked. The failure
of apparatus in no wise invalidates the divine call in that vision,
to which the whole church must respond."[26]

Everyone admitted the "failure of apparatus." Money had
been proved available, but it wrongly had all been directed to
denominational channels. Still convinced, therefore, that
friendly citizens as well as churchmen would answer the Interchurch's call for funds, the General Committee and denominational
board representatives resolved unanimously, first, to reorganize
the Interchurch World Movement and continue its operation at
least for another year on a greatly reduced budget of up to
$150,000 per month. Second, the participating denominations
would be notified to begin payment of their underwritings, while
the three million dollars already subscribed would be used to
finance the Movement during the next two months. Third, however,
a second campaign for ten million dollars--enough to repay the
denominations for their underwriting expenses and to finance the
Interchurch World Movement for another year--would begin immediately and last until July 15. Fourth, henceforth the denominations would be asked to help support the Interchurch World Movement directly on a monthly or yearly financial basis. The future
of the Movement depended largely upon the success or failure of
the last two resolutions--raising ten million dollars and securing denominational support.[27]

Interchurch leaders believed that the "friendly citizens"
fund had failed primarily because denominational allegiance and
pressure led canvassers to entice nominal Protestants to designate
their subscriptions to the denominations. According to Lyman L.
Pierce, campaign director, the "friendly citizens" fund actually
decreased in the daily reports by the fifth day of the campaign
as churches secured reversals in designations from the Interchurch
central treasury to their own denomination. The second campaign,
therefore, was not conducted through denominational channels at
all. Rather it was projected as "a quiet, effective, and tho
thorough-going still hunt for gifts to apply directly on the
program of the Interchurch World Movement [with] no national plan
of advertising and publicity . . . no public announced meetings."
Prospective givers of five thousand dollars or more, of one thousand to five thousand dollars, and of one hundred to one thousand
dollars were carefully separated, contacted first by letter, then
by phone, and finally by personal interview. It was assumed that

denominational forward movement leaders would realize their stake in this campaign and give it their full support.[28]

Despite all efforts, however, it soon became apparent that the second campaign was almost a total failure. When the General Committee met on June 18, only $125,000 had been pledged. A small committee of businessmen was appointed to consider the financial situation of the Interchurch World Movement and report to the Executive Committee ten days hence. This report could hardly have been more negative: the Interchurch debt was over $6,500,000; yet the original "friendly citizen" campaign had produced little more than one million dollars in cash, and of the ten million dollar goal for the second campaign, only six thousand dollars had been paid! "It is folly to blink at the facts," continued the report. "This campaign has not succeeded, and we are spending money for its maintenance far faster than we are getting it in." The report made no recommendation as to continuance of the Interchurch World Movement, but it concluded that unless the denominations decided to support it financially, including its indebtedness, the Interchurch World Movement would die of bankruptcy.[29]

Enthusiastic, generous denominational support, however, was sadly lacking. The second campaign came just as several key denominations held their annual meetings. Faced with the unexpected possibility of having to pay huge Interchurch debts, the denominations were now being asked to pledge additional financial support for the continuation of the Movement. By June 10, 1920, Interchurch leaders could announce that nine denominational judicatories had met and provisionally offered their continued support of the Movement--but none without much debate pro and con. The groundswell of enthusiasm for the Interchurch World Movement had vanished. The Methodist Episcopal General Conference, for example, on the last day of its month-long session (May 1-27), finally "reaffirmed approval of the aims of the Movement, and endorsed the plans for financing its immediate necessities, including the payment of the Methodist underwritings." But objections "to throwing good money after bad" were sounded, and the matter of relationship to the Movement was referred to the Board of Bishops meeting in the fall with full power to act.[30]

The Methodists had in fact put off making final commitments to the Interchurch World Movement until its financial stability would be known. The Disciples of Christ, among other denominations, held no annual meetings until the fall and thus could likewise hold back on making commitments until the Interchurch

World Movement had survived or perished in the storm. But the
Northern Presbyterians and the Northern Baptists, the other two
major components of the Interchurch World Movement, had their
annual meetings during the campaign period and literally held the
Movement's future in their hands.

On May 20, 1920, the Northern Presbyterian General
Assembly convened in Philadelphia anticipating a long, hard debate
over its relationship with the Interchurch World Movement. Five
days later, moderator John Willis Baer, a Pasadena, California
bank executive, presented the Executive Commission's report. The
business-oriented Executive Commission, now convinced that the
Interchurch World Movement had been grossly mismanaged and
excessively costly--in short, a bad business proposition costing
Presbyterians one million dollars, recommended that the denomination pay its underwriting debt and terminate relations with the
Movement, whereupon "a long and at times violent argument" en-
sued.[31] Chief spokesmen favoring the negative resolution were
pastors Maitland Alexander of First Church, Pittsburgh, and Mark
A. Mathews of First Church in Seattle. But they were outweighed
by Interchurch supporters. Layman James M. Speers, a prominent
New York business man who had replaced John R. Mott as chairman
of the Interchurch Executive Committee, frankly admitted that the
Movement had not been free from mistakes. But so had it raised
great sums of money for the churches, made important surveys, and
given a new vision of church unity. "Look at these values,"
counseled Speers, "and some of the acknowledged mistakes may not
appear so very important after all. We have at least been honestly trying to do a big thing for God and the need of the world
today." Speers opposed the recommendation to withdraw, arguing
that "all the enemies of religion and especially of Protestantism
will rejoice over such a failure of Protestant Churches to work
and stick together." Others likewise opposed the withdrawal,
including the influential Robert E. Speer, and it became apparent
that the Assembly was turning against the recommendation. The
whole matter was referred back to the Executive Commission for
further consideration.

Several days later, the Executive Commission presented a
compromise recommendation that, on the one hand, the General
Assembly "decline to incur any further financial obligation for
the Interchurch World Movement, as now organized and controlled;
that it terminate its relationship with said Movement and withdraw any representation it may have therein." On the other hand,

added the resolution, "realizing the deep and widespread feeling
in the Church that some definite agency of a cooperative character
should be in actual and efficient operation," the General Assembly
should contribute one hundred thousand dollars to the Interchurch
World Movement after its complete reorganization "so as to insure
an efficient and economical administration of its affairs." In
addition, in order for the Interchurch World Movement to receive
Presbyterian money, it would have to adopt a budget for the year
1920-1921 of no more than one million dollars. After six hours
of heated debate, the General Assembly finally passed this resolution. The compromise was publicized as a constructive move by
Presbyterians intended not to break the Interchurch World Movement
but to strengthen it. "The next move, so far as the renewal of
Presbyterian cooperation is concerned," explained John Willis
Baer, "is up to the Interchurch World Movement."[32]

The Presbyterian action, however, was a damaging blow to
the Interchurch World Movement. The General Committee had already
begun reorganization of the Movement on the basis of what seemed
a necessary budget of $150,000 per month--nearly twice what the
Presbyterians demanded as maximum. Moreover, the Presbyterian
attitude tended to force the Interchurch World Movement into a
position of complete capitulation to denominational controls
without liberty even to set its own budget. The obstacle which
Interchurch leaders had originally hoped to overcome with the new
Movement--that of having to wait for denominational action before
interdenominational decisions could be made--now seemed stronger
than ever. Furthermore, the Presbyterian action was widely interpreted to mean that this powerful denomination had entirely de-
serted the Interchurch World Movement, which weakened the Interchurch hold on other churches. For the time being, therefore,
Interchurch leaders made no further move; the Baptists had yet
to act.

On June 23, 1920, the Northern Baptist Convention assembled
in Buffalo for an explosive week-long session highlighted not only
by a fundamentalist-modernist scrimmage and the collapse of a
bleacher loaded with three hundred persons, but also by a major
action in the history of the Interchurch World Movement. Northern
Baptists had the largest financial stake in the Interchurch World
Movement of all denominations, with an underwriting debt of
$2,500,000--over one-third of the total Interchurch debt. To
some it seemed wise for Baptists to continue in the Movement,
hoping that somehow the denomination's debt might be relieved by

subsequent Interchurch income. Others vehemently advocated
immediate withdrawal from the Interchurch World Movement lest
further indebtedness strike the denomination. On June 23, retir-
ing Convention President D. C. Shull, a lawyer from Sioux City,
Iowa, spoke in favor of remaining in the Interchurch World Movement. His desires were countered by Cortland Meyers, pastor of
Boston's Tremont Temple, who called for burial of the Interchurch
World Movement in "a grave deep enough to keep it there so that
it shall never have a resurrection."[33]

The next day (June 24), John Y. Aitchison, Director of the
Baptist General Board of Promotion and a member of the Interchurch
Cabinet, submitted the following resolution:

> We declare our grateful belief that the Movement has
> accomplished some very desirable and far-reaching
> results under great difficulties and handicaps,
> but that our experience convinces us that our
> cooperative relationship cannot be adequately or
> satisfactorily expressed in this movement as now
> constituted, and that therefore our relations with
> the Interchurch World Movement should be dis-
> continued as of June 30, 1920.[34]

During the three hours of debate that followed, the resolution
was "greeted with joy and even noisy demonstrations by some," but
by others "with deep grief." According to *The Baptist* editor,
"there was a deep and ineradicable suspicion of the Interchurch
Movement and a feeling that even when reorganized, if it is, it
could not gain the confidence and cordial support which must be
had if the ends sought are to be attained."[35] Discussion continued; a substitute resolution was laid on the table; and
finally the decision to withdraw absolutely and unconditionally
was made as delegates passed the original resolution. Northern
Baptists would pay their underwriting debts immediately, but they
offered no further support to the Interchurch World Movement.

The actions of Northern Presbyterians and Northern Baptists made it practically impossible to continue the work of the
Interchurch World Movement. On July 28, 1920, the Executive
Committee voted to end the second financial campaign, to dismiss
the officers and staff of the Movement, and place the Interchurch
fate in the hands of the General Committee meeting July 8. But
even then, deeply in debt and without funds to continue active
operations, Interchurch leaders were determined to continue the
Movement. On July 8, the General Committee voted to reorganize
the Movement and continue operations for another year on a mere
seventy-five thousand dollar budget, appointing a Committee of

Fifteen to consider with the denominational and interdenominational agencies the future of the Interchurch World Movement and how its goals and achievements might be preserved. Meanwhile, Interchurch literature, surveys, and equipment were to be utilized and disposed of at no expense to the Interchurch World Movement, and the Interchurch headquarters in New York City was put up for lease.[36]

Some hoped that the Interchurch World Movement would weather the storm and eventually regain the support of the majority of Protestant churches. But, as one former Interchurch staff member wrote, there was a tendency to give up: "the crusaders for the ideal of associated action are sick at heart and slow of mind . . . . Many of those most active in Interchurch leadership seemingly have shell-shock." Those committed to the greatness of the Movement now felt compelled to judge it "the most colossal collapse in the church since the days of Pentecost. . . . the greatest blow to Protestantism since the Reformation," even "the greatest tragedy that has occurred in the history of the Christian Church."[37] The last great campaign had collapsed.

On April 8, 1921, the Committee of Fifteen made its final report to the General Committee, convinced that any new program under the Interchurch name could not gain denominational support. Completely reversing the Report of the Committee of Twenty made in January of 1919, the Committee of Fifteen now concluded that the various existing interdenominational agencies were adequate to handle cooperative Protestant work and that the Interchurch World Movement, no longer needed, should cease to exist. Liquidation of Interchurch resources, the winding up of its financial affairs, distribution of survey and other materials, and final discharge of the corporation were handled by a small group of businessmen which made its final report on November 20, 1923.[38] Thus ended one of the most dramatic religious events in American history.

The Interchurch World Movement was dead. Its brief life had touched solidly upon matters affecting the subsequent directions which organized Protestant Christianity would move in America. The problems of religious unity and diversity, of religious organization, and of religious involvement in social issues had assumed priority. But the problems of the new day were transcending the old rallying power of popular Protestantism, and the future loomed uncertain.

NOTES TO CHAPTER VII

1. *Missions*, X (December, 1919), p. 885.

2. *The Christian Advocate*, January 22, 1920, p. 123.

3. *Speakers' Manual, Nation-wide Campaign, Protestant Episcopal Church* (New York, 1919), p. 19.

4. *The Christian Advocate*, May 6, 1920, p. 617; and *The Baptist*, February 14, 1920, p. 80.

5. *The Christian Advocate*, March 6, 1919, pp. 290-291.

6. *Federal Council Bulletin*, II (December, 1919), p. 186.

7. *Interchurch Newsletter*, November 27, 1919, p. 1.

8. *New Era Magazine*, II (May, 1920), p. 328.

9. *New York Times*, April 21, 1920, p. 17:6; and *The Baptist*, May 1, 1920, p. 476.

10. *Missions*, XI (May, 1920), p. 279.

11. Cornelius H. Patton, *Christian America in the New World: An Interpretation of the Interchurch World Movement* (New York, 1920), p. 27.

12. "Some New Visions," *New Era Magazine*, II (January, 1920), p. 27.

13. *World Call*, II (May, 1920), p. 3.

14. From proposals made at the National Leaders' Training Conference, November 5-7, 1919, in *IWM Documents*, V, p. 20. Descriptions of the conference appear in *ibid.*, IV, pp. 58-125; and *Federal Council Bulletin* (April, 1920), p. 74.

15. Quotations on this point taken from *World Call*, I (January, 1919), p. 9; *The Christian Advocate*, March 13, 1919, p. 332; and R. E. Speer, *The New Opportunity of the Church* (New York, 1919), pp. 74-77.

16. *New Era Magazine*, II (March, 1920), p. 163.

17. Bishop Henderson to C. S. Macfarland, February 24, 1920. See also *Federal Council Bulletin*, III (April, 1920), p. 70.

18. See especially such pamphlets as *The Nineteen-twenty Evangelistic Campaign* (New York, 1920); *Lenten Campaign on Evangelism* (New York, 1920); *Work and Prayer for the*

Evangelistic Campaign (New York, 1920); and the account in *IWM Documents*, IV, pp. 10-19.

19. Executive Committee minutes, in *IWM Documents*, VI, pp. 14-15. See also *World Outlook*, VI (May, 1920), pp. 13, 59.

20. The campaign is discussed in *IWM Documents*, VI, pp. 30-34. For the Rockefeller tour, see *New York Times*, March 22, 1920, p. 14:7, and April 25, 1920, p. 10:1.

21. Quotations from *The Baptist Minute Man*, March 1, 1920, p. 2; *The Baptist*, April 24, 1920, p. 439; "General Letter to Intercessors," April 20, 1920. See also *Federal Council Bulletin*, III (April, 1920), p. 62; *New York Times*, April 26, 1920; and *IWM Documents*, VI, pp. 38-40.

22. Subscription progress, including the Rockefeller donations, were recorded in the *New York Times*, April 24, 1920, p. 14:6; April 26, 1920, p. 12:8; April 27, 1920, p. 18:1; April 28, 1920, p. 10:8; April 29, 1920, p. 13:3; April 30, 1920, p. 16:4; May 1, 1920, p. 14:8; May 2, 1920, p. 17:1; and May 3, 1920, p. 12:8.

23. *IWM Documents*, VI, p. 58.

24. On financial expectations and results, see *New York Times*, May 17, 1920, p. 14:8, and May 18, 1920, p. 17:8; and General Committee Minutes in *IWM Documents*, VI, p. 71.

25. Originally, after the World Survey Conference in January, 1920, the General Committee voted approval of a $12,000,000 Interchurch expense budget. This was later lowered to $8,000,000, figured at five per cent of $160,000,000 as a safe estimate of what might be raised by the united campaign, which had seemed quite reasonable assuming that $25,000,000 or so would go to the central treasury. The fact that Interchurch leaders had settled on $160,000,000 shows that the $200,000,000 or so actually subscribed more than fulfilled their minimum standard of success for the denominations. It was only the "friendly citizens" fund that anyone considered a failure. See Speers' statement to the General Committee, May 17, 1920, in *IWM Documents*, VI, pp. 63-64.

26. Quoted in "The Interchurch World Movement and the Denominations," a document issued by the Interchurch World Movement on June 10, 1920, containing several other similar statements by General Committee members.

27. See General Committee minutes, in *IWM Documents*, VI, pp. 70-75; and *New York Times*, May 19, 1920, p. 8:1.

28. See campaign reports in *IWM Documents*, VI, pp. 22, 59-61, 77-78.

29. *Ibid.*, VI, pp. 87, 94-97.

30. "Report to the Churches," issued by the Interchurch World Movement General Committee in May of 1920. See also *The Christian Advocate*, June 3, 1920, p. 750, and June 10, 1920, p. 801.

31. For accounts of the sessions, see *New York Times*, May 26, 1920, p. 17:1; and *New Era Magazine*, II (July, 1920), pp. 502-15.

32. "Official Interpretation of Assembly's Action on Interchurch," *New Era Magazine*, II (July, 1920), p. 516. For the full recommendation, see *Minutes of the General Assembly of the Presbyterian Church in the United States of America, 1920*, pp. 174-76. See also *New York Times*, June 13, 1920, VIII, p. 3:1.

33. For accounts of the sessions, see *New York Times*, June 24, 1920, p. 16:2; June 25, 1920, p. 10:8; June 26, 1920, p. 6:1; and *The Baptist*, July 3, 1920, p. 803.

34. The full resolution is in *Annual of the Northern Baptist Convention 1920*, pp. 121-22; and *The Baptist*, July 3, 1920, p. 810.

35. *The Baptist*, July 3, 1920, p. 798.

36. See Executive Committee minutes, in *IWM Documents*, VI, p. 98 and VIII, p. 15; and *World Call*, II (August, 1920), p. 41.

37. Quotations from John Ralph Voris, "Salvaging Co-operative Ideals," *The Baptist*, September 8, 1920, pp. 1165-66; and "Embarrassment of the Interchurch Movement," *The Literary Digest*, June 12, 1920, pp. 42-43.

38. See Reports in *IWM Documents*, VII, pp. 20-30, and X, pp. 1-18.

CHAPTER VIII

THE AFTERMATH: BIRTH PANGS OF A NEW ERA

Who in 1918 could have predicted the conflicts and ambi-
guities which would plague American Protestant churchmen two years
hence as they attempted to bring their ideals to fruition in
mission campaigns? In March of 1920, a young Detroit minister,
Reinhold Niebuhr, donned a prophet's robe to warn that "the
Christian church deceives itself in believing that the revival
of religious sentiment during the war . . . will secure it that
glorious destiny of prestige and power which religious leaders
are so confidently and so unanimously predicting." Having become
disillusioned with the easy reconciliation of Christian ethics
with the wartime politics he had endorsed in 1917, Niebuhr concluded that "the dictates of [the church's] conscience were
hardly ever unique enough (sic) to be distinguished from the dictates of national expediency."[1] Many American Protestants had
come to share Niebuhr's disappointment over the outcome of the
world war, but few were ready to accept his judgment of the
churches. Three months later, however, amid the ruins of the
Interchurch World Movement which dashed the fairest hopes of
progressive churchmen, even some of the most optimistic began to
feel that the church as well as the world had "gone crazy."

There were those, to be sure, who either ignored the signs
of the time or misjudged them and maintained an unperturbed optimism about the state of the world. "There never was an hour in
the history of the world when the Christian Church has had such
occasion for confidence and joy as just now," exclaimed a Methodist
bishop at the closing session of the General Conference on May 27,
1920. Lacking sympathy for "the dismal croakings of the chronic
pessimist," the bishop insisted that "this is the best day of the
best week of the best month of the best year of the best decade
of the best century that this world has ever seen. And tomorrow
will be every way better."[2]

But dismal croakings by far outweighed such cheery notes
after the collapse of the Interchurch World Movement in mid-1920.

157

Lofty idealism no longer carried the day even in the churches.
"There can be no question," admitted a Baptist from the Buffalo
Convention platform in June, "that a tremendous change for the
worse has come over our world since the armistice."

> From the lofty heights of spiritual vision and
> realization we have been slipping downward at a
> rapid pace. We are in an hour of spent enthusiasm.
> Perhaps the greatest disappointment the world has
> ever known, the deepest depression, is today upon
> us. Before two years have gone by, our enthusiasms
> have become so dead that even to mention the glow-
> ing ideals for which we fought brings a smile to
> men's faces.[3]

Those who had stoked the fires of wartime emotion with
religio-patriotic idealism could not curb the growing apathy of
the general public which smothered the battle flames as ideals
went unfulfilled in the post-war world. The war itself had not
produced the glorious, romantic adventure which had been dinned
into the minds of young American volunteers by Civil War songs
and Memorial Day parades. True, the comparatively brief fighting time for American soldiers, especially in proportion to their
emotional preparedness, left many of them with an unsatisfied
battle spirit--a spirit at times given unfortunate outlet in both
the fomenting and the quelling of social, labor, and racial
demonstrations, strikes, and riots. But more often American
soldiers, particularly those kept in Europe during the long and
tedious period of peace settlement, returned home battle-fatigued,
fed-up with war and the idealism upon which it had been projected,
vowing "never again" to leave American shores in supposedly
altruistic causes. Their families at home agreed. If, during
the months following the armistice, a millennial spirit swept
through various elements of American society hoping for complete
victory in their cause (laborites, social revolutionaries, red
hunters, religious progressives and fundamentalists, etc.), the
prevailing national mood now was becoming increasingly weary with,
disgusted by, and hostile toward crusades of all kinds. This
public reaction foreshadowed the end of the age of popular Protestant crusades, and a casualty as well as a signal of its demise
was the Interchurch World Movement. "The Interchurch came as the
last of many drives to a tired and indifferent nation," commented
the editor of *The Nation* perceptibly in July of 1920.[4]

The changing national temper which eventually found
Wilsonian idealism repugnant also put a damper on the spirit of
the Interchurch World Movement. Rising and flourishing during

the height of Wilson's popularity, receiving enthusiastic support
from all but deepest-dyed conservatives, the Interchurch World
Movement dropped just as rapidly and deeply into popular disfavor
as did the ailing President. As the election of 1920 became a
"solemn referendum" in which the nation disavowed the ideas for
which Wilson had stood, so the second (ten million dollar) Interchurch campaign was a decisive test of the Movement's support.
The test having failed, denominational leaders became thoroughly
disgusted with the "dead horse" (the epitaph of the Movement) and
looked for more likely vehicles of religious expression.[5] Many
yearned nostalgically for what they envisaged as religious normalcy, some mythological time of peaceful spirituality unaffected
by cultural change and social upheaval. "In some quarters," complained *The Baptist* editor, "people are becoming afraid of new
ideas. They are complaining of the prevalent restlessness and
longing for peace. It would be easier, they think, and more
comfortable, to settle back into the old ruts. Because the birth
pangs of the new order are severe, they are thinking lovingly of
the old."[6]

In this context of a yearning for some kind of normalcy in
the face of confused times, mounting opposition to the Interchurch World Movement spelled the doom of this great ecclesiastical
bubble and prefaced the stumbling (and abnormal) directions which
American Protestantism would take within the emerging twentieth
century national religious configuration.

The most damaging opposition came first from within the
ranks of the churches themselves--a bitter pill to swallow for
persons envisaging the unity of Protestant America. In his final
report as National Director of the Interchurch United Simultaneous
Financial Campaign, Lyman L. Pierce pointed to "active opposition"
as "the heartbreaking, soul-racking element in the campaign. In
city after city where unexpectedly strong committees of businessmen have been built up, they have lost heart because of the on-
slaughts of some leader of the church who has either damned with
faint praise or has penetrated the whole community by his unjust,
ill-advised and unfair public deliverances. . . . The load of
dissension," concluded Pierce, "has been too heavy to carry."[7]

Much of the dissension focused on issues brought to light
by the methods and organizational patterns programmed by the
Interchurch leaders who misjudged the diversity and uncertainties
within American Protestantism. The Interchurch World Movement
had set about to attain the impossible goal of maintaining an

abnormal wartime emotion and directing it into the regular ongoing
life of the churches. Its leaders presupposed the durability of
an atmosphere of crisis which had united the churches and
Americans-in-general in a common sense of mission, and which had
made possible the quick mobilization of men and materials by
means of large organizations and intense campaigns. But this
assumption caused Interchurch leaders to plunge into such an
immense program, to build such a tremendous organization at such
great cost and in such extreme haste, that increasing numbers of
churchmen feared that the Movement's goals were illusionary and
artificial. "It was replete with the infelicities of haste,"
wrote Federal Council of Churches General Secretary Charles F.
Macfarland years later, "attempting to unify sections of church
bodies without adequate relationship to them as a whole, bringing
men and groups together with a contrariety of motives and under-
standings, and, above all, impairing the financial stability of
the churches by highly speculative processes."[8] Macfarland
pointed to three basic failings--a lack of common understanding
of the nature and goals of the Interchurch World Movement, an
imprecise plan for relating the Movement to the churches (caused
partly by a misjudgment of church unity in America), and poor
financial procedure. These failings, which brought criticisms
from Interchurch members, also contributed to the decision by
such denominations as the Southern Baptist Convention and the
United Lutheran Church in America not to join the Movement.[9]

In one of the most judicious appraisals of the Interchurch
World Movement made by an insider, Robert E. Speer noted that the
Movement suffered from a lack of clearly thought out "principles
and province of the cooperation [it] proposed."

> Some joined the Movement with the understanding
> that it was temporary; others with the view that
> it was a beginning which must be carried forward
> into a new, permanent form. Some joined on the
> condition that it would be promotive only and
> not administrative; others saw in its a chance to
> displace old and, as they deemed them, slow and
> inadequate administrative agencies. Some based
> their cooperation on the assurance that denomina-
> tional interests and prerogatives would not be
> disturbed, and that the Movement could operate
> through denominational grooves; others deemed
> this an opportunity to transcend these. Sooner
> or later these and contrasted tendencies were
> sure to breed difficulty and misunderstanding.

Speer had long been sensitive to criticism of the Movement, men-
tioning at an Executive Committee meeting on May 1, 1919 that he
had "heard objection on the ground that we were launching an

indefinite undertaking, that once launched it would be beyond
our control, that it might grow to what no one now is prepared
to commit himself to."[10]

Many of the critics feared that the massive Interchurch
organization, and the speed with which it launched huge programs
purportedly for all of American Protestantism, threatened to make
it a super-church, seriously endangering the freedom and autonomy
of churches and denominations. Some critics eventually went so
far as to label the Interchurch World Movement a "Protestant
Papacy" and an undemocratic "Christian Soviet." Southern Baptists, as rigorous defenders of local church autonomy as churchmen could be, refused to join the Interchurch World Movement
partly because they believed "that Christianity is not safe under
any form of centralized ecclesiastical government." Their general hostility toward the Movement was captured in a poem entitled "That Interchurch Whale," which appeared in the *Baptist
Messenger*:

> A mammoth whale is on the sea,
> Oh, bigger'n any whale should be;
> He's spoutin' too, the grandest spout,
> As if he "knowed what" he's about.
> His name I hear is Interchurch!
> He aims to knock us off our perch;
> He thinks we Baptists all are shrimps
> To "sealler" or to put in crimps![12]

To a large extent, suspicion of the Interchurch leaders'
motives had been provoked by their unwise failure to wait, before
making startling announcements about policies and programs, until
denominational judicatories had discussed the Movement and elected
official representatives to its counsels. In the meantime, more
careful planning and delineation of policies and goals of the
Movement might have prevented many misunderstandings and criticisms. But the almost fanatical concern of Interchurch leaders
for speed, and their gross misjudgment of the readiness of
American Protestants for rapid advances in church unity, hindered
their ability to gain the profound support of the churches.

Leaders of the Interchurch World Movement were misled by
the display of unity shown by churchmen during the war. Even as
dissension among nations and among factions within the United
States after the war tore at the high aims of the League of
Nations, so a post-war flare-up of denominationalism countered
the very unity upon which the Interchurch World Movement had
meant to capitalize. The post-war recovery of denominational
feeling, due partly to the normal relaxation of superficially

imposed oneness among and within the churches by the national war
emergency, was one of the elements which the Interchurch Movement
faced, but which it had not really taken into account. The
simultaneous financial drive, in which each denomination strove
(in the public spotlight) to raise an unprecedented sum of money,
served as much to pit church against church in a great financial
contest as it served to further cooperative church action. "The
Methodist Centenary Fund of $105,000,000 has been all subscribed,"
warned a *New Era Magazine* editorial, "and certainly we Presbyterians do not want to lag behind our Methodist brethren in the
matter of benevolences."[13] Such apparently harmless statements
as this were common, but they were symptomatic of deeper "jeal-
ousies, intense bitterness of feeling which . . . resulted in
some deplorable recriminations, [and] fears for denominational
prestige" which badly hurt the Interchurch cause.[14]

The linkage of denominational consciousness with money was
in fact the most direct cause of the Interchurch World Movement's
collapse. The Interchurch World Movement received scattered, but
violent, criticism of its preoccupation with "the ring of the
coin," its "cheap, flippant, materialistic" advertising, its sug-
gestion that the keys to the Kingdom of God on earth were finance,
promotion, and publicity.[15] More problematic, rumors circulated
that the Interchurch World Movement was operating at heavy, undue
expense. But as long as most churchmen were convinced that the
Movement would cost their denominations little or nothing, they
generally endorsed its expense budget as reasonable in light of
the work it was doing. It is remarkable that they failed to comprehend the inherent financial instability of an organization
completely financed on borrowed money. The inevitable consequences
of their blindness for the Interchurch cause were realized too
late. "There was none too much unity among us anyway," reported
James M. Speers to the General on May 17, "and the lack of the
common binding force of a common responsibility for the expenses
of the work we were promoting was undoubtedly a weakness. Each
of the cooperating denominations went forward with concentrated
effort upon its own particular task without regard at all to our
mutual responsibility."[16]

When it became apparent that the Interchurch World Movement's expenses had turned into large denominational debts, denominational churchmen became bitter toward the Movement. They
accused Interchurch leaders of wild financial extravagance, of
drawing high salaries, and generally deplored what they now felt

to have been "a night's debauch of crazy money-spending."[17]
Handicapped by such hostile charges, unchecked by careful answers
by Interchurch leaders,[18] the second campaign for ten million
dollars stood no chance of success. Not only did the churches
feel double-crossed by being asked to pay their underwriting debts,
but by mid-1920 the words "debt" and "extravagance" had become,
temporarily at least, especially repugnant to the popular and
businessman's mind. The cost of living had risen steadily during
1919 and 1920, reaching the status of a mild depression by late
spring of 1920. Part of the Harding-led call "back to normalcy"
was the call to practice economy, which led to a veritable "vogue
of thrift" during the very period when the Interchurch World
Movement became suspected and accused of wild, wartime-like spending.[19] Hence the Movement's debts not only embittered those concerned for denominational budgets, but it ran against the grain
of public conscience during a time of financial difficulty. Too
few felt able, even if willing, to give any more money to the
Interchurch cause.

The Interchurch World Movement also suffered much opposition by persons who disagreed with its policies and programs.
It could not transcend or comprehend diverse Protestant conceptions of Christian life and thought; rather it became an occasion
for their clarification and overt manifestation. The post-war
years witnesses not only a disruptive rise in denominationalism,
but also an outbreak of extreme dissension within the denominations which became known as the modernist-fundamentalist controversy. Fundamentalists (a label coined in 1920 by *Watchman-
Examiner* editor, Curtis Lee Laws to designate those prepared to
battle for the fundamentals of the faith) represented a minority
of Protestants who for several decades had been increasingly
hostile toward "the new theology" or modernism and advocates of
all forms of religious liberalism. At the end of World War I,
the long-developing disaffection between these two segments of
Protestantism burst into a conflict which tore churches assunder
and hindered the overall Protestant prestige and influence in
America.

Probably the wartime spirit helped engender in fundamentalists a sense of decisive urgency similar to that which caused
Interchurch World Movement leaders to wage their fight to the
finish. But the Interchurch World Movement, representing a great
united campaign of those very progressive churchmen whom fundamentalists long had opposed, must itself be considered an

important factor in the fundamentalist uprising. "When they come together and coalesce in the Interchurch Movement they seem a great host," wrote a Northern Baptist with alarm, "and the apostasy of the church is seen to be on a scale not realized before when the denominations were each pursuing its (sic) own separate way."[20]

Their tendency being to lump all liberals or progressives into a single camp, fundamentalists continually accused the Interchurch World Movement of being "modern theology in the disguise of evangelical and missionary appeal."[21] Actually Interchurch leaders had refused to make doctrine any element whatsoever in the Movement; but this refusal, which prevented them from taking a position on fundamentalist doctrines, was enough to bring the charge of heresy and infidelity upon them. Fundamentalists did not recognize doctrinal neutrality; nor could they accept purely pragmatic Christian unity devoid of doctrinal agreement, as Curtis Lee Laws made clear in a *Watchman-Examiner* editorial:

> The Interchurch Movement has emasculated Christianity by eliminating all doctrinal emphasis from its pronouncements and appeals. It has no doctrinal basis, and yet it seeks to explain to the world the meaning of Christianity. It must offend no one, because it represents everyone. The real fundamentals of Christianity have had no emphasis in this Movement . . . . We believe in the union of the churches, but in the union that comes from doctrinal agreement rather than in the union that is urged with a view to saving coal next winter.[22]

Fundamentalists were correct in pointing out that the Interchurch World Movement, by the nature of its programs and goals, countered one of the basic doctrines of fundamentalism-- that the premillennial return of Christ rendered useless all attempts to Christianize the world in the meantime.[23] The fundamentalist critique chided Interchurch leaders for their optimistic determination to "capture the world for Christ," for their singing a "Lorelei song that the world is moving on to better and happier days," for their "socialistic, educational and ethical campaign" with "departments of exclusively world work" which "seek to save society rather than the individual." "Is the Interchurch Movement of God or Satan?", asked I. M. Haldeman, pastor of the First Baptist Church of New York City, answering in his May 3, 1920 sermon that it is "the slickest scheme the devil ever brought about." He had already charged that "the Interchurch Movement is the combined, aggressive effort of Post-millennialism to render meaningless the last promise of an ascended Lord: 'Surely I come quickly.'" Haldeman believed, as many fundamentalists did, that "it is not the work of the church to better the world, but to condemn it."[24] At stake was the whole conception of Christian mission, a problem destined to plague churchmen during the decades to follow.

The fundamentalist opposition to Christian social programs more often than not coincided with opposition to liberal social philosophies of all kinds. In some cases, conservative theology provided a powerful buttress to conservative politics, so that laissez-faire became a general principle to be applied to church and state alike. Furthermore, fundamentalists, being opposed to religious modernism and the social gospel in principle, doubtless found the post-war sentiment toward normalcy soothing to their natural bent and all tamperings with the social order--especially radical tamperings--anathema. The Interchurch World Movement's involvement in the steel strike, characteristically condemned as "the biggest piece of radical adventure that any organization of religious activity has ever attempted,"[25] became another reason for conservative hostility. Whereas it cannot be said that the Interchurch steel strike report was the major cause of the Movement's collapse, there can be no doubt that it added to the growing disenchantment of the churches with the Movement, which made its revivification impossible.[26]

Finally, the whole concept of "friendly citizens" supporting the church evoked much criticism, especially from fundamentalists. The old cry of "tainted money," and the familiar caution against preoccupation with money rather than with things of the spirit, constantly put Interchurch leaders on the defensive. *The Christian Advocate* noted criticisms to the effect that the Interchurch World Movement was "reversing the apostolic ambition to get men to give first their own selves to the Lord"--a procedure described by the Southern Baptist *Western Recorder* as going "to Satan's storehouse to replenish the Lord's treasury." According to C. H. Fountain, the Interchurch World Movement had chosen "to depend upon the world, the flesh and the devil for what God has promised to give in response to faith on the condition of sacrifice." After the Movement's collapse, John Roach Straton of New York City's Calvary Baptist Church declared that "the world has laughed us to scorn. Fancy Jesus Christ sending His disciples out to beg money from unbelievers for the establishment of His Kingdom in the world."[27] But by that time, Interchurch supporters as well as opponents had come to realize the error in thinking that a church program could be financed by persons whose concern for the church was too slight to cause them to join one.

The lessons for Protestant churchmen to learn from their crushing defeat in the Interchurch World Movement would prove to be far reaching. The new era so soon had loomed far more complex than they had anticipated. Crusading idealism had not made the world safe for democracy, had not brought the American people to a new level of world vision, had not even become the habitual temper of American Protestantism. The Protestant community, it seemed, would have to forge its way in the post-war world with uncertainty, disunity, and diminished vigor. "We must now settle down to the steady hum-drum and drudgery of common days," confessed a Presbyterian editorial, "and plod our way along in grim resolution and patience."[28]

Nothing would be common (or normal) about the 1920's, however. The churches emerged from the war and from the Interchurch World Movement ruins significantly altered, especially organizationally. They kept busy--often intensely busy--and many regained an optimistic outlook. The Interchurch World Movement made an impact on them greater than most dared or cared to admit. They could not pretend that there had been no Interchurch World Movement any more successfully than they could pretend there had been no world war.

To begin with, the churches benefited materially from their forward movement experience, although their gain was as much in the realm of wisdom and methods as in increased income. Despite the financial failure of the Interchurch World Movement itself, the tremendous sums pledged by church members awakened denominational leaders to the giving potential of their constituents. To be sure, the major denominations participating in the Movement failed to reach the amounts subscribed in the 1920 campaign, and some of them suffered greatly from the necessity to pay their underwriting debts.[29] In many cases, denominational spending for enlarged programs on the basis of unprecedented budgets which were never raised caused unhealthy indebtedness and the psychologically damaging necessity to cut-down on work already begun. In retrospect, therefore, it can be seen that 1920 marked an ab normal peak in Protestant giving for benevolences (non-congregational expenses); but it also is apparent that per capita giving remained higher throughout the 1920's in relation to the dollar value than ever before. Moreover, total church expenditures in 1926 had more than doubled those of 1916, as did the value of church property. Hence the churches shared in the prosperity of the post-war decade.[30]

The churches also learned much about the systematic formulation and promotion of budgets from their experience with the Interchurch World Movement. Many denominations learned that a consolidation of their various boards' budgets into one annual fund appeal not only brought a greater cohesiveness to the denomination, but it also increased promotional effectiveness while decreasing its overall cost. A more subtle lesson had also been learned from the Interchurch World Movement experience, namely that special drives, crash programs, and exaggerated goals do not form the best financial program for denominations. More systematic, business-like methods of raising realistic budgets became normative procedure during the 1920's.[31] Hence Northern Presbyterians set "a reasonable budget" for 1921, just half the "ideal but unattainable" budget of the previous, campaign year. "A church," they reasoned, "can acquire the habit of not reaching its goals. That we cannot afford. The wisdom of the $12,000,000 mark [for 1921] is therefore evident. In view of all the conditions, it is attainable. It is a practicable, not a visionary, budget."[32] Such was the changing temper of American Protestants—from idealistic vision to practical realism.

In a more comprehensive sense, the American churches entered the post-World War I world more intricately organized than before. Inspired by successful mass organization of the churches to meet the wartime emergency, the Interchurch World Movement set a pattern of bureaucratically structured religion for Modern America, highly centralized with closely knit links throughout the nation. The process of denominational and interdenominational organization and operation was becoming modeled after the development of secular business enterprises with little differences in technique among the denominations. During the 1920's, ecclesiastical polities and traditions would become increasingly irrelevant to the actual functioning style of organized church machinery. It would become clear that no large-scale organization of people, including the churches, could maintain programs in twentieth century America without utilizing the forms and methods operative in the technological society of military-industrial complex. Just how the bureaucracy could be made to facilitate the full dimensions of corporate religious life, much less distinctive ecclesiastical traditions, however, would prove to be a difficult problem. Frequently Protestant churchmen would rationalize their denominational affiliation in terms of practical convenience more than in terms of a distinctive ecclesiastical tradition.

The business-oriented organizational patterns of the churches
which tended to minimize operational differences among denominations of diverse traditions was complemented by the movement toward
interchurch cooperation. Despite resurgent denominational loyalties
and theological controversy after the war, conscious efforts toward
cooperative unity continued and even increased after the Interchurch
World Movement collapsed. The Interchurch vision remained, but a
more realistic understanding of how it might be attained resulted
from the Movement's downfall. The Federal Council of Churches,
which many thought had dragged its feet during the immediate post-
war period, emerged from the Interchurch experiment as the central
unifying agency of American Protestantism. The Interchurch World
Movement, according to Charles S. Macfarland, "was an effort to do
at one stroke what the Federal Council was seeking by patient,
slower, educational and evolutionary processes." The Federal Council philosophy won the day, as progressive churchmen began to
realize, with Robert E. Speer, that "all cooperative movements
must go more slowly than the fast are ready to go. If not, the
slow will not be carried along." Speer, who had been elected
president of the Federal Council for its fourth quadrennium (1920-
1924), represented to Protestant leaders what they expected of
the Federal Council: "He has visions, as a prophet should have,
but he keeps his feet upon the earth."[33]

If the Federal Council kept its feet on the ground, however, it also learned a good deal from the methods and program of
the Interchurch World Movement. Federal Council leaders became
more aware of the possibility of accomplishing large goals through
concerted, cooperative action by denominational boards. They also
discovered the necessity of seeking greater unity among the various
interboard agencies through one central organization. Above all,
they came to recognize the need to set the Federal Council on a
sound financial basis, a basis which in itself would exemplify
and further the spirit of cooperative unity among the churches.
At the Fourth Quadrennial Meeting in Boston, following the Interchurch World Movement collapse, the Federal Council voted to
enlarge the scope of its activities, to work toward a greater
unification of interboard agencies, to seek closer relationship
with its constituent bodies, and to solicit direct financial
support from the constituent bodies.[34]

On December 13, 1920, the Federal Council sponsored an
all-day conference of seventy representatives of the several
interboard agencies to consider the whole question of unity, and

especially to conserve the accomplishments toward that end made
by the Interchurch World Movement. It was "the sense of the
conference," according to resolutions adopted, that a "committee
on consultation" be formed representing the interboard agencies
"to consider matters of common interest," and to maintain some
correlation of the denominational forward movements.[35] A Consultative Committee of Interdenominational Agencies was subsequently
formed, which met periodically for the next several years. But
it was the Federal Council, mainly through its Administrative
Committee, which in the years to follow became the most important
centralizing agency of American Protestantism. In January of
1921, the Executive Committee of the Federal Council, in annual
session, voted to make the Administrative Committee "so constituted
as to be actually representative of and amenable to the constituent
denominations, and at the same time capable of correlating in a
comprehensive way the activities of the various interdenominational
agencies which need such a common sympathetic clearing house and
meeting ground."[36] In this way, the Federal Council tried to
assume some of the basic functions originally inspired by the
Interchurch World Movement.

The Federal Council also furthered some of the social
concerns of the Interchurch World Movement, especially in the
area of industrial problems. According to Federal Council General
Secretary Charles S. Macfarland, the Interchurch steel strike
report "made a strong moral impression."[37] The Federal Council
Commission on the Church and Social Service would resume the
Interchurch's battle against the Open Shop movement of 1921 and
against the abusive labor conditions in the steel industry. In
1923, the Commission would issue a study of the twelve-hour day
and call for its end, which would help to bring about that result.[38]
Throughout the 1920's, with popular social, economic, and political
conservatism contributing to the reduction of progressivism and
the social gospel to an unpopular minority undercurrent in America,
the Federal Council would stand out as a constant voice for social
reform--often being criticized, as was the Interchurch World Movement, for its stand on specific social issues and problems.

Whatever their views may have been about the Interchurch
World Movement as a whole, most Protestant leaders frankly admitted
the value of its accomplishments in the area of scientific reli-
gious-social surveys.[39] Interchurch leaders considered the surveys to have been "in many respects the richest contribution of
the Interchurch World Movement. . . . unique both for their

comprehensiveness, the scientific methods aimed at, and the great objectives sought."[40] Furthermore, the surveys demonstrated interdenominational cooperation in action. It was felt important, therefore, that the vast materials accumulated, and the unfinished projects begun by the Interchurch survey organization be preserved and utilized by the various Protestant agencies concerned. The conference of interboard agencies on December 13, 1920, encouraged the Interchurch World Movement to transfer its survey materials to these agencies (the Foreign Missions Conference of North America, the Home Missions Council, the Council of Women for Home Missions, the Federation of Women's Boards of Foreign Missions, the Council of Church Boards of Education, the Sunday School Council of Evangelical Denominations, the International Sunday School Association, and the Federal Council of Churches).[41]

By the spring of 1922, most of the survey material had thus been transferred to the interboard agencies. But its distribution had been taken over by the new Committee on Social and Religious Surveys, one of the most important outgrowths of the Interchurch World Movement. This committee, whose name was changed in 1923 to the Institute of Social and Religious Research, was organized on January 5, 1921, and financially supported by John D. Rockefeller, Jr., to complete the Interchurch surveys and project new research along the same lines. For the next fourteen years, the Institute, under the presidency of John R. Mott, sponsored and published many studies in a wide range of social-religious areas under the leadership of outstanding Protestant scholars and churchmen. The Institute also tried to foster cooperation and efficiency in the field of religious activity, without itself becoming the sponsor for specific programs. According to Mott, "the Institute constituted the first serious and extensive effort to apply to religious phenomena the methods of social research without the distorting influence of ecclesiastical or theological bias."[42] Just as important, the Institute provided much resource material to help guide the churches as they groped their way in a new era.

In the last analysis, however, the single most important impact of the Interchurch World Movement on religion in America was its demonstration that crusading Protestantism--indeed Protestantism-in-general--was losing its traditional hold on the American people as a whole and on the social and cultural tone of the nation. Not only did the Interchurch World Movement mark a transition within American Protestantism in such areas as mood and spirit, developments toward cooperative unity, utilization of business methods and organization, and changing attitudes toward church social involvement, but in its demise it also marked the changing status and role of American Protestantism itself as a religious force in America.

The collapse of the Interchurch World Movement, and especially the lack of response by so-called "friendly citizens" to the Movement's appeal for support, helped open Protestants' eyes to the fact that they and their churches no longer commanded the authority, power, influence, or even respect which they long had enjoyed in America. The long-developing pattern of a rising urban, secularized, religiously and culturally and racially pluralistic, American population, which had caused increasing alarm to Protestant leaders since the Civil War, had begun to come of age after World War I. Many church leaders had believed that the war effort would rejuvenate and preserve national unity based on the "one-hundred per cent Americanism" of old white stock Protestants, including, above all, the Puritan-Evangelical moral tradition. The Interchurch World Movement, its leaders hoped, would secure the preservation of this tradition. But disillusionment first with the war and then with the Interchurch World Movement, and the apparent wholesale rejection of the ideals behind them both by American people, shocked Protestant leaders to an awareness that the new era threatened the very existence of the tradition they had hoped to cement permanently in the nation and extend into the world. As the 1920's dawned, church leaders reaffirmed "the duty of American Christianity to form and guide public sentiment"; but they also recognized that Protestantism "must fight for its life."[43]

Much of the leadership of organized Protestantism, inheritors of the crumbling empire, would assume a defensive posture in the 1920's in a strenuous, at times almost desperate, attempt to maintain themselves as the dominant cultural-religious force in America. Some churchmen would battle against social and intellectual change, especially against changing patterns of moral behavior and the philosophical and psychological ideas critical of traditional American values. Social revolution was most pronounced in the large, increasingly secular urban areas, where material prosperity and leisure time spawned new forms of entertainment and self-indulgence quite contrary to the rigorous moral code of the sons of Puritanism. Hence the churches would lash out against all "modern evils." "The war has tremendously reenforced the powers of irreligion," complained *The Christian Advocate* in the Fall of 1920. "They are increasingly aggressive and arrogant, and claim the victory."[44]

Alcohol remained enemy number one. In its report to the Northern Baptist Convention at Des Moines, Iowa, in 1921, for example, the Social Service Commission of that denomination stressed more than any other topic the need "to ground the pro- hibition principle deep in the thought and custom of the people."[45] But second only to advocating strict enforcement of the Volstead Act, defending blue laws to protect the Christian Sabbath from "continental desecration" occupied the energies of church leaders who associated the quiet, devout Sunday with Christian Americanism. It is clear, from the following quotation from *New Era Magazine*, that the social-moral revolution struck the Protestant conscience hardest on the day of rest:

> Presbyterials all, Christians all, you have need to marshal all your forces, all your strength of prayer and works, to save the Christian Sabbath. The Christian Sabbath in America is doomed unless you act concertedly, unless you act at once. If the Christian Sabbath is once lost to America, America is doomed. America acquired world leadership through the faith and vision and fidelity of its Christian founders. Decay of other nations followed departure from sacred standards. The world war and its license, and the world's conse- quent moral lapse, have been seized by the forces of evil as their opportunity to debauch the Ameri- can nation, and their great strategic move is to despoil the Christian Sabbath. Terribly strong forces are at work, the combined forces of the rum hounds, the sport sharks, the movie vampires. These would commercialize the Sabbath, they would revolu- tionize the day and turn it into an orgy of base- ball, professionally exploiting seven days a week what has become one of the great gambling curses of the age, and into a saturnalia of sex-shows and murder-movies, corrupting the minds and morals of the youth of the land seven days a week, and they would rip the day wide open for other evils which modern methods have loosed from the pit. Cunningly the wicked ones have planned the downfall of the Christian Sabbath.[46]

The more the churches would look upon manifestations of change as enemies to be fought, however, the more enemies the churches in fact would acquire. And when not ridiculed by liter- ary artists and popular journalists, churchmen painfully would find themselves neglected by an indifferent public interested in anything but Protestant beliefs and traditions. Prohibition, celebrated by Protestants of nearly all stripes as their great victory for social salvation, would become instead the mark of

an anachronistic value system and fallen quasi-established religious culture. Sunday would become the regular public holiday
in which church worship and activity would find increasing compe-
tition from entertainment at the theater, the sports arena, and
wherever automobiles could travel. Among large segments of the
American public during the post-war decade, recalled Halford E.
Luccock in 1934, "organized religion simply did not register as
a field of interest."[47]

Then, as if acknowledging that American society-at-large
would no longer conform to the Protestant way, many churchmen
would try something apparently contradictory to social criticism
or to the Christianization of society. They would strive to
develop their churches into popular centers of social activity to
compete with the "worldly life" of the larger society they judged
degenerate. They would save souls out of the world and into the
churches which would become enclaves of religiosity. But in order
to sell religion, they would have to make it appealing, which would
lead churchmen to a *rapprochement* with secular tendencies and fads.
This attitude would allow for a relatively uncritical embracement
of the methods and goals of the business civilization for the promotion of religion. The church would become a business and evangelism the promotional department of a bureaucracy. Clever advertising, entertaining social programs, and promises of a healthy
prosperous life would become the marks of the church. This popular religion would feature a hedonistic indulgence in the new
prosperity by means of elaborate buildings and comfortable pews.

Such labors, however, finally would be in vain if the
purpose was either to re-Protestantize the social order or to
bring masses into the churches. Certainly churches reflecting
"the religion of prosperity" would make little ameliorative impact on the structures of society in which masses of American
citizens would continue to suffer economically.[48] Although they
would plunge into a spiritual depression of sorts beginning about
the mid-1920's, it would not be until the economic depression of
the 1930's that Protestant churches would begin to recognize the
extent to which the new era challenged their very existence. On
the eve of the stock market crash, Harry Emerson Fosdick, who as
a young Baptist minister a decade earlier had warned that the
visions of grandeur in the Interchurch World Movement might cause
disillusionment if the enterprise failed, would conclude now in
an essay ironically entitled "Recent Gains in Religion" that in
fact organized religion was losing ground.[49] By then the nation

would have become independent of the "great traditions" of evangelical piety. If Protestants would be wondering if they ever
again could "win America" or if Roman Catholicism might "win the
religious race in the United States,"[50] they would be expressing
the identity crisis shared by most American religious communities
during the following decades. The moment of truth had come:
henceforth American Protestantism, diversified in new ways, would
seek its identity within a society increasingly unbound by any
single historical religious tradition.

NOTES TO CHAPTER VIII

1.   "Religion's Limitations," *World Tomorrow*, III (March, 1920), p. 77.

2.   *The Christian Advocate*, June 10, 1920, p. 791.

3.   *The Baptist*, September 25, 1920, p. 1199.

4.   *The Nation*, July 10, 1920, p. 34.

5.   For example, see *New Era Magazine*, III (February, 1921), p. 82: "The horse is dead. Let us hasten to bury him lest he altogether defile the air." See also *World Call*, II (December, 1920), p. 5.

6.   *The Baptist*, May 1, 1920, p. 476.

7.   *IWM Documents*, VI, p. 22.

8.   Charles F. Macfarland, *Christian Unity in Practice and Prophecy* (New York, 1933), p. 69.

9.   The United Lutheran Church in America refused to participate in the Interchurch World Movement because, according to the editor of *The Lutheran*, in January of 1920, "The Interchurch World Movement is at its present stage of an emotional nature and without any defined policies and unable to answer, in an ecclesiastical sense, the question, 'what is your purpose?'" *The Lutheran*, January 15, 1920, p. 755. For a Southern Baptist judgment, see J. J. Taylor, *Religious Herald*, April 15, 1920, p. 11.

10.   Robert E. Speer, "The Present Situation in the Church as a Whole," *Christian Unity: Its Principles and Possibilities*, pp. 146-147; and Executive Committee minutes in *IWM Documents*, p. 3.

11.   For example, see *The Literary Digest*, April 17, 1920, p. 57; and *The Nation*, July 10, 1920, p. 34.

12.   *Baptist Messenger*, January 7, 1920, p. 1; E. Y. Mullins, "Current Tendencies Favorable and Unfavorable to the Baptist Position," *The Alabama Baptist*, April, 1920, pp. 5-6; and J. B. Gambrell, "The Interchurch World Movement in the South," *Western Recorder*, May 13, 1920, p. 8.

13.   *New Era Magazine*, II (January, 1920), p. 46.

14. Quoted in *The Literary Digest*, June 12, 1920, pp. 42-43.
     See also Clarence R. Athearn, *Interchurch Government* (New
     York, 1925), pp. 194-195.

15. For example, see C. H. Fountain, *The Interchurch World*
     Movement (Plainfield, N. J., 1920), pp. 9-20; and *New York*
     Times, July 5, 1920, p. 8:7.

16. From Speer's report, in *IWM Documents*, VI, p. 64.

17. *New Era Magazine*, II (December, 1920), p. 821.

18. S. Earl Taylor, for example, made a point-by-point answer
     to these charges in the *New York Times*, June 13, 1920,
     VII, p. 3:1.

19. The phrase comes from Mark Sullivan, *Our Times, the United*
     States, 1900-1925 (New York, 1935), pp. 164-165.

20. Fountain, *The Interchurch World Movement*, p. 27.

21. I. M. Haldeman, *Why I Am Opposed to the Interchurch World*
     Movement (n.p., n.d.), p. 53.

22. "Baptists and the Interchurch World Movement," *Watchman-*
     Examiner, June 10, 1920, pp. 751-752.

23. Fundamentalist doctrines, or tenets, were presented as
     "clear essentials" of the Christian faith in ten small
     volumes published in 1910 entitled *The Fundamentals*, trea-
     tises written by various men but edited by Amzi C. Dixon
     and Reuben A. Torrey, and financed by two wealthy Los
     Angeles laymen, Milton and Lyman Stewart. Over three mil-
     lion copies were distributed without charge to religious
     leaders across the nation.

24. Haldeman, *Why I Am Opposed to the Interchurch World Move-*
     ment, pp. 7-28; Fountain, *The Interchurch World Movement*,
     pp. 32-40; *The Baptist*, June 26, 1920, p. 763; and *Watch-*
     man-Examiner, June 10, 1920, p. 751.

25. H. H. Lewis, *The Facts in the Case of the Interchurch*
     World Movement (1920), p. 9. A pamphlet reprinted from
     Industry, July 5, 1920, p. 9.

26. No final judgment can be made on this point. Both *The*
     Nation, July 31, 1920, p. 120; and *The World Tomorrow*,
     III (August, 1920), p. 247, suggest strongly that the steel
     strike report turned the tables against the Interchurch
     World Movement. But the Movement had already collapsed
     financially before the steel strike report was published,
     though the report's general content may earlier have
     leaked out to some circles. Even the second campaign,
     which appealed mainly to "friendly citizens" of means

(the very businessmen most likely avidly to oppose the
steel strike report), had collapsed and ended before the
report was published. Yet the increasing suspicion that
the Interchurch World Movement had become sympathetic to
labor's cause probably caused many potential givers to
think twice.

27. Straton quoted in *New York Times*, July 5, 1920, p. 8:7.
     Other quotations from *The Christian Advocate*, April 15,
     1920, pp. 15-16; and *Western Recorder*, April 1, 1920, p.
     8; *Watchman-Examiner*, June 10, 1920, p. 751; and Fountain,
     The Interchurch World Movement, pp. 10-11.

28. *The Presbyterian Magazine*, III (November, 1921), p. 634.

29. Of the $100,000,000 five-year goal of Northern Baptists,
     for example, only $65,000,000 was ever subscribed, and of
     that only about $45,000,000 was finally collected. See
     Annual of the Northern Baptist Convention, 1924, p. 133.
     Likewise, the Methodists collected only about seventy-five
     per cent of the Centenary Movement subscriptions. See
     John Lankford, "Methodism 'Over the Top': The Joint Cen-
     tenary Movement, 1917-1925," *Methodist History* (October,
     1963-July, 1964), p. 36. Northern Presbyterians also fell
     far short of their grossly inordinate $20,000,000 goal for
     boards and agencies. See *Minutes of the General Assembly
     of the Presbyterian in the United States of America*, p.
     379; and *New Era Magazine*, II (November, 1920), pp. 753-
     754. By 1923, the Disciples' Men and Millions Movement
     had collected only $5,327,008 of the $6,000,000 goal. See
     Year Book, 1923, Organization of Disciples of Christ, pp.
     245-246. The Disciples perhaps suffered most from their
     $600,000 underwriting debt, being forced to wage two spe-
     cial and unpopular campaigns for the money (December of
     1920, and April through June of 1921). See *ibid.*, 1920-
     1921, pp. 200-201; and *World Call*, III (May, 1921), pp.
     6-7. But other denominations felt the pinch as well, such
     as the Northern Presbyterians who considered their
     $1,000,000 underwriting debt a "very grave financial
     emergency." See "Tasks Facing Our Church Now," *New Era
     Magazine*, II (November, 1920), pp. 753-754.

30. For a study of Protestant giving in the 1920's, see C. H.
     Fahs, *Trends in Protestant Giving* (New York, 1929), espe-
     cially the conclusions on pp. 65-67. For church expendi-
     tures, see *Religious Bodies*, 1926, Vol. I (Washington,

178

D. C., 1930), pp. 53-54. For an overall analysis of the churches' financial state between the World War and the economic depression of the 1930's, see Luther Fry, "Changes in Religious Organizations," in *Recent Social Trends in the United States* (New York, 1933), pp. 1009-1060.

31. For example, see *The Baptist*, July 2, 1921; and *World Call*, III (February, 1921), p. 43.

32. R. E. Vale, "The Ladder for Presbyterians," *New Era Magazine*, III (February, 1921), p. 82.

33. *The Baptist*, December 18, 1920, p. 1576. See Macfarland, *Christian Unity in Practice and Prophecy*, p. 67; and Speer, "The Present Situation in the Church as a Whole," *Christian Unity: Its Principles and Possibilities*, p. 148.

34. For a full report, see *Federal Council Bulletin*, IV (January, 1921), pp. 6-9. The Federal Council set a goal of $300,000 to be given annually by the constituent bodies. While this goal was never attained during the 1920's, there was a remarkable annual increase in denominational support which reached over $97,000 in 1927, as compared to about $13,000 in 1919. See *Twenty Years of Church Federation: Report of the Federal Council of the Churches of Christ in America, 1924-1928* (New York, 1929), p. 285.

35. See *Federal Council Bulletin*, IV (January, 1921), p. 27; and "Report of the Reorganization Committee of the Interchurch World Movement to the General Committee," April 8, 1921, in *IWM Documents*, VIII, pp. 20-22.

36. *Federal Council Bulletin*, IV (March, 1921), p. 32. See also "Future Policies in Cooperative Work," *United in Service: Report of the Federal Council of the Churches of Christ in America, 1920-1924*, pp. 59-70.

37. Macfarland, *Christian Unity in Practice and Prophecy*, p. 70.

38. *United in Service: Report of the Federal Council of the Churches of Christ in America, 1920-1924*, p. 116.

39. There were some who criticized the surveys for their hasty compilation, their unrealistic goals, and their pragmatic and promotional nature. For example, see Joseph H. Oldham, "The Interchurch World Movement," *The International Review of Missions* (London, 1920), p. 91.

40. "Report to the Churches," May, 1920, in *IWM Documents*, VII, p. 18.

41.   *Federal Council Bulletin*, IV (January, 1921), p. 27.

42.   Most of the original staff members of the Institute were
      former members of the Survey Department of the Interchurch
      World Movement, while subsequent members were drawn from
      university and other circles. A brief historical record
      of the Institute, including information about its chief
      contributors and a list of its many publications, is Galen
      M. Fisher, *The Institute of Social and Religious Research,
      1921-1934* (New York, 1934).

43.   *The Christian Advocate*, November 11, 1920, p. 1490; and
      The Presbyterian Magazine, III (November, 1921), p. 634.

44.   *The Christian Advocate*, October 7, 1920, p. 1330.

45.   *The Baptist*, July 9, 1921, p. 727.

46.   Walter Irving Clarke, "Christians, Save the Christian
      Sabbath!" *New Era Magazine*, III (March, 1921), p. 155.

47.   Luccock, *Contemporary American Literature and Religion*
      (New York, 1934), p. 43. By contrast, however, theological
      studies and the "scientific" study of religion had become
      popular in circles of higher education. As noted in the
      preface to this study (above, p. xi) creative Protestant
      theology and the public life of the churches had become
      relatively separated by the 1920's, theology being restricted
      increasingly to the classroom as the distance widened be-
      tween parish and academia, between clergy and professor.

48.   See Luccock's perceptive discussion of the Protestant
      situation in his *Jesus and the American Mind* (New York,
      1930), especially Chapter VI entitled "The Religion of
      Prosperity."

49.   *The Christian Advocate*, November 13, 1919, pp. 1342-1343;
      and Kirby Page (ed), *Recent Gains in American Civilization*
      (Chautauqua, N. Y., 1928), p. 238.

50.   See, for example, Conrad Henry Moehlman, *The Catholic-
      Protestant Mind* (New York, 1929); and Charles Clayton
      Morrison, *Can Protestants Win America?* (New York, 1948).

BIBLIOGRAPHY

Manuscripts

The most valuable single source for this study was a
collection of documents entitled "History of the Interchurch
World Movement," contained in the William Adams Brown Library of
Union Theological Seminary in New York City. Originally assembled
in manuscript form with editorial comment by the committee that
liquidated the movement, the collection now is on microfilm and
contained in the Yale Divinity School Library. The research
library and the archives of the National Council of the Churches
of Christ in the U. S. A., located at the Interchurch Center in
New York City, contains an important collection of correspondence
between leaders of the Federal Council of Churches and leaders
of the Interchurch World Movement, plus a wide variety of materials relevant to the post-World War I period. Two denominational
libraries provided especially helpful manuscript collections.
The library of the Methodist Board of Missions in New York City
contains unpublished "Minutes of the Centenary Commission"; and
The American Baptist Historical Society in Rochester, New York,
contains unpublished "Records of the General Board of Promotion
of the Northern Baptist Convention." Finally, the several Protestant archival collections contained within the Graduate Theological Union library in Berkeley, California, contributed a
variety of useful data.

Interchurch World Movement Publications

The Interchurch World Movement published a large volume
and variety of material. The results of the Interchurch surveys,
statistics of participating bodies, plus the movement's funda-
mental spirit and outlook are found in *World Survey by the Interchurch World Movement of North America, Revised Preliminary
Statement and Budget in Two Volumes*, New York: Interchurch Press,
1920. The *Interchurch Newsletter*, succeeded by the *Interchurch*

Bulletin, were the movement's weekly newspapers. They are held
by the Union Theological Seminary library in New York City.
Three magazines were published by the Interchurch World Movement:
Everyland, *La Nueva Democracia*, and *World Outlook*. Pamphlets,
leaflets, and bulletins dealing with all aspects of the movement's
work are too numerous to name (approximately two hundred were
examined). Large collections of them are available in the Union
Theological Seminary and the National Council of Churches libraries in New York City.

Newspapers and Periodicals

Newspaper publicity of the Interchurch World Movement was
large and continuous. The *New York Times*, for example, carried
between four and five times as many articles on the Interchurch
World Movement as it carried on the Federal Council of Churches
during 1919 and 1920. In addition to the *New York Times*, the
Interchurch Newsletter, and the *Interchurch Bulletin*, the following periodicals were studied thoroughly throughout the periods
indicated and were found to contain much of significance, especially in clarifying denominational perspectives on the Interchurch World Movement: *The Baptist* (1920-1921), *The Christian
Advocate* (New York edition, 1919-1921), *Federal Council Bulletin*
(1918-1921), *New Era Magazine* (1919-1921), *The Standard* (1919),
World Call (1919-1921), and *World Outlook* (1915-1920). Useful
articles dealing with the Interchurch World Movement appeared
during 1918-1921 in *The Alabama Baptist, The American Journal of
Sociology, The American Journal of Theology, The American Review
of Reviews, Baptist Messenger, Christian Century, The Christian
Herald, Christian Work, The Congregationalist and Advance, Cur-
rent Opinion, Homilectic Review, The Independent, Industry, The
International Review of Missions, Journal of Religion, Literary
Digest, The Missionary Review of the World, Missions, The New
Republic, Outlook, The Presbyterian, Watchman-Examiner, Western
Recorder, The World Tomorrow,* and *The World's Work.*

Official Reports

Formal and to some extent informal relations between the
Interchurch World Movement and other religious bodies are recorded
in many of the official reports published by the organizations
involved. Among denominational reports dealing with the Interchurch World Movement, the following are especially useful:

Annual of the Northern Baptist Convention (1918-1921); *Journal of the General Conference of the Methodist Episcopal Church* (1920, 1924); *Minutes of the General Assembly of the Presbyterian Church in the Presbyterian Church in the United States* (1918-1921); *Proceedings of the National Council of the Congregational Churches of the United States* (1917-1921); and *Year Book of Churches of Christ* (1918-1921). Many references to the Interchurch World Movement also appear in the *Annual Reports of the Federal Council of the Churches of Christ in America* (1918-1921), and in the Federal Council's *Quadrennial Reports* (1916-1920, 1920-1924, 1924-1928). Likewise *Proceedings of Annual Meetings of the Home Missions Council and Council of Women for Home Missions* (1918-1921), *Official Minutes of Annual Meetings and Annual Reports of the Federation of Woman's Boards of Foreign Missions of North America* (1915-1926), *Foreign Missions Conference of North America, Report of the Boards* (1919-1921), and *Foreign Missions Year Book of North America 1920* make significant references to the work of the Interchurch World Movement in relation to their respective programs.

Addresses

Baptist Fundamentals. Addresses Delivered at the Pre-Convention Conference at Buffalo, June 21 and 22, 1920. Philadelphia: Judson Press, 1920.

"Interchurch World Movement of North America First National Interboard Conference, Cleveland, Ohio, April 30th to May 1st, 1919." Unpublished Speeches.

Laidlaw, Walter (ed.). *The Moral Aims of the War*. Speeches Given at the April 4, 1918 International Clerical Conference, Promoted by the National Committee on the Churches and the Moral Aims of the War, under the Auspices of the New York Federation of Churches. New York: Fleming H. Revell Company, 1918.

Lynch, Frederick (ed.). *Mobilizing for Peace*. Addresses Delivered at the Congress on America and the Permanent Court of International Justice. New York: Fleming H. Revell Company, 1924.

Men and Religion. Addresses Delivered at the Buffalo Conference of the Men and Religion Forward Movement, October 25-26, 1910. New York: Young Men's Christian Association Press, 1911.

Mott, John R. *Addresses and Papers of John R. Mott*. 6 vols. New York: Association Press, 1947.

184

National Needs and Remedies. Discussions of the General Christian
Conference Held in Boston, Massachusetts, December 4th,
5th, and 6th, 1889 under the Auspices and Direction of the
Evangelical Alliance for the United States. New York:
Baker and Taylor, 1890.

National Perils and Opportunities. Discussions of the General
Christian Conference Held in Washington, D. C. under the
Auspices of the Evangelical Alliance for the United States.
New York: Baker and Taylor, 1890.

St. John, Burton (ed.). *North American Students and World
Advance*. Addresses Delivered at the Eighth International
Convention of the Student Volunteer Movement for Foreign
Missions, Des Moines, Iowa, December 31, 1919 to January
4, 1920. New York: Student Volunteer Movement for For-
eign Missions, 1921.

"Summary of Conference of Representatives of Promotional Organiza-
tions, Columbus, Ohio, November 1-2, 1922." Held under
Auspices of Federal Council of the Churches of Christ in
America. Unpublished Manuscript.

Books Written during the Period of 1880 to 1925

Abbott, Lyman. *The Twentieth Century Crusade*. New York: The
Macmillan Company, 1918.

Agar, Frederick A. *Church Finance: A Study of Wrong Methods
and the Remedy*. New York: Missionary Education Movement
of the United States and Canada, 1916.

Ainslie, Peter. *If Not a United Church--What?* New York: Fleming H. Revell Company, 1920.

_____. *Towards Christian Unity*. Baltimore, Md.: Associa-
tion for the Promotion of Christian Unity, 1918.

Athearn, Clarence R. *Interchurch Government*. New York: The
Century Co., 1925.

Barbour, Clarence A. (ed.). *Making Religion Efficient*. New
York: Association Press, 1912.

Barker, John Marshall. *The Social Gospel and the New Era*. New
York: The Macmillan Company, 1919.

Batten, Samuel Zane. *If America Fail: Our National Mission and
Our Possible Future*. Philadelphia: The Judson Press,
1922.

_____ (ed.). *The Moral Meaning of the War*. Philadelphia:
American Baptist Publication Society, n. d.

Bradshaw, Marion John (comp.). *The War and Religion, a Preliminary Bibliography of Material in English Prior to January
1, 1919*. New York: Association Press, 1919.

Brown, Arthur Judson. *The Why and How of Foreign Missions*. New
York: Young People's Missionary Movement of the United
States and Canada, 1908.

Brown, William Adams. *The Church in America*. New York: The Macmillan Company, 1922.

Cadman, S. Parkes. *Christianity and the State*. New York: The Macmillan Company, 1924.

Capen, Samuel B. *Foreign Missions and World Peace*. World Peace Foundation Pamphlet Series, Number 7, Part III. Boston: World Peace Foundation, October, 1912.

The Centenary Survey. 2 vols. New York: Methodist Home and Foreign Boards of Missions, 1918.

The Committee on the War and the Religious Outlook. *Christian Unity: Its Principles and Possibilities*. New York: Association Press, 1921.

_____. *The Church and Industrial Reconstruction*. New York: Association Press, 1924.

_____. *The Missionary Outlook in the Light of the War*. New York: Association Press, 1920.

_____. *Religion among American Men as Revealed by a Study of Conditions in the Army*. New York: Association Press, 1920.

_____. *The Teaching Work of the Church*. New York: Association Press, 1923.

Dennett, Tyler. *A Better World*. New York: George H. Doran, 1920.

Disciples of Christ. *The Whole Church Lifting the Whole Task*. Cincinnati, Ohio: Men and Millions Movement of the Disciples of Christ, 1914.

Duncan, John Wesley. *Our Christian Stewardship*. Cincinnati, Ohio: Jennings and Graham, 1909.

Ecumenical Missionary Conference, New York, 1900. 2 vols. New York: American Tract Society, 1900.

Eddy, Sherwood. *Facing the Crisis: A Study in Present Day Social and Religious Problems*. New York: George H. Doran, 1922.

Ellwood, Charles A. *The Social Problem: A Reconstructive Analysis*. Revised edition. New York: The Macmillan Company, 1924.

Ely, Richard T. *Social Aspects of Christianity*. New York: Thomas Y. Crowell and Company, 1889.

Faunce, W. H. P. *Christian Principle Essential to a New World Order*. New York: Association Press, 1919.

_____. *Religion and War*. New York: Abingdon Press, 1918.

Fleming, Daniel Johnson. *Marks of a World Christian*. New York: Association Press, 1919.

186

Foreign Missions Conference of North America. *Missionary Ammunition for the Exclusive Use of Pastors, Number IV: The War Test*. New York: Committee of Reference and Counsel, 1918.

_____. *Missionary Ammunition for the Exclusive Use of Pastors, Number VII: The Testimony of Government Officials to Missions and Missionaries*. New York: Committee of Reference and Counsel, 1920.

Fosdick, Harry Emerson. *The Church's Message to the Nation*. New York: Association Press, 1919.

_____. "Recent Gains in Religion," *Recent Gains in American Civilization*. Kirby Page (ed.). New York: Harcourt, Brace and Company, 1928.

Guild, Roy B. (ed.). *Community Programs for Cooperating Churches*. New York: Association Press, 1920.

_____. *The Manual of Inter-Church Work*. New York: The Commission on Inter-Church Federations of the Federal Council of the Churches of Christ in America, 1917.

_____. *Practicing Christian Unity*. New York: Association Press, 1919.

Harnack, Adolf, and Herrmann, Wilhelm. *Essays on the Social Gospel*. G. M. Craik (trans.). M. A. Canney (ed.). New York: Williams and Norgate, 1907.

Holmes, John Haynes. *New Churches for Old: A Plea for Community Religion*. New York: Dodd, Mead and Company, 1922.

Holt, Arthur E. *Social Work in the Churches*. Boston: The Pilgrim Press, 1922.

The Interchurch Emergency Campaign. New York: Campaign Headquarters, 1919.

Jefferson, Charles Edward. *What the War Has Taught Us*. New York: Fleming H. Revell Company, 1919.

Kelman, John. *Some Aspects of International Christianity*. New York: Abingdon Press, 1920.

Lynch, Frederick. *The Christian Unity Movement in America*. London: James Clarke and Co., Ltd., 1922.

_____. *The Christian in Wartime*. New York: Fleming H. Revell Company, 1917.

_____. *President Wilson and the Moral Aims of the War*. New York: Fleming H. Revell Company, 1917.

Macfarland, Charles S. *International Christian Movements*. New York: Fleming H. Revell Company, 1924.

_____. *The Progress of Church Federation to 1922*. New York: Fleming H. Revell Company, 1922.

Macintosh, Douglas Clyde. *God in a World at War*. London: George Allen and Unwin, 1918.

Mathews, Shailer. *The Social Teachings of Jesus*. New York: The Macmillan Company, 1897.

McConaughy, David. *Money the Acid Test*. New York: Missionary Education Movement of the United States and Canada, 1919.

McConnell, Francis J. *Church Finance and Social Ethics*. New York: The Macmillan Company, 1920.

_____. *Democratic Christianity: Some Problems of the Church in the Days Just Ahead*. New York: The Macmillan Company, 1919.

McGarrah, Albert F. *Practical Inter-Church Methods*. New York: Fleming H. Revell Company, 1919.

Merrill, William Pierson. *Christian Internationalism*. New York: The Macmillan Company, 1919.

Mott, John R. *The Decisive Hour of Christian Missions*. London: Young People's Missionary Movement, 1910.

_____. *The Evangelization of the World in This Generation*. New York: Student Volunteer Movement for Foreign Missions, 1900.

_____. *The Present World Situation*. New York: Student Volunteer Movement for Foreign Missions, 1914.

Murray, J. Lovell. *The Call of a World Task in War Time*. Revised edition. New York: Student Volunteer Movement for Foreign Missions, 1918.

Page, Kirby. *War: Its Causes, Consequences and Cure*. New York: George H. Doran Company, 1923.

Patton, Cornelius H. *World Facts and America's Responsibility*. New York: Association Press, 1919.

Powell, Lyman P. (ed.). *The Social Unrest: Capital, Labor, and the Public in Turmoil*. 2 vols. New York: The Review of Reviews Company, 1919.

Rauschenbusch, Walter. *Christianity and the Social Crisis*. New York: The Macmillan Company, 1907.

_____. *Christianizing the Social Order*. New York: The Macmillan Company, 1912.

_____. *A Theology for the Social Gospel*. New York: The Macmillan Company, 1917.

Renton, Margaret (ed.). *War-Time Agencies of the Churches-- Directory and Handbook*. New York: General War-Time Commission of the Churches, 1919.

Smith, Fred B. *Extracts of Letters from Mr. Fred B. Smith Relating to the World Tour of the "Men and Religion Forward Movement" Team*. Printed for Private Distribution by James G. Cannon, 1913.

Sneath, E. Hershey (ed.). *Religion and the War by Members of the Faculty of the School of Religion, Yale University.* New Haven: Yale University Press, 1918.

Speer, Robert E. *The New Opportunity of the Church.* New York: The Macmillan Company, 1919.

_____. *The War and the Religious Outlook.* Boston: The Pilgrim Press, 1919.

Stackhouse, Perry J. *The Sword of Christ and the World War.* Philadelphia: The Griffith and Rowland Press, 1917.

Strong, Josiah. *The New Era or the Coming Kingdom.* New York: The Baker and Taylor Company, 1893.

_____. *Religious Movements for Social Betterment.* New York: The Baker and Taylor Company, 1900.

Taylor, Alva W. *The Social Work of Christian Missions.* Cincinnati: The Foreign Missionary Society, 1912.

Taylor, Graham. *Religion in Social Action.* New York: Dodd, Mead, and Company, 1913.

Taylor, S. Earl, and Luccock, Halfrd E. *The Christian Crusade for World Democracy.* New York: The Methodist Book Concern, 1918.

Tippy, Worth M. *The Church and the Great War.* New York: Fleming H. Revell Company, 1918.

Ward, Harry F. *The New Social Order.* New York: The Macmillan Company, 1919.

_____. *The Opportunity for Religion in the Present World Situation.* New York: The Womans Press, 1919.

_____. *Social Evangelism.* New York: Missionary Education Movement of the United States and Canada, 1915.

Biographies and Autobiographies

Brown, Charles Reynolds. *My Own Yesterdays.* New York: The Century Company, 1931.

Brown, William Adams. *A Teacher and His Times: A Story of Two Worlds.* New York: Charles Scribner's Sons, 1940.

Eddy, Sherwood. *Eighty Adventurous Years: An Autobiography.* New York: Harper and Brothers, 1955.

Fisher, Galen M. *John R. Mott, Architect of Co-operation and Unity.* New York: Association Press, 1952.

Fosdick, Harry Emerson. *The Living of These Days.* New York: Harper and Brothers, 1956.

Fosdick, Raymond B. *John D. Rockefeller, Jr.: A Portrait.* New York: Harper and Brothers, 1956.

Lacy, Creighton. *Frank Mason North: His Social and Ecumenical Mission*. Nashville, Tenn.: Abingdon Press, 1967.

Latourette, Kenneth Scott. *Beyond the Ranges: An Autobiography*. Grand Rapids, Mich.: William B. Eerdmans, 1967.

Macfarland, Charles Stedman. *Across the Years*. New York: The Macmillan Company, 1936.

Mathews, Basil. *John R. Mott, World Citizen*. New York: Harper and Brothers, 1934.

Mathews, Shailer. *New Faith for Old*. New York: The Macmillan Company, 1936.

McConnell, Francis J. *By the Way: An Autobiography*. New York: Abingdon-Cokesbury Press, 1952.

McLoughlin, Jr., William G. *Billy Sunday Was His Real Name*. Chicago: The University of Chicago Press, 1955.

Nevins, Allan. *John D. Rockefeller, The Heroic Age of American Enterprise*. 2 vols. New York: Charles Scribner's Sons, 1940.

Niebuhr, Reinhold. *Leaves from the Notebook of a Tamed Cynic*. Sixth printing. Cleveland: The World Publishing Company, 1965.

Poling, Daniel A. *Mine Eyes Have Seen*. New York: McGraw Hill, 1959.

Sharpe, Dores Robinson. *Walter Rauschenbusch*. New York: The Macmillan Company, 1942.

Smith, Fred B. *I Remember*. New York: Fleming H. Revell, 1936.

Stelzle, Charles. *A Son of the Bowery*. New York: Doran, 1926.

Taylor, Graham. *Pioneering on Social Frontiers*. Chicago: The University of Chicago Press, 1930.

Thompson, Charles L. *Charles Thompson, An Autobiography*. New York: Fleming H. Revell Company, 1924.

Wheeler, W. Reginald. *A Man Sent from God: A Biography of Robert E. Speer*. Westwood, N. J.: Fleming H. Revell Company, 1956.

Studies in American Religious History

Abell, Aaron Ignatius. *American Catholicism and Social Action: A Search for Social Justice 1865-1950*. Garden City, N.Y.: Hanover House, 1960.

_____. *The Urban Impact on American Protestantism 1865-1900*. Hamden, Conn.: Archon, 1962.

Abrams, Ray H. *Preachers Present Arms*. New York: Round Table Press, 1933.

190

Addison, James Thayer. *The Episcopal Church in the United States, 1798-1931*. New York: Charles Scribner's Sons, 1951.

Ahlstrom, Sydney E. *A Religious History of the American People*. New Haven: Yale University Press, 1972.

_____ (ed.). *Theology in America*. New York: The Bobbs-Merrill Company, Inc., 1967.

Atkins, G. G., and Fagley, F. L., *History of American Congregationalism*. Boston: The Pilgrim Press, 1942.

Atkins, Gaius Glenn. *Religion in Our Times*. New York: Round Table Press, 1932.

Bailey, Kenneth K. *Southern White Protestantism in the Twentieth Century*. New York: Harper and Row, 1964.

Barnes, William Wright. *The Southern Baptist Convention, 1845-1953*. Nashville: Broadman Press, 1954.

Bass, Archer B. *Protestantism in the United States*. New York: Thomas Y. Crowell Company, 1929.

Benjamin, Walter W. "Bishop Francis J. McConnell and the Great Steel Strike of 1919-1920." *A Miscellany of American Christianity*. Edited by Stuart C. Henry. Durham, North Carolina: Duke University Press, 1963.

Brauer, Jerald C. *Protestantism in America*. Revised edition. Philadelphia: The Westminster Press, 1965.

_____ (ed.). *Reinterpretation in American Church History*. Chicago: University of Chicago Press, 1968.

Brown, William Adams. *Toward a United Church: Three Decades of Ecumenical Christianity*. New York: Charles Scribner's Sons, 1946.

Bucke, Emory Stevens, ed. *The History of American Methodism*. 3 vols. Nashville: Abingdon Press, 1964.

Buckham, John Wright. *Progressive Religious Thought in America*. Boston: Houghton Mifflin Company, 1919.

Carter, Paul A. *The Decline and Revival of the Social Gospel*. Ithaca, N.Y.: Cornell University Press, 1954.

_____. *The Spiritual Crisis of the Gilded Age*. DeKalb, Ill.: Northern Illinois University Press, 1971.

Cavert, Samuel McCrea. *The American Churches in the Ecumenical Movement, 1900-1968*. New York: Association Press, 1968.

_____. *Church Cooperation and Unity in America, A Historical Review: 1900-1970*. New York: Association Press, 1970.

Clebsch, William A. *From Sacred to Profane America*. New York: Harper and Row, 1968.

Cherry, Conrad, ed. *God's New Israel*. Englewood Cliffs, N.J.: Prentice-Hall, 1971.

Cole, Stewart G. *The History of Fundamentalism*. New York: R. R. Smith, 1931.

Cross, Robert D. *The Church and the City, 1865-1910*. Indianapolis: Bobbs-Merrill Co., 1967.

Douglass, H. Paul. *Church Unity Movements in the United States*. New York: Institute of Social and Religious Research, 1934.

Drummond, Andrew L. *Story of American Protestantism*. Edinburgh: Oliver and Boyd, 1949.

Fahs, Charles H. *Trends in Protestant Giving*. New York: Institute of Social and Religious Research, 1929.

Fisher, Galen M. *The Institute of Social and Religious Research, 1921-1934*. New York, 1934.

Fry, Luther. "Changes in Religious Organizations." *Recent Social Trends in the United States*. 2 vols. New York: McGraw-Hill Book Company, 1933. pp. 1009-1060.

_____. *The U. S. Looks at Its Churches*. New York: Institute of Social and Religious Research, 1930.

Furniss, Norman F. *The Fundamentalist Controversy, 1918-1931*. New Haven: Yale University Press, 1954.

Garrison, Winfred E. *Christian Unity and Disciples of Christ*. St. Louis: The Bethany Press, 1955.

_____. *The March of Faith: The Story of Religion in America Since 1865*. New York: Harper and Brothers, 1933.

Gatewood, William B., Jr., ed. *Controversy in the Twenties: Fundamentalism, Modernism, and Evolution*. Nashville: Vanderbilt University Press, 1969.

Gaustad, Edwin S. *A Religious History of America*. New York: Harper and Row Publishers, 1966.

Hall, Thomas C. *The Religious Background of American Culture*. Boston: Little, Brown, and Company, 1930.

Handy, Robert T. *A Christian America: Protestant Hopes and Historical Realities*. New York: Oxford University Press, 1971.

_____. *We Witness Together: A History of Cooperative Home Missions*. New York: Friendship Press, 1956.

Herberg, Will. *Protestant-Catholic-Jew: An Essay in American Religious Sociology*. Revised Edition. Garden City, N.Y.: Doubleday, 1960.

Hogg, William R. *Ecumenical Foundations: A History of the International Missionary Council and Its Nineteenth-Century Background*. New York: Harper and Brothers, 1952.

Hopkins, C. Howard. *History of the Y.M.C.A. in North America*. New York: Association Press, 1951.

Hopkins, C. Howard. *The Rise of the Social Gospel in American Protestantism 1865-1915*. New Haven: Yale University Press, 1940.

Hudson, Winthrop S. *American Protestantism*. Chicago: The University of Chicago Press, 1961.

_____. *The Great Tradition of the American Churches*. New York: Harper and Row, 1963.

_____, ed. *Nationalism and Religion in America*. New York: Harper and Row, 1970.

_____. *Religion in America*. New York: Charles Scribner's Sons, 1965.

Hughley, J. Neal. *Trends in Protestant Social Idealism*. Morningside Heights, N.Y.: King's Crown Press, 1948.

Hutchison, John A. *We Are Not Divided: A Critical and Historical Study of the Federal Council of the Churches of Christ in America*. Round Table Press, 1941.

King, William R. *History of Home Missions Council with Introductory Outline History of Home Missions*. New York: Home Missions Council, 1930.

Knebel, A. G. *Four Decades with Men and Boys*. New York: Association Press, 1936.

Latourette, Kenneth Scott. *The Christian World Mission in Our Day*. New York: Harper and Brothers, 1954.

Lee, Robert. *The Social Sources of Church Unity*. New York: Abingdon Press, 1960.

Littell, Franklin H. *From State Church to Pluralism*. Chicago: Aldine Publishing Company, 1962.

Macfarland, Charles S. *Christian Unity in Practice and Prophecy*. New York: The Macmillan Company, 1933.

_____. *Pioneers for Peace through Religion*. New York: Fleming H. Revell Company, 1946.

Marty, Martin E. *Righteous Empire*. New York: The Dial Press, 1970.

May, Henry F. *Protestant Churches and Industrial America*. New York: Harper and Brothers, 1949.

McLoughlin, William G., and Bellah, Robert N., eds. *Religion in America*. Boston: Houghton Mifflin Co., 1968.

Meyer, Donald. *The Protestant Search for Political Realism, 1919-1941*. Berkeley, Calif.: University of California Press, 1961.

Mead, Sidney E. *The Lively Experiment*. New York: Harper and Row, 1963.

Miller, Robert Moats. *American Protestantism and Social Issues, 1919-1939*. Chapel Hill: The University of North Carolina Press, 1958.

Mode, Peter G. *Source Book of American Church History*. Meanasha, Wisc.: Banta, 1929.

Moss, Leslie B. *Adventures in Missionary Cooperation*. New York: Foreign Missions Conference of North America, 1930.

Mott, John R. *Five Decades and a Forward View*. New York: Harper and Brothers, 1939.

Murch, James D. *Cooperation Without Compromise*. Grand Rapids, Mich.: W. B. Eerdmans, Co., 1956.

Nash, Arnold, ed. *Protestant Thought in the Twentieth Century*. New York: Macmillan, 1951.

Niebuhr, H. Richard. *The Kingdom of God in America*. Chicago: Willett, Clark and Company, 1937.

_____. *The Social Sources of Denominationalism*. Cleveland: The World Publishing Company, 1957 (original printing, 1929).

Olmstead, Clifton E. *History of Religion in the United States*. Englewood Cliffs, N. J.: Prentice-Hall, 1960.

Osborn, Ronald E. *The Spirit of American Christianity*. New York: Harper and Brothers, 1958.

Rowe, Henry K. *The History of Religion in the United States*. New York: Macmillan, 1924.

Salstrand, George A. *The Story of Stewardship in the United States of America*. Grand Rapids, Mich.: Baker Book House, 1956.

Sandeen, Ernest R. *The Roots of Fundamentalism, British and American*. Chicago: University of Chicago Press, 1970.

Sanford, Elias B. *Origin and History of the Federal Council of the Churches of Christ in America*. Hartford, Conn.: The S. S. Scranton Company, 1916.

Schneider, Herbert W. *Religion in Twentieth Century America*. Revised edition. New York: Atheneum, 1964.

Smith, Elwyn A. *Religious Liberty in the United States*. Philadelphia: Fortress Press, 1972.

Smith, H. Shelton, Handy, Robert T., and Loetscher, Lefferts A. (eds.). *American Christianity: An Historical Interpretation with Representative Documents*. 2 vols. New York: Charles Scribner's Sons, 1960.

Sontag, Frederick, and Roth, John K. *The American Religious Experience*. New York: Harper and Row, 1972.

Sperry, Willard L. *Religion in America*. Cambridge: The University Press, 1946.

194

Stewart, John T. *The Deacon Wore Spats: Profiles from America's Changing Religious Scene*. New York: Holt, Rinehard and Winston, 1965.

Stokes, Anson Phelps, and Pfeffer, Leo. *Church and State in the United States*. Revised one-volume edition. New York: Harper and Row, 1964.

Sweet, William W. *The Story of Religions in America*. New York: Harpers, 1939.

Torbet, Robert. *A History of the Baptists*. Philadelphia: Judson Press, 1950.

Visser 'T Hooft, Willem A. *The Background of the Social Gospel in America*. Haarlem: H. D. Tjeenk Willink and Zoon, 1928.